Routledge Revivals

The Plays of ARTHUR MURPHY

The Plays of ARTHUR MURPHY
VOLUME II

Edited with an introduction by
RICHARD B. SCHWARTZ

First published in 1979 by Garland Publishing, Inc.

This edition first published in 2018 by Routledge
2 Park Square, Milton Park, Abingdon, Oxon, OX14 4RN
and by Routledge
52 Vanderbilt Avenue, New York, NY 10017, USA

Routledge is an imprint of the Taylor & Francis Group, an informa business

© 1979 by Taylor and Francis

All rights reserved. No part of this book may be reprinted or reproduced or utilised in any form or by any electronic, mechanical, or other means, now known or hereafter invented, including photocopying and recording, or in any information storage or retrieval system, without permission in writing from the publishers.

Publisher's Note
The publisher has gone to great lengths to ensure the quality of this reprint but points out that some imperfections in the original copies may be apparent.

Disclaimer
The publisher has made every effort to trace copyright holders and welcomes correspondence from those they have been unable to contact.
A Library of Congress record exists under ISBN:

ISBN 13: 978-0-367-17414-9 (hbk)
ISBN 13: 978-0-367-17415-6 (pbk)
ISBN 13: 978-0-429-05662-8 (ebk)

EIGHTEENTH-CENTURY ENGLISH DRAMA

a comprehensive collection of over 200 representative plays, reproduced in facsimile in fifty-eight volumes with critical introductions by leading scholars

General Editor
PAULA R. BACKSCHEIDER

A GARLAND SERIES

The Plays of
ARTHUR MURPHY
VOLUME II

Edited with an introduction by
RICHARD B. SCHWARTZ

GARLAND PUBLISHING, INC.
New York & London
1979

For a complete list of the titles in this series see the final pages of volume 4

These facsimiles have been made from copies in the Yale University Library

Library of Congress Cataloging in Publication Data

Murphy, Arthur, 1727-1805.
   The plays of Arthur Murphy.

   (Eighteenth-century English drama)
   Reprint of nineteen plays from the 1786 ed. of The works, of Arthur Murphy printed for T. Cadell, London, together with the reprint of the 1798 ed. of Arminius, printed for J. Wright, London.
   I. Schwartz, Richard B. II. Murphy, Arthur, 1727-1805. Arminius. 1979. III. Series.
PR3605.M9A6   1979   822'.6   78-66610
ISBN 0-8240-3604-2

The volumes in this series are printed on acid-free, 250-year-life paper.
Printed in the United States of America.

The Plays of
Arthur Murphy

Volume I

The Orphan of China
Zenobia
The Grecian Daughter
Alzuma

Volume III

The Way to Keep Him
All in the Wrong
The Desert Island

Volume II

The Apprentice
The Upholsterer
The Old Maid
The Citizen
No One's Enemy but His Own
Three Weeks after Marriage

Volume IV

Know Your Own Mind
The School for Guardians
The Choice
News from Parnassus
The Rival Sisters
Arminius (London, 1798)

All of these plays except Arminius are in *The Works of Arthur Murphy, Esq.* In Seven Volumes (London, 1786)

THE WORKS
OF
ARTHUR MURPHY, Esq.

IN SEVEN VOLUMES.

VOL. II.

———

LONDON:
PRINTED FOR T. CADELL,
IN THE STRAND.

M DCC LXXXVI.

CONTENTS

OF THE

SECOND VOLUME.

	Page.
THE APPRENTICE, ni two Acts, - - -	5
THE UPHOLSTERER, in two Acts, - - -	79
THE OLD MAID, in two Acts, - - -	157
THE CITIZEN, in two Acts, - - - -	217
NO ONE'S ENEMY BUT HIS OWN, in two Acts, - - - - - - -	305
THREE WEEKS AFTER MARRIAGE, in two Acts, - - - - - -	365

The Apprentice

THE
APPRENTICE,
A
COMEDY,
In TWO ACTS.

Performed at the

THEATRE ROYAL

IN

DRURY-LANE.

-------- Non illo quisquam solertior alter
Exprimit incessus, vultumque modumque loquendi.
Ovid.

--------Tragicâ desævit & ampullatur in arte.
Hor.

PROLOGUE:

Written by DAVID GARRICK, Esq;

Spoken by Mr. WOODWARD.

*P*ROLOGUES *precede the piece in mournful verse,*
  As UNDERTAKERS *walk before the herse;*
Whose doleful march may strike the harden'd mind,
And wake it's feelings---for the dead behind.

  To-night no smuggled scenes from France we shew,
'Tis ENGLISH, ENGLISH, *Sirs, from top to toe.*
Though coarse the colours, and the hand unskill'd,
From real life our little cloth is fill'd.
The hero is a youth, by Fate design'd
For CULLING SIMPLES; *but whose stage-struck mind*
Nor FATE *could rule, nor his indentures bind.*
A place there is, where such young QUIXOTS *meet;*
'Tis called the SPOUTING-CLUB, *a glorious treat!*
Where PRENTICE KINGS *alarm the gaping street.*
There BRUTUS *starts and stares by midnight taper,*
Who all the day enacts---a Wollen-Draper.
There HAMLET'*s Ghost stalks forth with doubled fist,*
Cries out with hollow voice---" LIST, LIST, OH!
    LIST!"
And frightens Denmark's Prince,---a young Tobacconist.
The Spirit too, clear'd of his deadly white,
Rises a HABERDASHER *to the fight.*
Not young Attornies have this rage withstood,
But change their pens for TRUNCHEONS, *ink for*
    BLOOD,
And (strange reverse!) die for their Country's good.

B 2 PRO-

PROLOGUE.

To check these heroes, and their laurels crop,
To bring them back to REASON *and their* SHOP,
Our author wrote.---O you, Tom, Dick, Jack, Will!
Who hold the ballance, or who gild the pill;
Who wield the yard, and simp'ring pay your court,
And at each flourish snip an inch too short;
Let no false fire your heedless steps betray.
" Who can tread sure upon this slipp'ry way?"
Where, like to others, whom ambition calls,
Th' advent'rous youth, before he rises, falls!
The tinsel grandeur turns his giddy brain;
He strolls, and starves; he struts and frets in vain.

[Bell rings.

But soft;---the Prompter calls---brief let me be;
Would you no groanings hear, no apples see?
Nor yet be damn'd? fly hence; " farewell, remember
me."

Dramatis Personæ.

WINGATE,	MR. YATES.
DICK, *his Son*,	MR. WOODWARD.
GARGLE, *an Apotherary*,	MR. BURTON.
SIMON, *Servant to Gargle*,	MR. H. VAUGHAN.
CATCHPOLE, *a Sheriff's Officer*,	MR. W. VAUGHAN.
SCOTCHMAN,	MR. BLAKES.
IRISHMAN,	MR. JEFFERSON.
CHARLOTTE, *Daughter to Gargle*,	MISS MINORS.

MEMBERS *of the Spouting-Club*, WATCHMEN, &c.

THE APPRENTICE.

ACT the FIRST.

SCENE the FIRST.

Enter WINGATE *and* SIMON.

WINGATE.

HOLD your tongue, you blockhead, don't argue with me; don't think to impoſe upon me; I am convinced; I know it all; and if you imagine, varlet, that you are to trifle with me---- what right have you to trifle with me?---You are in the plot, you ſcoundrel, and if you don't diſcover all---

SIMON.

Dear heart, Sir, you won't give a body time.

WINGATE.

Tell me all you know this moment, or---zookers! a whole month miſſing, and no account of him far or near!---it is too much for a father: A vile, ungrateful prodigal!---Plague and diſtraction! where can the fellow be?---Look you, friend; don't you preſume---

SIMON

Simon.

Lord, Sir, you are so main passionate, you won't let a body speak.

Wingate.

Speak out then, and don't stand muttering.---- What a lubberly fellow you are! *(Looks at him and laughs)*---ha! ha! such a scare-crow figure! Why don't you speak out, you blockhead?

Simon.

Mercy on us!---your son to be sure is a fine young gentleman, and a sweet young gentleman; but lack-a-day, Sir, how should I know any thing of him?

Wingate.

Prevaricating booby! with more evasions than if you were before a Middlesex justice!---Has not he been apprentice to your master, my friend Gargle,--- who by the bye is as great a fool as yourself---Has not he been apprentice to him these three years? Have not you lived there all the time, and could you be so long in one house with my son, and not know all his haunts and all his ways? And then, you vagabond, you rascal, what are you lurking about my doors for? What brings you hither so often?

Simon.

My master Gargle and I, Sir, have been so uneasy about him, that I have been running all over the town ever since morning to enquire for him, every where, high and low; and so in my way, I thought I might as well call here.

WINGATE.

A villain, to give his father all this trouble! and so you have not heard any thing of him, friend?

SIMON.

Not a word, Sir, as I hope for mercy.

WINGATE.

You numſkull! you booby! why did not you tell me ſo at firſt?

SIMON.

I told you as ſoon as you would hear me; and as ſure as you are there, for all I know nothing, I believe I can gueſs what is come of him.

WINGATE.

Ay!---gueſs then, ſirrah; tell me as you gueſs.

SIMON.

As ſure as any thing, maſter, the gypſies have gotten hold of him, and we ſhall have him come as thin as a rake, like the young girl in the city, with living upon nothing but cruſts and water for ſix and twenty days.

WINGATE.

The gypſies have got hold of him!---get out of the room, you blockhead, you driveller, you nonſenſical---ha! ha! the gypſies got hold of him!--- Here, you, Simon---

SIMON.

Sir; anan---

WINGATE.

Where are you going in such a hurry?---Let me see; wounds! what must be done?---I'll plague myself no more; let him go on his own way.---An absurd, ridiculous, a silly, empty-headed coxcomb! with his *Cassanders*, and his *Cloppatras*, and his trumpery; with his Romances, and his damn'd plays, and his *Odyssey* Popes, and a parcel of fellows not worth a groat! wearing stone-buckles, and cocking his hat: What right has he to wear stone-buckles and cock his hat? But I'll not put myself in a passion---Death and fury! I never wear stone-buckles; never cock my hat. I think of nothing but the main chance; and-----Simon, do you step, and tell my friend Gargle that I want to speak to him. And yet, I don't know, why should I send for him? A sly, slow, hesitating, pedantic blockhead!---I send for such a fellow! a pestle-and-mortar, simple-squeezing, dry piece of formality, with his physical cant, and his nonsense!---Why don't you go, you booby, when I bid you?

SIMON.

Yes, Sir; I am gone, Sir.   [*Exit*.

WINGATE.

This son of mine will be the death of me. I can't sleep in my bed for thinking of him. He'll be undone; he'll be ruin'd;---well! it's his own fault; what care I? My advice is all lost. A scatter-brain puppy! to stand in his own light---Death and fire! that we can't get children, without having a regard for them! I have been turmoiling for him all my days, and now the villain is run away.----Suppose I advertise the dog, and promise a reward to any one that can give an account of him. There, more expence!

pence! why should I throw away money upon such a profligate? Why, as I don't say what reward, I may give what I please when they come. But then if the young rake-hell should deceive me, and happen to be dead? why then he tricks me out of three shillings for the advertisement; there's my money thrown into the fire. I'll think no more about him; let him follow his nose; it's nothing at all to me: what care I?---What do you come back for, friend?

Enter SIMON.

WINGATE.

Why don't you speak?

SIMON.

As I was going out, Sir, the post came to the door, and brought this letter.

WINGATE.

Let me see it---The gypsies have got hold of him! *(Looks at him and laughs)* ha! ha! what a conjure you are?---ha! ha!--why don't you go where I ordered you?

SIMON.

Yes, Sir, [*Exit.*

WINGATE.

Well, well; I'm resolved, and it shall be so; I'll advertise him to-morrow morning, and promise, if he comes home, that all shall be forgiven: If he bites at the hook then when I have him fast, I may do as I please. Ay, it shall be so; *(laughs)* I may then do as I please. Ha! ha! right! very good! Let me see, how must I describe him? He had on, a silver-

silver-looped hat; I never liked thofe damned filver-loops;---a filver-looped hat, and---and---confufion! what fignifies what he had on? I'll read my letter, and think no more about him. Hey! what in the name of wonder have we here? (*reads*) *Briftol!*---- how! what is all this?

Efteemed Friend,
Laft was 20*th ultimo, fince none of thine, which will occafion brevity. The reafon of my writing to thee at prefent, is to inform thee, that thy fon came to our place with a company of ftrolling players, who were taken up by the Magiftrate, and committed as vagabonds to jail.* That's good news; I am glad of it; let the villain lie there; let him beat hemp (*laughs*) What a fine figure he'll cut in the jail!---ha! ha! Alexander the Great at hard labour! I rejoice at this. Ha! ha! Let me fee, what more does he fay? (*reads*) *I am forry thy lad fhould follow fuch profane courfes; but out of the efteem I bear unto thee, I have taken thy boy out of confinement, and fent him off for your city in the wag-gon, which left this four days ago. He is configned to thy addrefs; being the needfull from thy friend and fervant,* *Ebeeneezer Broadbrim.*

My efteemed friend, Ebeeneezer Broadbrim, you are as great a fool as the reft of them: What did you take the puppy out of jail for? Could not you let him lie there?---Ha! ha! the fpirit moved him, I fuppofe.---Turned ftage-player! I'll never fee the villain's face. Who comes there?

Enter SIMON.

SIMON.
Our Cares are over.

WINGATE.
You lie, you blockhead: our cares are but juft begun.

SIMON.

SIMON.

All's safe and well, make us thankful for it. I met Mr. Gargle on the way, and he has got such news for you, and he is coming as fast as he can, and here he is.

WINGATE.

Let him come in, and do you go and recover your breath, you gapeing, stareing, open-mouthed, fly-catching son of a-----

SIMON.

We're all alive and merry. [*Exit.*

Enter GARGLE.

WINGATE.

So, friend Gargle, here's a fine piece of work. Dick's turn'd vagabond.

GARGLE.

He must be put under a proper regimen directly. He arrived at my house within these ten minutes, but in such a trim! I brought him with me; he is now below stairs. I judged it proper to leave him there, till I had felt your pulse, and in due course prepared you for his reception.

WINGATE.

Death and fire! what could put it into his head to turn buffoon?

GARGLE.

Nothing so easily accounted for: when he ought

to be reading the Dispensatory, there was he constantly poreing over plays, and farces, and *Shakespeare*.

WINGATE.

Ay, that damn'd *Shakespeare!* I hear the fellow was nothing but a deer-stealer in *Warwickshire*. If he had sold the venison, there would have been some sense in that; he would have made money by it; a better trade than writing plays. Zookers! if they had hanged the fellow out of the way, he would not now be the ruin of honest men's children. What right has my son to read Shakespeare? I never read Shakespeare. Wounds! I caught the rascal, myself, reading that Bartholomew-fair play of *Hamlet*, Prince of----I don't know what, not I---*Sweden* I believe---and there was the Prince keeping company with strollers and vagabonds. A fine example, master Gargle!

GARGLE.

His disorder is of the malignant kind, and my daughter has taken the infection from him. Bless my heart! she was as innocent as water-gruel, till he spoiled her. I caught her the other night in the very fact.

WINGATE.

Zookers! you don't say so! caught her in the fact?

GARGLE.

As sure as you are there, he has debauched the poor girl.

WINGATE.

Debauched your daughter?

A COMEDY.

GARGLE.

Even so.

WINGATE.

I don't much wonder at that, friend Gargle. (*Looks at him and laughs*) The boy has good blood in his veins.

GARGLE.

Poor Charlotte! I caught her in the very fact, reading a play-book in bed.

WINGATE.

Is that the fact?

GARGLE.

Yes, and bad enough of all conscience.

WINGATE.

Why, you metaphorical blockhead, why could not you say so at first?

GARGLE.

That was my meaning; but I have done for my young madam; I have locked up all her books, and confined her to her room.

WINGATE.

You have served her right. Look you here, friend Gargle; I'll never see the villain's face; let him follow his own courses; let him bite the bridle.

GARGLE.

Lenitives, Mr. Wingate, lenitives are properest

at

present. His habit requires gentle alteratives: Leave him to my management: Twenty ounces of blood, a cephalic tincture, and a cool regimen, will bring him to himself, and then he may do very well.

WINGATE.

Pho! truce with your jargon: Where is the scoundrel?

GARGLE.

Dear Sir, moderate your anger. Harsh language may---

WINGATE.

Harsh language! If he behaves like a profligate shan't I tell him of it?

GARGLE.

Violence may inflame: gentle means may work a reformation: the boy has good sentiments.

WINGATE.

Sentiments! don't tell me of sentiment; what have I do with sentiment?---Let the booby mind his business, learn how to get money, and never miss an opportunity. I never missed an opportunity; got up at five in the morning; struck a light; made my own fire; worked my fingers ends; and this vagabond is now going to destruction. Let him have his full swing. Let him go on: A ridiculous---

GARGLE.

Ay; ridiculous indeed! For a long time past he could not converse in the language of common sense.

A COMEDY.

Afk him a trivial queftion, he gave you a cramp anfwer out of fome of his plays, that are always running in his head. No underftanding a word that he fays!

WINGATE.

Death and fury! this comes of his keeping company with wits, and be damned to 'em for wits.---ha! ha! wit is a fine thing indeed. I never knew one of your men of genius worth fixpence. There's my friend Bookworm; he has parts and talents; every body fays fo; we went to fchool together; he ftudied well. *(laughs)* Ha! ha! yes, he ftudied well! he made Verfes, and I learned Vulgar Fractions. Where is he now? Looking through iron bars at the King's Bench prifon.---Ha! ha! wit is the moft rafcally, contemptible, beggarly thing on the face of the earth.

GARGLE.

Would you believe it, Mr. Wingate? I have found out that your fon went three times a week to a fpouting club.

WINGATE.

A fpouting club, friend Gargle! what's a fpouting club?

GARGLE.

A meeting of prentices, and clerks, and giddy young men, all intoxicated with plays! and fo they meet at public houfes, and there they repeat fpeeches, and alarm the neighbourhood with their noife, and neglect their bufinefs, aud defpife the advice of their friends, and think of nothing but of becoming actors.

Wingate.

You don't tell me so! a spouting club! zookers! they are all mad.

Gargle.

Ay, mad, indeed, Sir: madness is occasioned in a very extraordinary manner; the spirits flowing in particular channels---

Wingate.

'Sdeath! you are as mad yourself as any of them.

Gargle.

And continuing to run in the same *ducts*---

Wingate.

Ducks!---what *ducks?* roast *ducks* for supper?

Gargle.

No, sir, no; but the finer juices running in the same capillary ducts or vessels, the texture of the brain becomes disordered.

Wingate.

Friend Gargle, don't plague me. *(walks away)* Who's below there?

Gargle. *(following him)*

And by the pressure on the nervous system, the head is disturbed: obstructions are formed, and thus your son's malady is contracted.

Wingate. *(walking away)*

Will nobody answer? Who is below?

A COMEDY.

GARGLE. *(following him)*

But I shall alter the morbid state of the juices, correct his blood, sweeten the humours, and produce laudable CHYLE.

WINGATE.

Produce a laudable fortune; that's the true use of GUILE. Who's below there? Tell that fellow to come up.

GARGLE.

Nay, be a little cool: inflammatories may be dangerous. He may reform; there is now some prospect of it.

WINGATE.

Po! none of your prospects; give me a prospect of gain. Prithee, don't teaze me, man; here the rascal comes.

Enter DICK.

DICK.

(Walking slow and sullen, with his arms folded: he looks at his father, then fixes his eyes on the ground)

There's an attitude! If I had chains on, BAJAZET could not do it better. *(Aside.)*

WINGATE.

Did you ever see such a fellow? So friend!

DICK.

" Now, my good father, what's the matter?"

WINGATE.

You have been upon your travels, have you?---you have had your frolick?---Look you, young man, I'll not put myfelf in a paffion; but death and fire! you fcoundrel, what right have you to plague me in this manner? Do you think I am to fall in love with your face? Muft I bear with you, becaufe I am your father?

DICK.

" A little more than kin, and lefs than kind."

WINGATE.

What a pretty figure you cut now? *(ftands laughing at him)* fuch a poverty-ftruck rafcal I never faw! Why don't you fpeak you blockhead? have you nothing to fay for yourfelf?

DICK. (*afide*)

Nothing to fay for yourfelf? What an old prig it is!

WINGATE.

Mind me, friend; I have found you out. How often muft I tell you that you will never come to good? Turn ftage-player! wounds! you'll not have an eye in your head in a month. (*Looks at him, and laughs*) Ha! ha! you'll have 'em knocked out of the fockets with withered apples. Remember I tell you fo, friend.

DICK.

A critic too! (*whiftles*) well faid old fquare-toes.

WIN-

A COMEDY.

WINGATE.

Look you, young man; my advice is all thrown away upon you. But once for all, mind what I say. I made my own fortune, and I could do the same again. Wounds! if I were placed at the bottom of Chancery-lane with a brush and blackball, I know the world, and could make my own fortune again. You read Shakespeare! get Cocker's Arithmetic; you may buy it for a shilling upon a stall; the best book that ever was wrote.

DICK. (*aside*)

Pretty well that! Ingenious, truly! Egad, the old buck has a pretty notion of letters.

WINGATE.

Can you tell me how much is *five eights of three sixteenths of a pound?*---I see you are a blockhead. Five eights of three sixteenths of a pound! you can't tell me; I would not give a farthing for all you know. If you have a mind to thrive in this world, study figures, and make yourself usefull.

DICK.

" How weary, stale, flat and unprofitable seem to
" me all the uses of this world!"

WINGATE.

Mind the scoundrel now!

GARGLE.

Do, Mr. Wingate, let me speak to him. Softly, softly; I'll touch him with a gentle hand. Come, young man, lay aside this sulky humour, and speak as becomes a son.

DICK.

Dick.

" O Jeptha, judge of Ifrael, what a treafure hadft
" thou!"

Wingate.

What does the fellow fay?

Gargle.

He relents, Sir; come, come, young man, make peace with your father.

Dick.

" They fool me to the top of my bent." Egad, I'll bamboozle 'em, and fo get out of the fcrape.---
" A truant difpofition, good my lord."---No, no, ftay, ftay, that's not right: my friend *Ranger* can fupply a better fpeech.---" It is as you fay, when
" we are fober, and reflect but ever fo little on our
" follies, we are afhamed and forry; and yet, the
" very next minute, we rufh again into the very
" fame abfurdities."

Wingate.

Well faid, lad, well faid; that's very good fenfe; I like you when you talk fenfe. Liften to me, friend: commanding our own paffions, and artfully taking advantage of other peoples, is the fure road to wealth. And without wealth, what is life?---Die a beggar, rather than live a beggar. A man fhould always have a thoufand pounds at his banker's. Wounds! it's ridiculous not to have a thoufand pounds at your banker's.

Dick.

Without doubt, Sir. *(ftifling a laugh)*

Win-

WINGATE.

I'll tell you what, friend; I have a great regard for you in the main. What do I mind my bufinefs for, and get up at five in the morning? Is not it all for you? I never loft an opportunity in my life. There was my friend Barlow, I knew he could not live; he drank brandy in a morning; I faw it; fixed my eye upon him; fold him an annuity: he did not live to receive the firft quarter. Ha! ha! ---my poor friend Barlow!---I knew what I was about: and is not all that for you? Mind me friend: if I abufe you, it is beaufe I wifh you well. Death and fire! do you think I'd call you a fcoundrel, if I had not a regard for you?

DICK.

To be fure, Sir.

WINGATE.

You don't hear me call a ftranger a fcoundrel.

DICK.

No bad mark of prudence.

WINGATE.

Prudence!---what do I care for a ftranger? Mind me, and I'll make a man of you. If you want any thing, you fhall be provided: have you any money in your pocket? Not a fixpence, I warrant. (*looks at him and laughs*) There is nothing I hate like poverty. Let me fee, if I have any money in my purfe. How is this? A ten pound note! Now if I was to give you a bank-note---no; I'll keep it for you; that will do better; and fo mind what I fay, and go and make yourfelf ufefull.

DICK.

Dick.

" Elfe, wherefore breathe I in a Chriftian land?"

Wingate.

Very well; I like that: you had better ftick to your bufinefs, than turn mountebank, and get truncheons broke upon your arm, and tumble about upon carpets.

Dick.

" I fhall in all my beft obey you, Sir."

Wingate.

Very well; very well faid. You may do very well: I'll fay no more to you now: go change your drefs; make yourfelf fit to be feen, and go home to your bufinefs. And let me fee no more play-books: let me never hear that you wear a laced waiftcoat: what right have you to wear a laced waiftcoat? I never wore a laced waiftcoat; never wore one till I was forty. But I'll not put myfelf in a paffion; go, and remember what I have faid to you.

Dick.

I fhall, Sir.
 " I muft be cruel only to be kind;
 " Thus bad begins, and worfe remains behind."
Cocker's Arithmetic, Sir?

Wingate.

Ay, Cocker's Arithmetic: ftudy figures; figures and the true Italian method of book-keeping will carry you through the world.

Dick.

Dick.

Yes, Sir. (*stifling a laugh*) Cocker's Arithmetic!
[*Exit.*

Wingate.

Let him mind me, friend Gargle, and I'll make a man of him.

Gargle.

Ay, Sir, you know the world. Your son will do very well: I wish he were out of his time; he shall then have my daughter.

Wingate.

Yes, but not a stiver of her fortune; I must touch the cash myself; he shan't finger it during my life. I must keep a tight hand over him. (*Goes to the door*) Do you hear, friend? Mind what I say, and go home to your business immediately.---Friend Gargle, let him follow my directions, and I'll make a man of him.

Enter Dick.

Dick.

" Who call'd on Achmet? Did not Barbarossa require me here?"

Wingate.

What's the matter now? Barossa! wounds! what's Barossa? Does the fellow call me names? What makes the booby stand in such confusion?

Dick.

" That Barbarossa should suspect my truth."

Wingate.

Mad, stark staring mad!---Get out of the room, you villain, get out of the room.

Dick.

I thought you called me back, to give me the bank-note, Sir.

Wingate.

Give you a bank-note!---Death and confusion! you oaf; you scrub; you ridiculous coxcomb; give you a bank-note! the more you expect it, the less I'll give it. What right have you to expect it?

Dick.

If you had not mentioned it yourself, Sir---

Wingate.

I mention it!

Dick.

I thought so, Sir; and as your word is as good as your bond---

Wingate.

There now I see you're a blockhead: my word as good as my bond! you fool, you numskull, you'll never succeed in the world. Death and fire! how is my word as good as my bond? My word is one thing, and my bond is another; all the world knows that. Let me hear such another word out of your mouth, and I'll turn you out of my house immediately. My word as good as my bond. Wounds!

I have

I have a mind never to fee your face. I hate poverty and nonsense: never say that to me again.

Gargle.

Come, young man, every thing was quietly settled: do as your father bids you, and don't spoil all again. Be advised by me: go, make yourself clean, and then come home to your business.

[*He pushes* Dick *out.*

Dick.

"Oh! I am Fortune's fool." [*Exit.*

Wingate.

I can be very peremptory, friend Gargle: if he vexes me once more, I'll have nothing to say to him. But I still have hopes; he can do very well: and now I think of it, I have *Cocker*'s Arithmetic below stairs in the counting-house. I'll step and get it for him, and he shall take it home with him.

Gargle.

Mr. Wingate, I wish you a good evening. I have a slow fever in the neighbourhood, that I must pay a visit to. You'll send him home to his business. [*Exit.*

Wingate.

He shall follow you directly. *Five-eights of the three-sixteenths of a pound!*---Multiply the numerator by the denominator; five times sixteen, is ten times eight; ten times eight is eighty; and then---a---five and carry one. [*Exit.*

Scene changes to another Apartment.

Enter DICK *and* SIMON.

DICK.

Simon, did you ever fee fuch a queer old putt as my father?

SIMON.

Good enough when he is pleafed; but main choleric; mercifull! how he ftorms and raves! blows up like gunpowder.

DICK.

His character will do for the ftage, and I'll act it myfelf.

SIMON.

Lord love you, mafter, I am fo glad you are come home; but methinks we had better get away from this houfe; all fifhing in troubled waters here; much quieter at Mr. Gargle's

DICK.

No, no, Simon; ftay a moment. This is but a fcurvy fort of a coat I have on: I know old fquaretoes has always fomething fmart locked up in his clofet; I know his ways; he takes them in pawn; never parts with a guinea without a good pledge in hand.

SIMON.

Odds my life, take care; as fure as a gun he'll hear you. Hufh! I believe he's coming up ftairs.

DICK. (*goes to the door and liftens*)

No---no---no---he is going down ftairs, growling and

and grumbling---" fcoundrel, rafcal---bite the bridle
---" make yourfelf ufefull---fix times twelve is fe-
" venty two"---All is fafe, Simon; he is gone down;
we have nothing to fear. Stand you there, and I'll
difpatch this bufinefs in two minutes " by Shrewf-
" bury clock."

Simon.

Bleffings on him, what is he about?---Why, the
clofet door is locked, mafter.

Dick.

I know it, Simon, but I can unlock it.---You fhall
fee me do it with as much dexterity as any *Sir John
Brute* of 'em all.---This right leg here is the beft
lockfmith in England. Come, furrender up your
truft--- (*Kicks the door open and goes in*)

Simon.

He is at his plays again: odds my heart, he is
wondrous comical; pure diverting; he will go
through with it, I warrant him. Old Drybeard
muft not fmoke that I have any concern. I muft be
main cautious. What's he about? Blefs his heart,
he is to teach me to act Scrub. He began with me
long ago, and I got as far as the Jefuit before he
went out of town. " Scrub!---coming Sir---why
" Scrub!---Ma'am---Lord Ma'am, I have a whole
" packet full of news; fome fay one thing, and
" fome another, but for my part, Ma'am, I believe
" he is a Jefuit."---That's main pleafant---" I be-
" lieve he is a Jefuit."

Enter Dick.

Dick.

" I have done the deed; didft thou not hear a
noife?"

Simon.

No, mafter; don't look fo frightened; not a moufe ftirring; all fnug.

Dick.

This coat will do charmingly. I have outwitted the old gentleman nicely. " In a dark corner of his " cabinet I found this paper; what it is this light " will fhew." (*reads*) *I promife to pay*---ha!---*I promife to pay to Mr. Moneytrap or order on demand---* " 'tis his hand; a note of his;---yet more"---*the fum of feven pounds fourteen fhillings and feven pence, value received by me, London, this* 15*th June* 1775. " 'Tis " wanting what fhould follow; his name fhould fol- " low, but 'tis torn off, becaufe the note is paid."

Simon.

Oh! Lud! dear heart, I'm frighted out of my fenfes. You'll fpoil all; I wifh we were well out of the houfe. Our beft way, mafter, is to make off directly.

Dick.

I'll do it; we'll found a retreat in a moment; but firft help me on with this coat. (*puts it on*) Simon, you fhall be my dreffer, when I am a great actor; you'll be pure happy behind the fcenes.

Simon.

As happy as the day is long, mafter. I fhall like of it hugeoufly. I have been behind the fcenes in the country, when I lived with the man that fhewed wild beaftices.

Dick.

Dick.

Hark ye, Simon; when I am playing some deep tragedy, and " cleave the general ear with horrid speech," you must stand at the side of the scenes, and cry bitterly. (*Teaches him*) Oh!---it's so moving, I can't stand it.

Simon.

Yes, I'll do it; I am rare one to cry.

Dick.

And when I am playing a gay, sprightly, genteel part in comedy, you must be ready to crack your sides with laughing. (*Teaches him*) I shall be damned pleasant.

Simon.

Never doubt me, master. (*Both laugh*)

Dick.

Very well; now go and open the street door; I'll steal down, and we'll leave old Multiplication Table to himself.

Simon.

Ay, so best: we are dancing upon thorns here: I am gone to serve you, master.

Dick.

" To serve thyself; for look, when I am Manager,
" claim thou of me the care o' th' wardrobe, with all
" those moveables whereof the property-man now
" stands possest."

Simon.

I does not underſtand it, but I likes to hear you talk. Huſh! I am gone.

Dick.

Hold, hold; Simon, come hither. " What " money have you about you, Maſter Matthew?"

Simon.

But a teſter.

Dick.

A teſter!---ſomething of the leaſt, Maſter Matthew. Let me ſee it.

Simon.

You have had fifteen ſixpences now.

Dick.

Never mind; I'll pay you all at my benefit.

Simon.

I does not fear you. Huſh!---I'll go and open the door. [*Exit.*

Dick, *ſolus.*

" Thus far we run before the wind."---An apothecary! make an apothecary of me! what cramp my genius over a peſtle and mortar, or mew me up in a ſhop with an " alligator ſtufft, and a beggarly ac- " count of empty boxes!" To be culling ſimples, and conſtantly adding to the bills of mortality. No, no, I'll add to the Play-bills rather: it will be much better to be paſted up in capitals, *The part of Romeo by a young gentleman who never appeared upon any ſtage*

be-

before!---My ambition fires at the thought. But hold, hold; may'nt I run some chance of failing in my attempt? Hissed, pelted, laughed at, not admitted into the Green-room! That will never do;" " down busy devil, down, down."---Take it t'other way---Loved by the women, envied by the men, applauded by the pit, clapped by the gallery, admired by the boxes; " Colonel, is not he a charming crea- " ture?---My Lord, don't you like him of all " things? Makes love like an angel---What an eye " he has? The sweetest figure!---I'll certainly go " to his benefit." Celestial sounds!---and then I'll get in with all the painters, and have myself put up in every shop;---in the character of Macbeth, " This is a sorry sight." (*stands in an attitude*) In the character of Richard, " Give me another horse, " bind up my wounds; have mercy"---Oh! it will do rarely; and then the chance of some great fortune falling in love with me---" O glorious thought! By " Heav'n, I will enjoy it, though but in fancy; ima- " gination shall make room to"---I wonder what o'clock it is: (*looks at his watch*) sdeath! almost ten. I'll away at once; this is club-night; the spouters will be all met. I'll make one among 'em. Little do they think I am in town; they will be surprized to see me; I'll beat up their quarters, and then for my assignation with my master *Gargle*'s daughter. Poor Charlotte! by her letter I find she is locked up, but I shall contrive means to favour her escape. I'll carry her off. A pretty theatrical genius. If she flies to my arms " like a hawk to it's perch," it will be so rare an adventure, and so dramatic an incident! as my friend POLYDORE says,

" Limbs do your office, and support me well;
" Bear me but to her, then fail if you can."

End of the FIRST ACT.

ACT the SECOND.

Scene discovers the Spouting Club: the Members seated, and roaring out BRAVO, *while one stands at a distance, acting* PIERRE.

FIRST MEMBER.

" CURS'D be your senate; curs'd your consti-
"   tution;
" The curse of growing factions and divisions
" Still vex your councils"---

SECOND MEMBER.

Don't you think his action rather confined?

FIRST MEMBER.

Confin'd!---don't you know that I am in chains? you know nothing of the stage. A blockhead!

SECOND MEMBER. *(advancing to him)*

Blockhead, say you?---I know more of the stage, than such upstarts as you can pretend to. Blockhead!---Was not I the first that took compassion on you, when you lay, like a sneaking fellow, under the counter, and swept your master's shop in a morning? When you read nothing but *The Young Man's Pocket Companion,* or *The True Clerk's Vade Mecum,* did not I shew you the way to the upper gallery? teach you the use of a catcall, and put *Chrononhotonthologos* into your hand?

All.
Well argued; bravo! bravo!

President.
Come, gentlemen; no disputes; no quarrelling. Consider where you are: This is the honourable society of Spouters; and so to put an end to all animosities, read the seventh rule of this society.

Third Member. *(reads)*
That business, or want of money, shall not be received as an excuse for non-attendance; nor the anger of Parents, Masters, Guardians, *or* Relations, *be a restraint to genius; to the end that this Society may boast it's own mimic heroes, and be a seminary of young actors, to grace the sock and buskin, in spite of the low mechanic notions of people fit only for the drudgery of trade and business.*

President.
That is not the rule I meant to read. But come---
" Fill a measure the table round"---" Now good digestion wait on appetite, and health on both"---

All.
Huzza! huzza! huzza!

Scotchman.
What say you, lads?---Now I'll gee you a touch of *Macbeeth*.

First Member.
Well done highlander; let us have it.

Scotchman.

What do'ft leer at, mon? I have had muckle applaufe at *Edinburgh*, when I enacted in the *Reegiceede*. I now intend to do *Macbeeth*. I feed the *degger* yefterneet, and I thought I fhould ha' killed every one that came athwart my gate.

Irishman.

Arrah, ftand out of the way, my boys, and you fhall fee me give a touch of Othollo, my dear. Now for the truth of it. *(Burns a cork, and blacks his face)* The devil burn the cork, it would not do it faft enough.

First Member.

Here, here; I'll lend you a helping hand.

(a rap at the door.)

Second Member.

" Open locks, whoever knocks."

Enter Dick.

Dick.

" How now, ye fecret, black, and midnight *wags!*
" what is't you do?"

All.

Ha! the genius! the genius come to town!---the genius!---huzza!

Dick.

" How fare the honeft partners of my heart?"
Natt Pigtail, give us your hand; *Jack Oakftick*, yours; *Bob Nankeen*, how goes it my boy? *Billy Saplin*, I
re-

joice to fee you.---Gentlemen, I rejoice to fee you all. But come the news; the news of the town, for I am but juft arrived. Has any thing been damned? Any new performer this winter? How often has Romeo and Juliet been acted? What new plays on the ftocks? Come, my bucks, inform me; for I want news.

FIRST MEMBER.

Bravo, Sir Harry! yon fhall know all in good time: but prithee, my dear boy, how was it? you played at Briftol: the firft dafh is over with you: come, let us hear.

SECOND MEMBER.

Ay, the particulars, my dear Dick.

DICK.

Look you there now; as *Ranger* fays, let us have it, dear boy, and dear Dick.

FIRST MEMBER.

Nay, nay, let us hear; how was you received?

DICK.

Romeo was my part: I touch'd 'em to the quick. Every pale face from the Wells was there. Not in the leaft frightened; on I went. Eafy at firft; came to the Garden-fcene: Juliet thought to have it hollow! fhe tuned her filver pipe: are you at that work fays I? three ftrides to the ftage door, turned fhort, and here goes. I gave 'em a volley. I tickled 'em, as you will fee in the papers. But come, "What "bloody fcene has Rofcius now to act?"

FIRST MEMBER.

All well ftudied; ready in feveral characters. But
Genius,

Genius, why come among us fo late? Why was not you here in the beginning of the night?

Dick.

Why, *ſtap* my vitals, I longed to fee you all; but whom ſhould I meet in my way but my friend *Catcall*? a deviliſh good critic. He has been in at the death of many a piece. He and I went together, and had our pipe, " to cloſe the orifice of the ſtomach you know," and what do you think I learned of him?

First Member.

Something deep.

Dick.

" Not as deep as a well, but it will do." Can you tell whether the *emphaſis* ſhould be laid upon the *epitaph* or the *ſubſtantive?*

First Member.

The *epitaph*, or the *ſubſtantive!*

Dick.

Ever while you live, lay your *emphaſis* upon the *epitaph*.

Irishman.

Arrah, my dear, what is that fame *epitaph* now?

Dick.

Arrah, " my dear Couſin Macſhane, won't you " put a remembrance upon me?"

Irishman.

But is it mocking me you are?---I believe it's a knock

knock you have a mind to take. Hark you, my jewell; if you'd be taking me off---don't you call it taking off?---By my fhoul, I would be making you take yourfelf off.---What?---don't you like it?---If you are for a carte over the arm, I would not matter you three fkips of a *flay*.

Dick.

Nay, prithee, no offence: I hope we fhall be brother players.

Irishman.

Ow! then we'd be very good friends; for you know two of a trade can never agree, my dear.

Scotchman.

Locke is certainly *reet* in his chapter aboot innate ideas; for this mon was born without any at all. A fheet of blank paper: *Tabula rafa*: and t'other mon yonder---I ken not his name; they call him the Genius; I doot he has no great heed-piece.

Dick.

What character do you intend to appear in?

Irishman.

Othollo, my dear. Let me alone: you'll fee how I'll *bodder* 'em. Though by my fhoul, myfelf does not know but I would be frightened, when every thing is in a *bub-bub*, and nothing to be heard, but " Throw him over"---" Over with him"---" Off, off, off the ftage"---" Mufic"---" Wont y' ha' fome orange chips"---" Ha! fome nonpareils"---" Prologue"---" Hornpipe"-- " Roaft beef"---My dear, it is not like going to the *fod*: A body could do that, frefh and fafting in a morning, without fee or reward;

ward; *becaze*, why? you are as terrible yourself as your enemy.---But the critics have the advantage---Ow! never mind that; who knows but the dear *craturs* in the boxes will be *lucking* at my legs? To be sure! the Devil burn the *luck* they'll give 'em.

SCOTCHMAN.

By St. Andrew, the *cheeld* of *North-Britain* has taken that trade out of your hands.

IRISHMAN.

That trade out of our hands, is it?---Why sure, my dear, the *legs* are the manufacture of Ireland. Ow! never fear it. Let me alone, my jewel; may be I would see a little round face from Dublin in the pit; may be I would.

SCOTCHMAN.

For the elocution you will see that we have the preference: I'll gee you a specimen.

DICK.

What with that impediment?

SCOTCHMAN.

Impeediment! what impeediment? I do not *leefp*, do I? I do not *fqueent*. I am well *leem'd*, am I not?

IRISHMAN.

Why then, if you go to that, I am as well *timber'd* myself as any of them; and by and by you will see what a figure I will make in *genteel* and *top* comedy.

SCOTCH-

Scotchman.

Out a waw! ftand clear, mon, and I'll *gee* you a touch of *Macbeeth*. (*repeats.*)
"Is this a dagger that I fee before me?
"The haundle tow'rds my haund!"

Irishman. (*collaring him*)

"Villain, be fure you prove my
"Love a whore"   (*repeats the reft of the fpeech.*)

Third Member.

(*With his face powder'd, and a pipe in his hand.*)
"I am thy father's fpirit;
"Doom'd for a certain time to walk the night---"

Dick.

Po! Prithee, man; you are not fat enough for a ghoft.

All.

No, no; it ftands to reafon that a ghoft fhould be the fatteft actor on the ftage.

Third Member.

I intend to make my firft appearance in the Ghoft: but I am little puzzled about one thing. The audience, you know, allways applaud a man at his firft appearance: now I want to know, when I come on, and they all fall a clapping, whether I fhould make a bow to the pit and boxes?

Irishman.

To be fure you would; and then if you are *damned*, being a ghoft, you are at home you know, my dear.

Second

Second Member.

Now gentlemen for the true way of dying--(*spreads a blanket*) you muſt ſuppoſe me wounded---(*falls*)
" Oh! Altamont, thy genius is the ſtronger;
" Thou haſt prevail'd---"

Watchman. (*within*)

Faſt five o'clock, and a cloudy morning.

Dick.

How! paſt five o'clock!---ſdeath! I ſhall miſs my appointment with Charlotte---" I have ſtaid too " long, and I ſhall loſe my proſelyte."---Come, my boys, let us ſally out.

All.

Ay! let us adjourn; let us beat the rounds.

Irishman.

Ow! never fear me; I am ready for any thing, my dear; though if they had ſtaid, I ſhould have *boddered* 'em finely in *Othollo*.

Scotchman.

I ſhould have *ſheened* in *Macbeth*. But never mind it now. I'll go to my friend the bookſeller, and tranſlate *Cornelius Tacitus*, or *Grotius de Jure Belli*.

All.

Huzza! huzza! huzza!

Dick.

We'll ſcower the watch---" Confuſion to Mora-
" lity! I wiſh the conſtable was married"---Huzza!

IRISHMAN.

Why then, myself did not care if I was well married too; a wife with a good fortune would be hindering me from going on the stage. Ow! no matter; I may meet with a willing *cratur* somewhere.

[*Exit singing.*

DICK.

Now for the *Montagues* and the *Capulets,* and if they bite their thumbs at me──── [*Exit.*

ALL.

Huzza! huzza! huzza! [*Exeunt omnes.*

Scene a STREET.

Enter WATCHMAN.

WATCHMAN.

Past five o'clock, and a cloudy morning.────All mad I believe in this house. This is their trade three nights in the week, I think.───Past five o'clock, and a cloudy morning.

ALL. (*within*)

Huzza! down with the watch: I wish the constable was married.

WATCHMAN.

What in the name of wonder are they about now?

Enter the SPOUTERS.

DICK.

" Angels and ministers of grace defend us."

First Member.
" By Heav'n, I'll tear thee joint by joint, and ftrew
" This hungry church-yard with your limbs."

Dick.
" Avaunt, and quit my fight: thy bones are mar-
    " rowlefs;
" There's no fpeculation in thofe eyes, that thou
    " doft glare withall."

Watchman.
You are difpofed to be merry, mafter.

Second Member.
" Be fure you write him down an afs."

Dick.
" Be alive again
" And dare me to the defert with thy pole."

First Member.
" Approach thou like the rugged Ruffian bear"

Second Member.
" The arm'd rhinoceros, or Hyrcanian tyger"---

Dick.
" Take any fhape but that, and my firm nerves
" Shall never tremble"---

Watchman.
Soho! foho!

Enter

Enter Watchmen from all parts, some drunk, some coughing, and many standing at a distance.

Second Watchman.

What's the matter here?

First Watchman.

I charge 'em all in the King's name; they have broke the peace; they have committed burglary.

Watchmen.

Down with 'em; bring 'em along.

Dick.

" Unmanner'd slave!
" Advance your *lanthorn* higher than my breast,
" Or by St. Paul, I'll strike thee to my foot,
" And spurn the beggar for this insolence."

Watchmen.

Upon 'em; fall on; to the round-house. *(They fight; Dick falls; several run away; Watchmen follow.)*

Dick.

" I am not valiant neither.
" Man but a rush against Othello's breast,
" And he retires. Where should Othello go?"

Go! where should I go?---To my little Charlotte to be sure. Egad, I'll make my escape. Now Love direct me, " Like the surest arrow from your " quiver." [*Exit.*

Enter WATCHMEN *and several* SPOUTERS.

FIRST WATCHMAN.
Bring 'em along.

SECOND WATCHMAN.
Ay, ay; bring 'em along; they shall answer this.

FIRST MEMBER.
" Good ruffians, hold a while."

FIRST WATCHMAN.
Hold 'em fast.

SECOND MEMBER.
" I am unfortunate, but not asham'd of being so."

SECOND WATCHMAN.
No, asham'd of nothing, I'll warrant.

FIRST MEMBER.
Rascals! here is the most prevailing, powerful rhetoric. *(throws money down.)*

FIRST WATCHMAN.
Stay, stay; the money need not be lost.

SECOND WATCHMAN.
We came honestly by it, whatever they did. *(Watchmen pick up the money, and the Spouters run away.)*

FIRST WATCHMAN.
Come, neighbour; no bad booty.
[*Exeunt Watchmen.*

Scene

A COMEDY.

Scene, Another STREET.

Enter DICK, *with a Lanthorn and Ladder.*

DICK.

All's quiet here; the coaſt clear. Now for my adventure with Charlotte. This ladder will do the buſineſs; though it would be more theatrical if it was a ladder of ropes. That does not ſignify much: I have ſeen it done this way in one of the pantomimes.---This is my maſter Gargle's. " I remember an apothecary, and hereabout he dwells."---Not being yet broad day, " the beggar's ſhop is ſhut."--- What ho! apothecary!---Soft; " what light breaks from yonder window?- -

" It is the Eaſt, and Juliet is the Sun.
" Ariſe, fair Sun, and kill the envious Moon"---

CHARLOTTE. *(at the window.)*

Who's there? my Romeo?

DICK.

" The ſame, my love, if it not thee diſpleaſe."

CHARLOTTE.

Not ſo loud; be a little natural now; you'll wake my father.

DICK.

" Alas! there's more peril in thy eye,"
Than twenty of his gallypots.

CHARLOTTE.

Pſhaw! how can you? don't be in heroics now;
never

never mind poetry and plays. How could you ſtay ſo long?

DICK.

" Chide not, my fair, but let the god of love
" Laugh in thy eyes, and revel in thy heart."

CHARLOTTE.

As I live and breathe, you'll ruin every thing. I ſhall be diſcovered. Be ſilent; make no noiſe, and I'll come down to you.

DICK.

No, no; not ſo faſt; let us act the *Garden-ſcene* firſt.

CHARLOTTE.

And my next ſcene will be a priſon ſcene. My father will lock me up, where I ſhall have no poſſibility of eſcaping. Have patience, and I'll be with you in a moment.

DICK.

Nay, then, I'll act Ranger: " Up I go, neck or " nothing."

CHARLOTTE.

Was there ever ſuch a man? You are enough to fright a body out of one's wits. I have ſettled every thing with Simon: he is going to open ſhop, and has promiſed to let me out that way. Can't you ſtay where you are? Don't come up. I tell you there is no occaſion for the ladder.

DICK.

But I tell you, I would not give a farthing for it
                                                    without

without the ladder. " Up I go: If it was as high
" as the garret, I should mount."

Enter SIMON, *at the Door.*

SIMON.

Sir, Sir; master, madam---

DICK. (*Going up the ladder*)

Prithee be quiet, Simon. I am ascending " the
" high top-gallant of my joy."

SIMON.

Always some new comical notion in his head.
An't please you, master, my young mistress may
come through the shop: I am going to sweep it out,
and she may pass that way safe and fast enow.

CHARLOTTE.

That will be the best way: do you go down
again; stay at the door, and be ready to receive
me. [*She goes in.*

DICK.

But I tell you that will not do: you shan't hinder
me from going through my part. (*Goes up and looks
in at the window*) " A woman by all that's lucky;
" neither old nor crooked;" in I go. (*Gets in*)
And for fear of my master *Gargle,* and the pursuit of
the family, I'll make sure of the ladder.
(*Pulling up the ladder*)

SIMON.

Hist! hist! master; leave the ladder; it may save
me from being suspected. I can say that young
mistress got out of the house that way.

DICK.

Dick.

Very true, Simon: take care of a single rogue: I'll leave the ladder, aud be with you in a moment.
[*He goes in*.

Simon.

Lord love him, how pleasant he is!---it will be fine diversion for me, when we are all playing the fool together in the stage-play, to call him Brother Martin---" Brother Martin; Brother Martin."

Enter Charlotte.

Charlotte.

Dear me! I am frighted out of my senses: where is he?

Simon.

He is a coming, ma'am---." Brother Martin."

Enter Dick.

Dick.

" Cuckold him, ma'am, by all means: I'm your " man."

Charlotte.

Well, I protest and vow, I wonder how you can serve a body so. Feel how my heart goes, thump, thump: it flutters like a bird in a cage.

Dick.

" 'Tis an alarm to love."---But stay; I have not done my part right: here has been no rapture at our
meet-

meeting---Quick let me snatch thee to thy Romeo's arms."

Charlotte.
Hush! don't you consider the danger?

Dick.
But I tell you, in spite of all danger we should indulge our rapture. It is not dramatic otherwise. (*Embraces her*) " Curls like a vine, and touches " like a god."

Watchman. (*Within*)
Past six o'clock, and a cloudy morning.

Charlotte.
As I live and breathe, we shall be discovered and taken. We have not a moment to lose: if you love me, let us make our escape without more foolery.

Watchman. (*Within*)
Past six o'clock, and a cloudy morning.

Charlotte.
It comes nearer and nearer: let us get away.

Dick.
Give me your hand, my fair adventurer, I attend you. " He must fight damn'd hard that takes you " from me now."
" Yes, my dear Charlotte, we will go together;
" Together to the Theatre we'll go;
" There to their ravish'd eyes our skill we'll shew,
" And point new beauties---to the Pit below.
[*Exit with* Charlotte.

Simon.

Heaven blefs the couple of 'em!---Lud! fome
body coming!---hufh; I muft get out of the way.
[Goes in and fhuts the door.

Enter Catchpole *and his* Follower.

Catchpole.

That's he yonder, as fure as you're alive. Yes,
yes; 'tis he. And by that token there *(pointing to
the ladder)* he has been about fome mifchief.

Follower.

Yes, it is; no, no: that an't he. That one has a
laced coat on him: thoff I can't fay---yes, it is---as
fure as a gun it is he.

Catchpole.

Ay, I fmoked him at once.---Do you run that
way, and ftop at the bottom of *Catherine-ftreet*; I'll
turn into *Drury-lane*, and between us both, it's odds
but we *nab* him.   *[Exeunt.*

Enter Watchman.

Watchman.

Paft fix o'clock---a troublefome riotous night I
have had of it---hey! what's here? A ladder at
mafter Gargle's window! I muft alarm the family.
Ho! ho! mafter Gargle! *(raps at the door)*

Gargle. *(at the window)*

What's the matter? How comes this window to
be open? Ha!---a ladder: who's below there?

Watch-

A COMEDY.

WATCHMAN.

Good morning, master Gargle: you an't robbed, I hope: going my rounds I found a ladder here, and saw that window open.

GARGLE.

My mind misgives; some misfortune has happened; that young Graceless has been at work, I fear. Take away the ladder: where is Charlotte? my daughter, Charlotte---
[*He goes in.*

Enter SIMON *imitating* SCRUB.

SIMON.

" Thieves! murder! thieves! robbery! popery!"

WATCHMAN.

What's the matter with the man? Are you crazy?

SIMON. *(with his coat half off)*
" Spare all I have, and take my life,

WATCHMAN.

Any mischief within?

SIMON.

" They broke in with fire and sword. " They'll " be here in a moment---five and forty!"---this will do---young master taught me this: I should not know what to say but for he: this will deceive em all. Five and forty, Sir; with sword and pistol!

WATCHMAN.

Robbers in the house?

Simon.

"With sword and pistol---Five and forty, I saw 'em all."

Watchman.

Nay, an that be the case, it's time for me to march off: I may happen to have the worst on't, and so I'll go and sleep in whole bones---Half an hour past six o'clock. [*Exit.*

Simon.

If it was not for my friend Scrub I don't know what I should do.

Enter Gargle.

Gargle.

She's gone; the villain has robbed me; my daughter is run away; he has carried her off; Simon, I say, Simon; where is the fellow?

Simon.

Down o' your knees; down o' your marrowbones; five and forty! robbers, villains, thieves, murderers, with sword and pistol; down o' your marrowbones.

Gargle.

What a fright the poor fellow is in?---Get up Simon. My daughter is lost; I am ruined.

Simon. (*Aside*)

He does not suspect me: young master has taught me rarely, blessings on him for it. (*to Gargle*) "Spare all I have, Sir, and take my life."

Enter.

Enter WINGATE, *with a News-paper.*

WINGATE. (*Reading*)

" *Wanted on good security*, FIVE HUNDRED
" POUNDS, *for which lawful interest will be given,*
" *and a* GOOD PREMIUM : *Whoever this may suit,*
" *enquire for* S. T. *at the* CROWN AND ROLLS *in*
" *Chancery-lane. Nota-Bene* ; *The utmost secrecy may*
" *be depended upon.*"---This may be worth looking
after. If the fellow's a fool, I'll fix my eye upon
him. Other peoples follies are an estate to the man
who knows how to make himself usefull. Hey!
whom have we here?---Friend Gargle!---up early I
see; nothing like it; nothing to be got by lounging
in bed, like a great lubberly fellow. What's the
matter with you? You look as if you had been taking your own physic.

GARGLE.

No wonder; no wonder; my daughter Charlotte!

WINGATE.

Your daughter! what signifies a foolish girl?

GARGLE.

Poor girl! out at that window there!

WINGATE.

Fallen out of the window! If she is dead, she is
provided for. Here, I have brought the book; I
could not find it last night. Here it is; more sense
in it than in all their *Macbeths* and their trumpery:
(*reads the title page*) Cocker's Arithmetick; let that
booby son of mine study this, and he will know how
to fight his way in the world. Look you here now:

suppose

suppose you have a sixteenth part of a ship, and I buy one fifth of you; what share of the ship do I buy?

Gargle.

Dear heart! dear heart! mine is a melancholy case.

Wingate.

So it is, if you can't answer the question. Why should not a man know every thing? How can you settle partnership accounts? One fifth of one sixteenth, what share of the whole do I buy? Let me see; I'll do it a short way.

Gargle.

To lose my daughter in this manner! seduced out of my house! She is gone, beyond redemption.

Wingate.

Zookers! be quiet man; you put me out. Can't you hold your tongue? Five times sixteen is equal to ten times eight; ten times eight is eighty. Wounds! I'll give the book to that ignorant scoundrell, though, for aught I see, you are as ignorant yourself.

Gargle.

Deliver me! I don't know which way to turn myself. Your son is returned to his old tricks.

Wingate.

His old tricks! what, on the stage again?

Gargle.

I suppose so; and he has carried off poor Charlotte.

Win-

A COMEDY. 55

WINGATE.

Carried off your daughter! how did the rascall contrive that?

GARGLE.

Oh! I am distracted. The watch alarmed us a little while ago, and I found a ladder at the window. I wish I had never taken him into my house. He may debauch the poor girl.

WINGATE.

Suppose he does; what then? She's a woman, is not she? The fellow will have sense enough for that, I warrant him.---Ha! ha! and that's what she wants I suppose.

GARGLE.

I never suspected her: their intrigue was all a secret to me.

SIMON. (*Aside*)

Now I may venture to speak------" Secrets! " Secrets!"

WINGATE.

What does the fellow say?---Are you in the secret, rascall?

SIMON.

" There be secrets in all families, but for my part " I'll not speak a word *pro* or *con* till there's a peace."

WINGATE.

You won't speak, sirrah? Speak out this moment you villain; do you know any thing of this plot?

SIMON

Simon.

Who, I Sir? Not I, Sir, I know no secret, Sir; he came home last night from your house, and went out again directly.

Wingate.

You saw him then?

Simon.

Yes, Sir; I saw him to be sure, Sir. He made me open the shop-door for him: he stopt on the threshold, and looked as if he saw something, and pointed at one of the clouds, and asked if it was like an ouzel.

Wingate.

Like an ouzel! wounds! what's an ouzel?

Gargle.

And then he came back in the dead of the night, and stole away my daughter.

Wingate.

Po! what signifies your daughter? All women are ruined some time or other. Wounds! I'll not put myself in a passion: what right has the scoundrell to put me in a passion? Ill think no more about him. Let him bite the bridle. I'll go and mind my business, and not lose an opportunity for such a worthless numskull.

Gargle.

What shall I do? Mr. Wingate, do not leave me in this affliction. Consider, Sir, Sir, when the animal

mal spirits are properly employed, the whole system is exhilarated; a proper circulation in the smaller ducts or capillary vessels.

WINGATE.

Look you there now; the fellow is at his *ducks* again. Ha! ha! what a mountebank of a doctor you are!

GARGLE.

But when the spirits are under undue influence---

WINGATE.

Po! you are as mad with your physical jargon as my son is with his *Shakespeare*, and his ridiculous beggarly poets.

GARGLE.

Dear Sir, let us go in quest of him. He shall be well phlebotomized, and for the future I will keep his solids and fluids in a proper ballance.

WINGATE.

Don't tell me of solids. The blockhead will never be solid. I'll mind my own affairs. What care I for him? Let me see; my chap is at (*reads the news-paper*) ay, at the *Crown and Rolls*. Friend Gargle, make your mind easy: go and study vulgar fractions. Arithmetical proportion is when the antecedent and the consequent---

Enter a PORTER.

WINGATE.

Who are you, friend? What do you want?

Porter.
Is one Mr. Gargle here?

Gargle.
My name is Gargle: any body taken sick?

Porter.
Here's a letter for you.

Gargle.
Let me see it. What can this be? *To Mr. Gargle at the Pestle and Mortar*---A letter from your son, Mr. Wingate; this is his hand.

Wingate.
Let me see it (*snatches it*) this will unravel all, I suppose---his writing sure enough: what can the villain say for himself (*reads*)

To Mr. Gargle.
Most potent, grave, and reverend Doctor, my very noble and approved good master---The fellow is mad: what a reverend doctor you are! (*looks at Gargle and laughs*) ha! ha! you look like a mummy---(*reads*) *That I have ta'en away your daughter it is most true; true I will marry her. 'Tis true 'tis pity, and pity 'tis 'tis true.* I never read such nonsense in my life. His friend Shakespeare has taught him this. (*reads*) *I have done your shop some service, and you know it; no more of that. Yet I could wish, that at this time, I had not been this thing.* What does the scoundrel mean? (*reads*) *For time may have yet one fated hour to come, which wing'd with liberty, may overtake occasion past.*--- His poets have taught him that too, and it's all flat nonsense: time and tide wait for no man, (*reads*) *Here is a ruffian making villainous jests at my undoing. Even the lewd rabble, when they beheld him seizing me,*
grumbled

grumbled pity. I could have hugged the greasy rogues; they pleased me. I expect redress from thy noble sorrows. Farewell, remember me. *Richard Wingate.*

I don't understand a word of it. Mad as a March hare; stark staring mad.

PORTER.

An't please ye, I fancy's the gentleman is a little beside himself. He took me hold by the collar, and called me villain, and bid me prove his wife a whore. Lord help him! I never feed the gentleman's spouse in my born days before.

GARGLE.

Is she with him now?

PORTER.

There's a likely young woman with him, all in tears.

GARGLE.

My daughter to be sure.

WINGATE.

Let him stay there. Wounds! I would not go the length of my arm to save the villain from the gallows. Where was he, friend, when he gave you this letter?

PORTER.

I fancy the gentleman's in troubles: I brought it from a spunging-house.

WINGATE.

A spunging-house!

PORTER.

Porter.

Yes, Sir---Mr. Catchpole's in *Gray's Inn Lane.*

Wingate.

Let him lie there; I am glad of it.

Gargle.

Let us go to him, Mr. Wingate, I intreat you; we may save him from ruin.

Wingate.

No; let him suffer for it. This it is to have a genius---ha! ha! Genius is a fine thing indeed!

Gargle.

We may still do some good. We may retrieve him. Step into my house. I'll slip on my coat. This honest porter will shew us the way.

Wingate.

Come in, and I'll talk to you: but I will have nothing to do with the scoundrell--- [*Exit.*

Gargle.

Honest friend come with us; I shall be ready in a moment. Simon, do you stay and take care of the house. [*Exit.*

Simon.

Oh! I understand it now: my poor young master shut up in a jail. I have three shillings, and a tester,

and

and I fhould like to give it to him all, an it would do him any good.

GARGLE. (*within*)

Simon, Simon.

SIMON.

Anan; I'm a coming. [*Exit.*

Scene a SPUNGING-HOUSE.

DICK *and* CATCHPOLE *at a table*; CHARLOTTE *fitting in a difconfolate manner.*

CATCHPOLE.

Here's my fervice to you, young gentleman. Don't let your fpirits fink. The debt is no fuch great matter. Why fo fad?

DICK.

"Becaufe captivity has robbed me of a juft and "dear revenge."

CATCHPOLE.

Never look out of humour at me. I never ufes any body ill. No complaints of my houfe. Come, this has been many a good man's lot. Don't be dejected. I have taken a liking to you. Your look befpeaks fomething. My heart warms, to you, methinks. Here's my fervice to you. Hey! the liquor out. Come, we'll have t'other bowl.

DICK.

Dick.

" I've now not fifty ducats in the world ; yet
" Still I am in love, and pleas'd with ruin."

Catchpole.

What do you fay ? You have fifty fhillings I hope.

Dick.

" Now thank Heav'n, I'm not worth a groat."

Catchpole.

Not worth a groat !---Then there's no credit here; I can tell you that. You muft get bail, or go to Newgate. The county jail is the place for the like of you. Who do you think is to pay houfe-rent for you? I faw fomething fneaking in you at the firft caft of my eye. I knew you was nobody. My heart turned againft you at once. Such poverty-ftruck devils as you have no bufinefs in my houfe.

Dick.

" The infolence of office, and the fpurns that pa-
" tient
" Merit from th' unworthy takes !"

Catchpole.

Merits ! The plaintiff will fhew you that he has merits, I warrant him. And you fee your friends won't come near you. They have all anfwered in the old cant, " I've promifed my wife never to be " bail for any body"---" I have fworn not to be fe- " curity"---I would lend you the money, if I had it, " but I defire to be excufed from juftifying bail"--- And the porter you fent but juft now will bring the fame anfwer. Don't think to ftay fnivelling here.
You

You shall go to *quod* I can tell you that. *(knocking at the door.)* Coming, coming; I'm a coming. I shall lodge you in *Newgate* before night. Not worth a groat!---I'll keep no such low-lived company in my house. *(knocking at the door)* Knock the house down, do, will you? A parcel of actor-folks coming I suppose. None but players will come after you. I'll take none of 'em for bail. They shan't jibe me, I promise you. [*Exit.*

Dick.

" Has this fellow no feeling in his business, that " he laughs in making prisoners?" Come, clear up, Charlotte; never mind this; let us act the Prison-scene in the *Mourning-Bride.*

Charlotte.

How can you think of acting plays now, when we are in such distress?

Dick.

Why that's the time to imitate great examples. " Unbend that brow and look more kindly on me." Come, we'll practice an attitude. How many of 'em have you?

Charlotte.

Oh! attitudes enough, if that would pay the debt. Let me see; one, two, three, and then in the fourth act, and then---as I live and breathe, I believe, I have ten at least.

Dick.

That will do swimmingly. I believe I have a round dozen myself.

Enter

Enter WINGATE *and* GARGLE.

GARGLE.

Hush! let us listen to him. I dare say he repents.

WINGATE.

Wounds! what cloaths are those he has on? The villain has robbed me.

DICK.

Ay, we will shew 'em attitudes enough. Let us try, Charlotte. Come; you fancy me dead, and I think the same of you. (*They stand in attitudes*)

WINGATE.

The fellow ought to be in a strait waistcoat--- there, there; mind him now.

DICK.

" Oh! thou soft fleeting form of Lindamira!"

CHARLOTTE.

" Illusive shade of my beloved lord!"

DICK.

" She lives, she speaks, and we shall still be happy."

WINGATE.

You lie, you villain, you shan't be happy.
(*Knocks him down.*

DICK. (*On the ground*)
" Perdition catch thy arm, the chance is thine."

GARGLE.

A COMEDY.

Gargle.
So, young madam, I have found you again.
(*Seizes* Charlotte.

Dick.
"Capulet forbear; Paris let loose your hold;
"She is my wife; our hearts are twin'd together."

Wingate.
Sirrah! villain! I'll teach you what it is to torment your father. (*striking him*)

Dick.
"Parents have flinty hearts; no tears can move
"'em; children must be wretched."

Wingate.
Get off the ground; rise up this moment, or—

Dick. (*Rising*)
A pity there are no scene-drawers to carry me off.

Wingate.
What a vile profligate! Where did you get that coat? Rascal, I have a mind to break your head.

Enter Catchpole, *listening at a distance.*

Dick.
What, like this? (*Pulls off his wig, and shews two patches on his head*)

Wingate.
Have not I told you what your follies would bring you to? Can nothing sting you to reflection? A thou-

thousand circumstances might before now have touched you to the quick. Your own sufferings; a sense of filial duty; the ingratitude that marks your conduct, and the certain ruin that must be the consequence of irregular and wild pursuits.

CATCHPOLE. (*aside*)

Vastly well! he speaks more naturally than any of them.

DICK.

Sir, with your permission, " Rude am I in my " speech, and little shall I grace my cause in speak- " ing for myself, yet by your gracious favour"---

CATCHPOLE. (*aside*)

No; that won't do; sad stuff and ill spoken.

WINGATE.

What do you deserve for this behaviour? Where do you think it will end? Without experience and knowledge of the world, must you presume to judge for yourself? Is there nothing due to your superiors? No deference to authority? By persisting in a wild career of error and dissipation, you may plant thorns upon a father's pillow, but the uneasiness you give him will only serve to embitter your own reflections, when you are left in ruin and distress to think of what you have done.

CATCHPOLE.

Very good! (*goes up to Wingate and claps him on the shoulder*) I like to hear you: you are the best actor among them. (*embraces him*)

WINGATE.

What does the fellow mean?

CATCHPOLE.

You do it admirably: give us another speech. You have a good salary, I warrant you.

WINGATE.

Zookers! do you take me for a mountebank? Mighty well, young man; you see what disgrace you bring upon your father. Wounds! friend Gargle, I have done with him. I made my own fortune, and sooner than he shall spend a shilling of my money, I'll take a boy out of the *Blue-coat Hospital*, and give him all I have. The scoundrell has robbed me, and so Mr. CATCHPOLE you may take him to *Newgate*.

CATCHPOLE.

Well, I thought I never heard a better actor in my life. I'll take him if you be so minded, and are in good earnest.

GARGLE.

If you go to that extremity, Mr. Wingate, then you know the fortune I intended to give my daughter must go into another channel.

WINGATE.

How is that?---I must not lose the handling of his money---Why you know, friend Gargle, I am not hard-hearted in the main.

GARGLE.

Very true, Sir, and if you'll make the young gentleman

tleman serve out the last year of his apprenticeship, I shall be giving over business; he may then set up for himself, and have all my practice into the bargain.

Wingate.

Right, you are right---I don't like to lose an opportunity: If the blockhead would get as many crabbed physical phrases from your *Hippocrites and Allen*, as he has from his plays and farces, I don't know, between you and me, but he may pass for a good physician.

Dick.

" And must I leave thee Juliet?

Charlotte.

Have done with speeches now: you see we are in the last distress: you had better make it up.
(*aside to Dick*)

Dick.

Why, for your sake, I could almost find it in my heart---(*aside*)

Wingate.

You'll settle your money on your daughter?

Gargle.

You know it was always my intention.

Wingate.

I must not let the cash slip through my hands. (*aside*) Look ye here, young man: I am the best natured man in the world.---Mr. Catchpole, how much is the debt?

CATCHPOLE.

The gentleman gave his note at *Briſtol*, I underſtands, where he boarded: 'Tis but twenty pounds, debt and coſts. I have treated him kindly, as I always do to every body, and ſo what you pleaſe for civility money.---The gentleman knows I have been very civil.

WINGATE.

Twenty pounds! what right have you to owe twenty pounds? Why don't you ſend for your friend *Shakeſpeare* to bail you?---ha! ha! I ſhould like to ſee *Shakeſpeare* attempt to juſtify bail---Mr. Catchpole, will you take bail of *Ben Thompſon*, and *Shakeſpeare*, and *Odyſſey Popes*?

CATCHPOLE.

No ſuch people have been here. Are they houſekeepers?

DICK.

" You do not come to mock my miſeries?"

GARGLE.

Huſh! you'll ſpoil all *(takes him by the hand)* Bleſs me! you are in a high fever. When you come home, I'll adminiſter a gentle febrifuge.

DICK.

" Throw phyſic to the dogs, I'll none of it."

WINGATE.

What does he ſay, Gargle?

GARGLE.

Gargle.

He repents; he promises to reform.

Wingate.

That's right, lad; now you are right. Serve out your time, and my friend Gargle will make a man of you. Wounds! you'll have his daughter and all his money; and if I hear no more of your trumpery, and you mind your business, and stick to my little Charlotte, and make me a grandfather in my old days, why then, you will have all my money too, that is, when I am dead.

Dick.

And then, Charlotte, we may go to the play as often as we please. *(aside)*

Charlotte.

That will be the purest thing in the world, and we may see *Romeo and Juliet* every time its acted.
(aside)

Dick.

So we may: I'll buy a renter's share. And besides, it will look like a play now, if I reform in the end---*(aside)*---Sir *(to Wingate)* " free me so " far in your most generous thoughts that I have shot " my arrow o'er the house, and hurt my brother."

Wingate.

What do you say? speak out friend.

Charlotte.

Tell him in plain English. *(aside to Dick)*

Dick.

DICK.

I will: he knows nothing of metaphors. Sir, you shall find for the future that we will both endeavour to give you all the satisfaction in our power.

WINGATE.

Very well; that's right. You may still do very well. Friend Gargle, I am overjoy'd.

GARGLE.

Chearfulness is the principal ingredient in the composition of health.

WINGATE.

Wounds! no more of your physic. Here young man, put this book in your pocket, and let me see how soon you'll be master of vulgar fractions. Mr. Catchpole, step home with me, and I'll pay you the money. You seem a notable sort of a fellow, Mr. Catchpole, and I dare say mind your opportunities. Could you *nab* a man for me?

CATCHPOLE.

Ay, fast enow, when I have the writ.

WINGATE.

Very well, step with me. I lent a young gentleman a hundred pounds. A cool hundred he called it---ha! ha!---it did not stay to cool with him. I touched a *præmium* there; but I shan't wait a moment. Come, young man; do you know any body that will give you twenty pounds? I never was obliged to my family for twenty pounds. But I'll say no more. If you have a mind to thrive in the world, make yourself usefull; that's the only rule I know, and it's the *golden rule*.

DICK.

Dick.

Charlotte, as you are to be my reward, I intend now to be a new man.

Charlotte.

And now I shall see how much you love me.

Dick.

It shall be my study to deserve you. And since we don't go on the stage it is some comfort that " the world's a stage, and all the men and women " merely players."

Some act the upper, some the under parts,
And most assume what's foreign to their hearts.
Thus life is but a tragi-comic jest,
And all is FARCE and MUMMERY at best.

EPILOGUE:

Written by Mr. CHRISTOPHER SMART.

Spoken by Mrs. CLIVE.

Enters reading the Play Bill.

A Very pretty Bill, as I'm alive!
 The part of---Nobody---by Mrs. Clive!
A paltry, scribbling fool! to leave me out!
He'll say, perhaps, he thought I could not spout.
Malice and envy to the last degree!
And why?---I wrote a farce as well as he.
And fairly ventur'd it, without the aid
Of Woodward *dress'd in black, and Face in masquerade.*
Poor soul, such canting stuff will never do,
Unless, like Bayes, *he brings his hangman too.*
But granting that, from these same obsequies,
Some pickings to our youthful bard arise;
Should your applause to joy convert his fear,
As Pallas turns to feast Lardella's *bier;*
Yet 'twould have been a better scheme by half
T'have wrote for me, and made his audience laugh.
I could have shewn him, had he been inclin'd,
A spouting junto of the female kind.
There dwells a Milliner in yonder row,
Well dress'd, full voic'd, and nobly built for shew,
Who, when in rage, she scolds at Sue *and* Sarah,
Damn'd, damn'd dissembler!---thinks she's more than
  ZARA.

EPILOGUE.

She has a daughter too that deals in lace,
And sings---O ponder well---and Chevy Chase,
And fain would fill the fair Ophelia's *place.*
And in her cock'd up hat, and gown of camblet,
Presumes on something---touching the Lord Hamlet.
A cousin too she has, with squinting eyes,
With wadling gait, and voice like London Cries;
Who, for the stage too short by half a story,
Acts Lady Townly---thus---in all her glory.
And, while she's traversing the scanty room.
Cries---" Lord, my Lord, what can I do at home!"
In short, there's girls enough for all the fellows,
The ranting, whining, starting, and the jealous,
The Hotspurs, Romeos, Hamlets, and Othellos.
Oh! little do those silly people know,
What dreadful trials actors undergo.
Myself, who most in harmony delight,
Am scolding here from morning until night.
Then take advice from me, ye giddy things,
Ye royal Milliners, ye apron'd Kings;
Young men beware, and shun our slipp'ry ways,
Study arithmetic, and burn your plays;
And you, ye girls, let not our tinsel train
Enchant your eyes, and turn your madd'ning brain;
Be timely wise, for oh! be sure of this!
A shop with virtue is the height of bliss.

The Upholsterer

THE
UPHOLSTERER;
OR
WHAT NEWS?
A
COMEDY,
In TWO ACTS.

Performed at the

THEATRE ROYAL
IN
DRURY-LANE.

------------O Bone (nam te
Scire, Deos quoniam propius contingis, oportet)
Num quid de Dacis audisti?
Hor.

PROLOGUE.

Spoken by Mr. MOSSOP.

THE love of news, now grown the ruling passion,
   In ev'ry age has been the gen'ral fashion.
'Twas so at Athens :---when in evil hour
Ambition aim'd at universal pow'r;
When the fierce man of Macedon began
Of a new monarchy to form the plan;
Each Greek (as fam'd Demosthenes relates)
Politically mad! wou'd rave of states!
And help'd to form, where'er the mob could meet,
A band of Senators in ev'ry street.
What news, what news? was their eternal cry;
Is Philip sick! then soar'd their spirits high;
Philip is well!---dejection in each eye.
Athenian coblers join'd in deep debate,
While gold in secret undermin'd the state;
Till Wisdom's bird the vulture's prey was made;
And the sword gleam'd in Academus' shade.

   Now modern Philips threaten this our land,
What say Britannia's sons?---along the Strand
What news? ye cry---with the same passion smit;
And there at least you rival attic wit.
A Parliament of porters here shall muse
On state affairs, "swall'wing a taylor's news;"
For ways and means no starv'd projector sleeps;
And ev'ry shop some mighty statesman keeps;
He Britain's foes, like Bobadil, can kill;
Supply th' EXCHEQUER, and neglect his till.
In ev'ry alehouse legislators meet;
And patriots settle kingdoms in the Fleet.

   To shew this phrenzy in its genuine light,
A modern newsmonger appears to night!

PROLOGUE.

Trick'd out from Addison's *accomplish'd page,*
Behold th' Upholsterer *ascends the stage.*

No Minister such trials e'er hath stood;
He turns a BANKRUPT *for the public good!*
Undone himself, yet full of England's *glory!*
A politician!---neither Whig nor Tory!
Nor can ye high or low the Quixote *call;*
" He's Knight o' th' Shire, and represents ye all."

As for the Bard, to you he yields his plan;
For well he knows, you're candid where you can.
One only praise he claims; no party stroke
Here turns a public character to joke.
His Panacæa is for all degrees,
For all have more or less of this disease.
Whatever his success, of this he's sure,
There's merit even to attempt the cure.

Dramatis Personæ.

QUIDNUNC, *the Upholsterer,*	MR. YATES.
PAMPHLET, *a Political Writer,*	MR. GARRICK.
RAZOR, *a Barber,*	MR. WOODWARD.
FEEBLE,	MR. BLAKES.
BELLMOUR,	MR. PACKER.
ROVEWELL,	MR. USHER.
CODICIL, *a Serjeant at Law,*	MR. TASWELL.
BRISK,	MR. VERNON.
WATCHMAN.	

WOMEN.

HARRIET,	MRS. YATES.
TERMAGANT,	MRS. CLIVE.
BETTY,	MISS COCKAYNE.

THE UPHOLSTERER;

OR

WHAT NEWS.

ACT the FIRST.

SCENE Bellmour's *Lodging*.

Enter Bellmour *beating* Brisk.

Brisk.

MR. Bellmour,---let me die, Sir,---as I hope for mercy, Sir---

Bellmour.

Sirrah! rogue! villain!---I'll teach you, I will, you rascal, to speak irreverently of her I love.

Brisk.

As I am a sinner, Sir, I only meant---

Bellmour.

Only meant! you could not mean it, varlet, you had no meaning, booby.---

Brisk.

Brisk.

Why no, Sir, that's the very thing, Sir, I had no meaning.

Bellmour.

Then, firrah, I'll make you know your meaning before you give a loofe to your tongue for the future.

Brisk.

Yes, Sir, to be fure, Sir, and yet upon my word if you would be but a little cool, Sir, you would find I am not much to blame. Befides, mafter, you can't conceive the good it would do your health, if you would but keep your temper a little.

Bellmour.

Mighty well, Sir, give your advice.

Brisk.

Why really now this fame love hath metamorphofed us both very ftrangely, mafter; for to be free, here have we been at this work thefe fix weeks, ftark-ftaring mad in love with a couple of baggages not worth a groat: and yet, Heav'n help us! they have as much pride as comes to the fhare of a lady of quality before fhe has been caught in the fact with a handfome young fellow; or indeed after fhe has been caught, for that matter.

Bellmour.

You won't have done, rafcal?

Brisk.

In fhort, my young miftrefs and her maid have as much

much pride and poverty as---as---no matter what, they have the devil and all, when at the same time every body knows the old broken Upholsterer, Miss Harriet's father, might give us all he has in the world, and not eat the worse pudding on a Sunday.

Bellmour.

Insolent, scurrilous wretch! detract from that heaven of beauty! I'll reform your notions, I will, thou profligate, abandoned, vile blasphemer!

(*striking him*)

Brisk.

Hold, hold, Sir; for mercy-sake, a little patience; not so hard, Sir.

Enter Rovewell.

Rovewell.

Bellmour, your servant. What at loggerheads with my old friend Brisk!

Bellmour.

Confusion! Mr. Rovewell, your servant. This is your doing, hang-dog.---Jack Rovewell, I am glad to see thee.

Rovewell.

Brisk used to be a good servant: he has not been destroying the game, instead of springing it for his master, has he?

Bellmour.

Do you know, Rovewell, that he had the impudence to talk detractingly and prophanely of the idol of my heart?

Brisk.

Brisk.

For which, Sir, I have suffered in a most inhuman and unchristian-like manner, I assure you, Sir.

Bellmour.

Will you leave prating, booby?

Rovewell.

Well, but Bellmour, where does she live?---I'm but just arrived you know: don't grudge your friend a little intelligence: I may have occasion to beat up her quarters.

Bellmour.

Beat up her quarters!---
(looks at him, then half aside)

" Favours to none; to all she smiles extends,
" Oft she rejects, but never once offends."
(stands musing)

Rovewell.

Hey! what fallen into a reverie!---Prithee, Brisk, what does all this mean?

Brisk.

Why, Sir, you must know, I am over head and ears in love.

Rovewell.

But I mean your master; what ails him?

Brisk.

That's the very thing I am going to tell you: as
I said,

I said, Sir, I am over head and ears in love with a whimsical, queer kind of an odd piece of affectation here in the neighbourhood, and so nothing can serve my master, but he must fall in love with the mistress. Look at him now, Sir.

(Bellmour *continues musing and talking to himself*)

Rovewell.

Ha, ha, ha,---poor Bellmour, I pity thee with all my heart---(*strikes him on the shoulder*)

" Ye Gods, annihilate both space and time,---
" And make two lovers happy."

Bellmour.

My dear Rovewell, such a girl!---ten thousand Cupids play about her mouth, you rogue.

Rovewell.

Ten thousand pounds had better play about her pocket? What fortune has she?

Brisk.

Heaven help us, not much to crack of.---

Bellmour.

Not much to crack of, Mr. Brazen! Prithee, Rovewell, how can you be so ungenerous as to ask such a question? You know I don't mind fortune, though by the way she has an uncle who is determined to settle very handsomely upon her; and on the strength of that expectancy, does she give herself as many airs, as the most finished coquette that ever fluttered in a side box.

Rovewell.

Fortune not to be minded!---I'll tell you what,

Bellmour, though you have a good one already, there's no kind of inconvenience in a little more. I'm sure if I had not minded fortune, I might have been in Jamaica still, not worth a sugar-cane; but the widow Molosses took a fancy to me; heaven or a worse destiny has taken a fancy to her: and so, after ten years exile, and being turn'd adrift by my father, here I am again a warm planter, and a widower, most woefully tired of matrimony. But, my dear Bellmour, we were both so overjoyed to meet one another yesterday evening, just as I arrived in town, that I did not hear a syllable from you of your love fit: how, when, and where did this happen?

BELLMOUR.

Oh! by the most fortunate accident that ever was. I'll tell thee, Rovewell: I was going one night from the tavern, about six weeks ago; I had been with a parcel of blades, whose only joy is centered in their bottle, and 'faith till this accident I was a mere town-rake myself. But from that time I am grown a new man.

ROVEWELL.

Ay, a new man indeed!---Who in the name of wonder would take thee, sunk as thou art into a musing, moping, melancholy lover, for the gay Charles Bellmour, whom I knew in the West-Indies?

BELLMOUR.

Poh, the West Indies! the object there was to kill time, you know. What could I do? My father took me against my will from the University, and consigned me over to the academic discipline of a man of war; so that to prevent a dejection of spirits, I was obliged to run into the opposite extreme, as you yourself were wont to do.

ROVEWELL.

Why, yes, I had my moments of reflection; thoughts were uneasy, and I was glad to dissipate them. You know I always told you there was something extraordinary in my story; and so there is still; I suppose it must be cleared up in a few days. I'm in no hurry about it; I must see the town a little this evening, and have my frolick first. But to the point, Bellmour; you was going from the tavern you say.

BELLMOUR.

Yes, Sir, about two in the morning, and I perceived an unusual blaze in the air: I was in a rambling humour, and so resolved to know what it was.

BRISK.

I and my master went together.

BELLMOUR.

Oh! Rovewell! my better stars ordain'd it to light me on to happiness; by sure attraction led, I came to the very street where a house was on fire: water-engines playing, flames ascending, all hurry, confusion, and distress; when on a sudden the voice of despair, silver sweet, came thrilling down to my heart; poor dear, lovely angel, what can she do! cried the neighbours. Again she scream'd, the fire gathering force, and gaining upon her every instant. Here, ma'am, said I, leap into my arms, I'll be sure to receive you; and wou'd you think it? down she came,---my dear Rovewell, such a girl! I caught her in my arms, you rogue, safe, without harm. The dear naked Venus, just risen from her bed, my boy! Her slender waist, Rovewell, the downy smoothness

of

of her whole person, and her limbs "harmonious, "swell'd by Nature's softest hand."

ROVEWELL.

Raptures and Paradise!---What Seraglio in Covent Garden did you carry her to?

BELLMOUR.

There again now! Do, prithee correct your way of thinking: take a *quantum sufficit* of virtuous love, and purify your ideas. Her lovely bashfulness, her delicate fears, her beauty heightened and endeared by distress, dispersed my wildest thoughts, and melted me in tenderness and respect.

ROVEWELL.

But, Bellmour, surely she has not the impudence to be modest after you have had possession of her person?

BELLMOUR.

My views are honourable I assure you, Sir; but her father is absurdly positive. The man's distracted about the balance of power, and will give his daughter to none but a politician. When there was an execution in his house, he thought of nothing but the camp at *Pyrna*; and now he's a bankrupt, his head runs upon ways and means, and schemes for paying off the national debt: the affairs of *Europe* engross all his attention, while the distresses of his lovely daughter pass unnoticed.

ROVEWELL.

Ridiculous enough! But why do you mind him? Why don't you go to bed to the wench at once? Take her into keeping, man.

BELLMOUR.

How can you talk so affrontingly? Have not I told you, though her father is ruin'd, that she has great expectancies from a rich relation?

ROVEWELL.

Then what do you stand watering at the mouth for? If she is to have money enough to pay for her china, her gaming debts, her dogs, and her monkeys, marry her at once, if you needs must be ensnar'd; amuse yourself in a fool's paradise for a honey-moon, then come to yourself, wonder at what you've done, and mix with honest fellows again. Carry her off I say, and never stand whining for the father's consent.

BELLMOUR.

Carry her off! I like the scheme: will you assist me?

ROVEWELL.

No, no; there I beg to be excused. I'll have no hand in that business. My friend may marry if he will, but he shall never say that I helped to fasten the noose. Don't you remember what the satyrist says,---" Never marry while there's a halter to
" be had for money, or a bridge to afford a con-
" venient leap."

BELLMOUR.

Prithee leave fooling.

ROVEWELL.

I am in serious earnest I assure you; I'll drink with you, game with you, go into any scheme or frolic with you, but war matrimony. Nay, if you'll
come

come to the tavern this evening, I'll drink your miftrefs's health in a bumper; but as to your conjugal
fcheme, I have no relifh for that bufinefs. It is not
my talent. I will ferve my friend with all my heart,
but will do no mifchief.

BELLMOUR.

Well, well, I'll take you at your word, and meet
you at ten exactly, at the fame place where we fpent
laft night; then and there I'll let you know what
further meafures I have concerted.

ROVEWELL.

Till then, farewell; *a-propos*,---do you know that
I've feen none of my relations yet?

BELLMOUR.

Time enough to-morrow.

ROVEWELL.

Ay, to-morrow will do,---well, your fervant. If
you muft marry, bon voyage! [*Exit*.

BELLMOUR.

Rovewell, yours,---Brifk do you come to me in
my ftudy, that I may give you a letter to Harriet;
and hark you Sir,---be fure you fee Harriet yourfelf,
and let me have no meffages from that officious go-
between, her maid,---Mrs. Termagant, I think you
call her.

BRISK.

Yes, Sir, Mrs. Termagant. You know by experience that love fpies certain perfections in the object of it's efteem, which nobody elfe can difcover,
and

and I may possibly be in the same case with the maid, as you are with Miss Harriet.

BELLMOUR.

Again taking liberties!---Rascal! your Mrs. Termagant is the veriest blunderer that ever perverted the use of language. Another Mrs. SLIPSLOP! with an eternal fund of unintelligible jargon, and a medley of words, of which she neither knows the meaning nor the pronunciation. Go, and order a coach.

BRISK.

Yes, Sir.--- [*Exit.*

BELLMOUR.

I'll write to Harriet this moment; acquaint her with the soft tumult of my desires, and, if possible, make her mine this very night.

"Love first taught letters for some wretch's aid,
"Some banish'd lover, or some captive maid."

[*Exit.*

Scene the UPHOLSTERER'S HOUSE.

Enter HARRIET *and* TERMAGANT.

TERMAGENT.

Well, but Ma'am, he has made love to you six weeks *successfully*; he has been as constant in his *'moors* poor gentleman, as if you had the *subversion* of *'state* to settle upon him---and if he slips thro' your fingers, now Ma'am, you have nobody to *depute* it to but yourself.

HARRIET.

My gracious! how you run on!-- I tell you, Termagant

magant, my pride was touched, becaufe he feemed to
prefume on his opulence, and my father's diftreffes.

TERMAGANT.

La, Mifs Harriet, how can you be fo *paradropfical*
in your *'pinions?*

HARRIET.

Well, but you know, though my father's affairs
are ruin'd, I am not in fo defperate a way; confider,
my uncle's fortune is no trifle, and I think that profpect entitles me to give myfelf a few airs before I
refign my perfon.

TERMAGENT.

I grant ye, Ma'am, you have very good pretenfions; but then it's waiting for dead men's fhoes:
I'll venture to be perjur'd Mr. *Bellmour* ne'er *dif-
claim'd* an *idear* of your father's diftrefs.

HARRIET.

Suppofing that.

TERMAGANT.

Suppofe, Ma'am---I know it *difputably* to be fo.

HARRIET.

Indifputably I guefs you mean;---but I'm tired of
wrangling with you about words.

TERMAGANT.

By my troth you're in the right on't;-----there's
ne'er a fhe in all Old England, (as your father calls
it) is miftrefs of fuch *phifiology*, as I am. Incertain
I am, as how you does not know nobody that puts
their words together with fuch a *curacy* as myfelf.
I once

I once lived with a *miſtus*, Ma'am,---*miſtus*!---ſhe was a lady; a great tallow-chandler's wife! and ſhe wore as fine cloaths as any perſon of quality, let her get up as early as ſhe will; and ſhe uſed to call me ---Tarmagant, ſays ſhe, what's the *ſignification* of ſuch a word? and I always told her; I told her the *importation* of all my words, though I could not help laughing, Miſs Harriet, to ſee ſo fine a lady, ſuch a downright *ignoranimus*.

HARRIET.

Well,---but pray now, Tarmagant, would you have me directly upon being aſked the queſtion, throw myſelf into the arms of a man?

TERMAGANT.

O' my conſcience you did throw yourſelf into his arms with ſcarce a ſhift on, that's what you did.

HARRIET.

Yes, but that was a leap in the dark, when there was no time to think of it.

TERMAGANT.

Well, it does not ſignify *argifying*, I wiſh we were both warm in bed, you with Mr. Bellmour, and I with his coxcomb of a man; inſtead of being *mi-nured* here with an old crazy fool---*axing* your pardon, Ma'am, for calling your father ſo---but he is a fool, and the worſt of fools, with his *policies*, and his news, and his pamphlets, and his one ſide of the queſtion, and then t'other ſide, when all the time his houſe is full of *ſtatues of bankreſſy*.

HARRIET.

It is too true, Termagant; but he is my father ſtill,

still, and I must always think of him with respect, with gratitude and love.

TERMAGANT.

Love! I should not have though of that. He is an *anecdote* against love.

HARRIET.

Hush! here he comes.

TERMAGANT.

No, it's your uncle Feeble. Poor gentleman, I pity's him, eaten up with *infirmaries,* and yet always taking pains about a crack-brained politician, asking your pardon, Madam.

Enter FEEBLE.

HARRIET.

Well, uncle, have you been able to console him?

FEEBLE.

He wants no consolation child. Lackaday! I am so infirm I can hardly move. I found him tracing in the map, Prince Charles of Lorraine's passage over the Rhine, and comparing it with Julius Cæsar's.

TERMAGANT.

An old blockhead! I've no patience with him, with his fellows coming after him every hour in the day with news. Well now, I wishes there was no such thing as a news-paper in the world, with such a pack of lies, and such a deal of good authority to day, and such flat contradiction tomorrow, that there is no such a thing as believing a word they say.

FEEBLE.

FEEBLE.

Ay, there were three or four fhabby fellows with him when I went into his room. I can't get him to think of appearing before the Commiffioners tomorrow, to difclofe his effects; but I'll fend my neighbour Counfellor Codicil to him. Don't be dejected, Harriet; my poor fifter, your mother, was a good woman; I love you for her fake, child, and all I am worth fhall be your's. But I muft be going; I find myfelf very ill; good night, Harriet, good night. [*Exit* Feeble.

HARRIET.

You'll give me leave to fee you to the door, Sir.
[*Exit* Harriet.

TERMAGANT.

O' my confcience this mafter of mine within here, might have pick'd up his crumbs as well as Mr. Feeble, if he had any *idear* of his bufinefs. I'm fure if I had not hopes from Mr. Feeble, I fhould not tarry in this houfe. By my troth, if all who have nothing to fay the *'fairs* of the nation, would mind their own bufinefs; and thofe who fhould take care of our *'fairs*, would mind their bufinefs too, I fancy poor Old England (as they call it) would fare the better among 'em. This old crazy pate within here! playing the fool, when the man is paft his grand *clytemnefter*. [*Exit* Termagant.

SCENE *difcovers* QUIDNUNC *at a Table, with News-Papers, Pamphlets, &c. all around him.*

QUIDNUNC.

Six and three is nine; feven and four is eleven,
and

and carry one. Let me see, one hundred and twenty-six million, one hundred and ninety-nine thousand, three hundred and twenty-eight: and all this with about---where, where's the amount of the specie? Here, here; with about fifteen million in specie, all this great circulation! good, good; why then how are we ruined?---how are we ruined? What says the land tax at four shillings in the pound? two million! now where's my new assessment?----- here, here, the 5th part of twenty, five in two I can't, but five in twenty *(pauses)* right, four times: why then upon my new assessment there's four million. How are we ruined?-----What says malt, cyder, and mum? eleven and carry one, nought and go two---good, good, malt, hops, cyder, and mum; then there's the wine licence, and the gin act. The gin act is no bad article. If the people will shoot fire down their throats, why in a Christian country they should pay as dear as possible for suicide. Salt! good; sugar! very good; window lights! good again! stamp duty! that's not so well; it will have a bad effect upon news-papers, and we shan't have enough of politics. But there's the lottery: where's my new scheme for a lottery?---Here it is----Now for the amount of the whole: how are we ruined? seven and carry nought; nought and carry one.

Enter TERMAGANT.

TERMAGANT.

Sir, Sir,---

QUIDNUNC.

Hold your tongue, you baggage, you'll put me out. Nought and carry one.

Termagant.
Counsellor Codicil will be with you presently.

Quidnunc.
Prithee be quiet, woman. How are we ruined?

Termagant.
Ay, I'm *confidous* as how you may thank yourself for your own *ruination*.

Quidnunc.
Ruin the nation!---hold your tongue, you jade, I am raising the supplies within the year. How many did I carry?

Termagant.
Yes, you've carried your pigs to a fine market.

Quidnunc.
Get out of the room, huffey; you trollop, you jade, you baggage, get out of the room.
[*turns her out.*

Enter Razor, *with a Shaving Bason in his Hand.*

Quidnunc.
Friend Razor, I am glad to see thee. Well, hast got any news?

Razor.
A budget! I left a gentleman half shaved in my shop over the way; it came into my head of a sudden, so I could not be at ease till I told you.

THE UPHOLSTERER;

QUIDNUNC.

That's kind, that's kind, friend Razor: never mind the gentleman, he can wait.

RAZOR.

Yes, so he can, he can wait.

QUIDNUNC.

Come, now let's hear, what is it?

RAZOR.

I shav'd a great man's butler to day.

QUIDNUNC.

Did ye?

RAZOR.

I did.

QUIDNUNC.

Ay!

RAZOR.

Very true. *(both shake their heads)*

QUIDNUNC.

What did he say?

RAZOR.

Nothing.

QUIDNUNC.

Hum---how did he look?

RAZOR.

RAZOR.

Full of thought.

QUIDNUNC.

Ay! full of thought! What can that mean?

RAZOR.

It muſt mean ſomething. *(ſtaring at each other)*

QUIDNUNC.

Mayhap ſomebody may be going out of place.

RAZOR.

Like enow: there is always ſomething at the bottom when a great man's butler looks grave. Things can't hold out in this manner, maſter Quidnunc!---Luxury will be the ruin of us all, it will indeed.---Kingdoms riſe and fall! *(ſtares at him)*

QUIDNUNC. *(ſtaring at* RAZOR*)*

So they do.---They riſe and fall like the Stocks. ---Here to-day, gone to-morrow. Pity! great pity!

RAZOR.

Yes, yes; the more the pity. *(both ſtand muſing)*

QUIDNUNC.

Pray, friend Razor, do you find buſineſs as current now as before the war?

RAZOR.

No, no: I have not made a wig the Lord knows when

when. I can't mind it for thinking of my poor country.

QUIDNUNC.

That's generous, friend Razor.

RAZOR.

Yes, I can't gi'my mind to any thing for thinking of my country. When I was in Bedlam, it was the same; I cou'd think of nothing else in Bedlam, bu poor Old England, and so they said as how I was incurable for it.

QUIDNUNC.

Ay! and so they laugh at all virtue, and true patriotism. They might as well say the same of me.

RAZOR.

So they might. Well, your servant, Mr. Quidnunc, I'll go now and shave the rest of the gentleman's face.---Poor Old England!

(sighs and shakes his head going)

QUIDNUNC.

But hark ye, friend Razor, ask the gentleman if he has got any news.

RAZOR.

I will---I will.

QUIDNUNC.

And d'ye hear, come and tell me if he has.

RAZOR.

I will, I will---poor Old England! *(going returns)* O, Mr. Quidnunc, I want to ask you---pray now---

Enter

Enter TERMAGANT.

TERMAGANT.

My ſtars! O gemini! Are you mad? How can a man have ſo little *difference* for his cuſtomers?

QUIDNUNC.

I tell you, Mrs. Malapert---

TERMAGANT.

And I tell you, the gentleman keeps ſuch a bawling yonder; for ſhame, Mr. Razor; you'll be a *bankrupper* like my maſter, with ſuch a houſe full of children as you have, pretty little things---that's what you will.

RAZOR.

I'm a coming, I'm a coming, Mrs. Termagant--- I ſay, Mr. Quidnunc, I can't ſleep in my bed for thinking what will become of the Proteſtants, if the Papiſts ſhould get the better in the preſent war.

QUIDNUNC.

I'll tell you---The geographer of our coffee-houſe was ſaying the other day, that there is an huge tract of land about the Pole, where the Proteſtants may retire, and that the Papiſts will never be able to beat 'em thence, if the Northern Powers hold together, and the Grand Turk make a diverſion in their favour.

RAZOR.

That makes me eaſy---I'm glad the Proteſtants will know where to go, if the Papiſts ſhou'd get the better. *(going returns)* Oh! Mr. Quidnunc---hark'ye ---India Bonds are riſen.

Quidnunc.
Are they?---how much?

Razor.
A Jew Pedlar said in my shop as how they are risen three sixteenths.

Quidnunc.
Why then that makes some amends for the price of corn.

Razor.
So it does, so it does; if they but hold up, and the Protestants know where to go, I shall then have a night's rest mayhap. Poor Old England!
[*Exit* Razor.

Quidnunc.
I shall never be rightly easy till those careening wharfs at Gibraltar are repaired.

Termagant.
A fiddle for you *dwarfs, impair* your ruin'd fortune, do that.

Quidnunc.
If only one ship can heave down at a time, there will be no end of it---and then, why should watering be so tedious there?

Termagant.
Look where your daughter comes, and yet you'll be *ruinating* about *Give-a-halter*, while that poor thing is breaking her heart.

Enter

Enter HARRIET.

QUIDNUNC.

It's one comfort, however, they can always have fresh provisions in the Mediterranean.

HARRIET.

Dear papa, what's the Mediterranean to people in our situation?

QUIDNUNC.

The Mediterranean, child? Why if we should lose the Mediterranean, we're all undone.

HARRIET.

Dear Sir, that's our misfortune; we are undone already.

QUIDNUNC.

No, no,---here, child; I have raised the supplies within the year.

TERMAGANT.

I tell you, you're a *lunadic* man.

QUIDNUNC.

Yes, yes, I'm a lunatic to be sure---I tell you, Harriet, I have saved a great deal out of my affairs for you.

HARRIET.

For Heav'n sake, Sir, don't do that: you must give up every thing; my uncle Feeble's lawyer will be here to talk with you upon that subject.

THE UPHOLSTERER;

QUIDNUNC.

Poh, poh, I tell you, I know what I am about. You shall have my books and pamphlets, and all the manifestoes of the powers at war.

HARRIET.

And so make me a politician, Sir?

QUIDNUNC.

It would be the pride of my heart to find I had got a politician in petticoats. A female Machiavel! S'bodikins, you might then know as much as most people that talk in coffee-houses; and who knows but in time you might be a Maid of Honour, or Sweeper of the Mall, or---

HARRIET.

Dear Sir, don't I see what you have got by politics?

QUIDNUNC.

Pshaw! my country's of more consequence to me; and let me tell you, you can't think too much of your country in these worst of times; for Mr. *Monitor* has told us, that affairs in the North, and the Protestant interest, begin to grow *ticklish*.

TERMAGANT.

And your daughter's affairs are very ticklish. Poor thing to be in such *jeopardy*.

HARRIET.

Prithee Termagant---

TERMAGANT.

Nay, I must speak to him---I know you are in a *ticklish* situation, Ma'am.

QUID-

QUIDNUNC.

I tell you, Trull---

TERMAGANT.

But I am convicted it is so---and the posture of my affairs is very ticklish too; and so for my part I *imprecate* that Mr. Bellmour may come, and---

QUIDNUNC.

Mr. Bellmour come! I tell you, Mrs. Impudence, that my daughter shall never be married to a man, that has not better notions of the balance of power.

TERMAGANT.

But what *purvision* will you make for her now, with your balances?

QUIDNUNC.

There again now!---Why do you think I don't know what I'm about? I'll look in the papers for a match for you, child; there's often good matches advertised in the papers. Evil betide it, evil betide it!---I once thought to have a struck a great stroke, that would have astonished all Europe.---I thought to have married my daughter to Theodore King of Corsica.

HARRIET.

What, and have me perish in a jail, Sir!

QUIDNUNC.

S'bodikins my daughter would have had her Coronation Day; I should have been allied to a crowned head, and been FIRST LORD of the TREASURY of COR-

Corsica!---But come,---now I'll go and talk over the *London Evening*, till the *Gazette* comes in. I shan't sleep to-night unless I see the *Gazette*.

Enter Serjeant Codicil.

Codicil.

Mr. Quidnunc, your servant. Your street door was open, and I entered upon the *premises*. I am just come from the great hall of Pleas.

Quidnunc.

This man is come to keep me at home. What from the Hall at this late hour in the evening?

Codicil.

Yes; afternoon sittings have detained me. Upon my word Miss Harriet is as pretty a young lady as a man would desire to have and to hold. Ma'am your most obedient; I have drawn my friend Feeble's will, in which you have all his goods and chattles, lands, tenements and hereditaments.

Harriet.

I thank you, Sir, for the information.

Codicil.

And I hope soon to draw your marriage settlement for my friend Mr. Bellmour.

Harriet.

Hush, dear Sir; not a word of that before my father. I wish you'd try, Sir, to get him to think of his affairs.

Codicil.

Why yes, I have inftructions for that purpofe. Mr. Quidnunc, I am inftructed to expound the law to you.

Quidnunc.

What, the law of nations? Termagant, get out of the room; Harriet, leave me with this gentleman ---I fay, Termagant, begone and leave me. Leave me this moment. (*puts them both out*)

Codicil.

I am inftructed, Sir, that you're a bankrupt; *quafi bancus ruptus*; *banque route faire*. And my inftructions fay further, that you are fummoned to appear before the Commiffioners to-morrow.

Quidnunc.

That may be, Sir, but I can't go to-morrow, and fo I fhall fend 'em word. I am to be to-morrow at Slaughter's coffee-houfe with a private committee, about bufinefs of great confequence to the affairs of Europe.

Codicil.

Then, Sir, if you don't go, I muft inftruct you, that you'll be guilty of a felony: it will be deem'd to be done *malo animo*; it is held fo in the Books; and what fays the Statute? By the 5th *George* 2d, *Cap.* 30. Not furrendering or imbezzling is felony without benefit of Clergy.

Quidnunc.

Ay;---you tell me news.

Codicil.

Give me leave, Sir,---I am instructed to expound the law to you; felony is thus described in the Books; *felonia*, saith *Hotoman, de verbis feudalibus, significat capitale facinus*, a capital offence.

Quidnunc.

You tell me news, you do indeed.

Codicil.

It was so apprehended by the *Goths* and the *Longobards*, and what saith Sir Edward Coke? *Fieri debeat felleo animo.*

Quidnunc.

You've told me news: I did not know it was felony; but if the Flanders mail should come in while I am there, I shall know nothing at all of it.

Codicil.

But why should you be uneasy? *Cui bono*, Mr. Quidnunc, *cui bono?*

Quidnunc.

Not uneasy! If the Papists should beat the Protestants in the present war.

Codicil.

But I tell you, they can get no advantage of us. The laws against the further growth of Popery will secure us. There are provisoes in favour of Protestant purchasers under Papists---10th Geo. I cap. 4. and 6th Geo. II. cap. 5.

Quidnunc.

Ay!

Codicil.

And befides, Popifh recufants can't carry arms, fo can have no right of conqueft, *vi & armis*.

Quidnunc.

That's true; that's true; I'm eafier in my mind.

Codicil.

To be fure: what are you uneafy about? The Papifts can have no claim to Silefia.

Quidnunc.

Can't they?

Codicil.

No, they can fet up no claim. If the Queen on her marriage had put all her lands into *Hotchpot*, then indeed---and it feemeth, faith *Littleton*, that this word *Hotchpot* is in Englifh a Pudding.

Quidnunc.

You reafon very clearly, Mr. Codicil, upon the rights of the powers at war, and fo now if you will, I am ready to talk a little of my affairs.

Codicil.

Nor does the matter reft here; for how can fhe fet up a claim, when fhe has made a conveyance to the Houfe of Brandenburgh? The law, Mr. Quidnunc, is very fevere againft fraudent conveyances.---

QUIDNUNC.

S'bodikins, you have satisfied me.

CODICIL.

Why therefore then, if he will levy fines and suffer a common recovery, he can bequeath it as he likes in *feodum simplex,* provided he takes care to put in *ses Heres.*

QUIDNUNC.

I'm heartily glad of it; so that with regard to my effects---

CODICIL.

Why then suppose she was to bring it to a trial at bar---

QUIDNUNC.

I say with regard to the full disclosure of my effects---

CODICIL.

What wou'd she get by that? At common law she would have no chance, and as to equity---

QUIDNUNC.

Pray, must I now surrender my books and my pamphlets?

CODICIL.

What wou'd Equity do for her? Equity can't relieve her; she might be kept at least twenty years before a Master to settle the account.

Or, WHAT NEWS? 109

QUIDNUNC.

You have made me easy about the Proteſtants in this war, you have indeed; ſo that with regard to my appearing before the Commiſſioners---

CODICIL.

And as to the *Ban of the Empire*, he may demur to that. For all Tenures by *Knight's Service* are aboliſhed, and the Statute 12 Char. II. has declared all lands to be held in *Common Socage*.

QUIDNUNC.

To the point, Mr. Serjeant. Why will you ramble thus? I want to hear about my own affairs. To the point. Is there no way of compelling the creditors to grant my certificate?

CODICIL.

Why therefore then, if they're held in *Common Socage*, I ſubmit it to the Court, whether the Empire can have any claim to *Knight's Service?* They can't call upon him for a ſingle man for the war.

QUIDNUNC.

But I ſay as to my certificate.

CODICIL.

They can't demand *Unum Hominem ad Guerram*;--- for what is *Common Socage?---Socagium idem eſt quod Servitium ſocæ*, the ſervice of the plough.

QUIDNUNC.

I tell you I am willing to attend the Commiſſioners.

sioners. But pray now,---It is of great consequence to me to know this point. I say, Mr. Serjeant---

Codicil.

A number of cases may be cited---

Quidnunc.

Truce with your cases. I say, when my certificate is signed, may not I then---Hey! (*starting up*) hey! ---What do I hear?

Codicil.

I apprehend, I humbly conceive, when your certificate is signed---

Quidnunc.

Hold your tongue, man---did not I hear the Gazette?

Newsman. (*within*)

Great news in the London Gazette.

Quidnunc.

Yes, yes it is---it is the Gazette---Termagant, Termagant; I say, Termagant; where is the jade? Stop the Newsman; he is going by now; Termagant, I say. (*stands bawling at the side of the scene*)

Codicil.

The law in that case, Mr. Quidnunc, *prima facie*,

Quidnunc.

I can't hear you now; I have not time. Termagant, run, fly, make haste; get me the Gazette; bring it directly.   (*stamping violently*)

CODICIL.
I say it is held in the Books---

QUIDNUNC.
I care for no Books; I want the Papers---
(stamping)

CODICIL.
It is held throughout the Books, that your certificate, if not obtained by fraud---

QUIDNUNC.
You shan't defraud me of my Newspaper. Where is it? Bring it this moment.

Enter TERMAGANT.

TERMAGANT.
What do you keep such a bawling for?

CODICIL.
Non compos, that's his case. Mr. Quidnunc, your politicks---

QUIDNUNC.
Mr. Serjeant, your Cases, and your Statutes, and your musty old Books---

CODICIL.
Bo! as mad as any man in Bedlam. Have you no such thing as a strait waistcoat in the house?

QUIDNUNC.
Give me the news, I say.

CODI-

Codicil.

There again! His friends, instead of a commission of bankrupts, should take out a commission of lunacy. [*Exit.*

Termagant.

He is an old *Don Quickset* sure enough. The Newsman says as how the Emperor of *Molocco* is dead.

Quidnunc.

The Emperor of Morocco!

Termagant.

Yes, him.

Quidnunc.

The Emperor of Morocco had a regard for the Balance of Europe, (*sighs*) well, well, come, come, give me the Paper.

Termagant.

The Newsman would not trust, because you're a *bankrupper*, and so I paid two-pence halfpenny for it.

Quidnunc.

Let me see; let me see.

Termagant.

Give me the money first. (*running from him*)

Quidnunc.

Give it me this instant, you jade, (*after her*)

TERMAGANT.

Give me the money, I say. (*from him*)

QUIDNUNC.

I'll teach you, I will you baggage. (*after her*)

TERMAGANT.

I won't part with it till I have the money.
(*from him*)

QUIDNUNC.

I'll give you no money, huffey. (*after her*)

TERMAGANT.

Your daughter shall marry Mr. Bellmour.
(*from him*)

QUIDNUNC.

I'll never accede to the treaty. (*after her*)

TERMAGANT.

Go, you old fool. (*from him*)

QUIDNUNC.

You vile minx, worse than the Whore of Babylon.
(*after her*)

TERMAGANT.

There, you old crack'd brain politic! there's your paper for you. (*throws it down and exit.*

QUIDNUNC. (*sitting down.*)

Oh! Heavens!---I am quite out of breath. A jade, a vile baggage, to keep my news from me.

What does it say? (*Reads very faſt*) "Whereas a commiſſion of bankrupt is awarded and iſſued forth againſt Abraham Quidnunc, of the pariſh of St. Martin in the Fields, Upholſterer, Dealer, and Chapman, the ſaid Bankrupt is hereby required to ſurrender himſelf." Po, what ſignifies this ſtuff? I don't mind myſelf, when the balance of power is concerned. However, I ſhall be read of in the ſame paper, in the London Gazette, by the powers abroad; together with the Pope, and the French King, and the Mogul, and all of 'em. Good, good, very good! here's a pow'r of news,---let me ſee, (*reads*) "Letters from the Vice Admiral, dated Tyger, off Calcutta."---(*mutters to himſelf very eagerly*) Oddſheart, thoſe baggages will interrupt me, I hear their tongues a-going, clack, clack, clack; I'll run into my cloſet, and lock myſelf up. A vixen! a trollop! to want money from me, when I may have occaſion to buy The State of the Sinking Fund, or Faction Detected, or The Barrier Treaty, ---or---and beſides, how could the jade tell but tomorrow we may have a Gazette Extraordinary?

[*Exit.*

End of the FIRST ACT.

ACT the SECOND.

Scene the UPHOLSTERER'S HOUSE.

Enter QUIDNUNC.

QUIDNUNC.

WHERE, where, where is he?---Where's Mr. Pamphlet?---Mr. Pamphlet!---Termagant, Mr. a---a---Termagant, Harriet, Termagant, you vile minx, you faucy---

Enter TERMAGANT.

TERMAGANT.

Here's a racket indeed!

QUIDNUNC.

Where's Mr. Pamphlet? You baggage, if he's gone---

TERMAGANT.

Did not I *intimidate* that he's in the next room? Why fure the man's out of his wits.

QUIDNUNC.

Shew him in here then. I would not mifs feeing him for the difcovery of the North-Eaft paffage.

TERMAGANT.

Go you old Gemini Gomini!

[*Exit* Termagant.

Quidnunc.

Shew him in I say. I had rather see him than the whole state of the Peace at *Utrecht*, or ' the *Paris A-la-main*,' or the Votes, or the Minutes, or---Here he comes, the best political writer of the age.

Enter Pamphlet.

(With a surtout coat, a muff, a long campaign wig out of curl, and a pair of black garters, buckled under the knees.)

Quidnunc.

Mr. Pamphlet, I am heartily glad to see you; as glad as if you were an express from the Groyn, or from Berlin, or Zell, or from Calcutta over land, or from---

Pamphlet.

Mr. Quidnunc, your servant. I am come from a place of great importance.

Quidnunc.

Look ye there now! Well, where, where?

Pamphlet.

Are we alone?

Quidnunc.

Stay, stay, till I shut the door. Now, now, where do you come from?

Pamphlet.

From the Court of Requests.
(laying aside his surtout coat)

QUIDNUNC.
The Court of Requeſts! (*whiſpers*) Are they up?

PAMPHLET.
Hot work.

QUIDNUNC.
Debates ariſing may be?

PAMPHLET.
Yes, and like to ſit late.

QUIDNUNC.
What are they upon?

PAMPHLET.
Can't ſay.

QUIDNNNC.
What carried you thither?

PAMPHLET.
I went in hopes of being taken up.

QUIDNUNC.
Lookye there now. (*ſhaking his head*)

PAMPHLET.
I have been aiming at it theſe three years.

QUIDNUNC.
Indeed! (*ſtaring at him*)

Pamphlet.

Indeed: sedition is the only thing an author can live by now. Time has been I could turn a penny by an earthquake; or live upon a jail-distemper; or dine upon a bloody murder; but now that's all over; nothing will do now but roasting a Minister; or telling the people that they are ruined (*whispers*); the people of England are never so happy as when you tell 'em they are ruined.

Quidnunc.

Yes, but they an't ruined: I have a scheme for paying off the national debt.

Pamphlet.

Let me see it; let me see. (*puts on his spectacles*) Well enough! well imagined,----a new thought this; I must make this my own. (*aside*) Silly, futile, absurd, abominable, this will never do---I'll put it in my pocket, and read it over in the morning for you. Now look you here; I'll shew you a scheme (*rummaging his pockets*) no that's not it---that's my Conduct of the Ministry, by a Country Gentleman---I proved the nation undone here; this sold hugely---and here now, here's my answer to it, by a Noble Lord;---this did not move among the trade.

Quidnunc.

What, do you write on both sides?

Pamphlet.

Yes, both sides. I have two hands Mr. Quidnunc, always impartial, *ambo dexter*.----Now here, here's my Dedication to a Great Man-----touched twenty

twenty for this! and here,----here's my libel upon him.

QUIDNUNC.

What, after being obliged to him?

PAMPHLET.

Yes, for that reason: it excites curiosity. Whitewash and blackball, Mr. Quidnunc! *in utrumque paratus*---no thriving without it.

QUIDNUNC.

What have you here in this pocket?
(prying eagerly)

PAMPHLET.

That's my account with Jacob Zorobabel, the Broker, for writing paragraphs to raise or tumble the stocks, or the price of lottery tickets, according to his purposes.

QUIDNUNC.

Ay, how do you do that?

PAMPHLET.

As thus,---To day the Protestant interest declines, Madrass is taken, and England's undone; then all the long faces in the Alley look as dismal as a blank, and so Jacob buys away and thrives upon our ruin. ---Then to-morrow, we're all alive and merry again, Pondicherry's taken; a certain Northern Potentate will shortly strike a blow, to astonish all Europe, and then every true born Englishman is willing to buy a lottery ticket for twenty or thirty shillings more than it is worth; so Jacob sells away, and reaps the fruit of our success.

QUIDNUNC.
What, will the people believe that now?

PAMPHLET.
Believe it!---believe any thing; no swallow like a true born Englishman's: a man in a quart bottle, or a victory, it's all one to them,---they give a gulp, and down it goes,---glib, glib, they swallow all.

QUIDNUNC.
Yes, but they an't at the bottom of things.

PAMPHLET.
No, not they; they dabble a little, but can't dive.

QUIDNUNC.
Pray now, Mr. Pamplet, what do you think of our situation?

PAMPHLET.
Bad, Sir, bad, and how can it be better?----the people in power never send to me, never consult me; it must be bad. Now here, here, (*goes to his loose coat*) here's a manuscript!---this will do the business, a master-piece! I shall be taken upon up for this.

QUIDNUNC.
Shall ye?

PAMPHLET.
As sure as a gun I shall. I know the Bookseller's a rogue, and will give up his author.

QUIDNUNC.

But pray now what shall you get by being taken up?

PAMPHLET.

I'll tell you---(*whispers*) in order to make me hold my tongue.

QUIDNUNC.

Ay, but you won't hold your tongue for all that.

PAMPHLET.

No, no, not a jot the more for that: abuse them the next day.

QUIDNUNC.

Well, I wish you success. But do you hear no news? Have you seen the Gazette?

PAMPHLET.

Yes, I've seen it. Great news, Mr. Quidnunc: but harkye!---(*whispers*) and kiss hands next week.

(*Each in deep thought without looking at the other.*)

QUIDNUNC.

Ay!

PAMPHLET.

Certain.

QUIDNUNC.

Nothing permanent in this world.

PAMPHLET.
All is vanity.

QUIDNUNC.
Ups and downs.

PAMPHLET.
Ins and outs.

QUIDNUNC.
Wheels within wheels.

PAMPHLET.
No smoak without fire.

QUIDNUNC.
All's well that ends well.

PAMPHLET.
It will last our time.

QUIDNUNC.
Whoever lives to see it, will know more of the matter.

PAMPHLET.
Time will tell all.

QUIDNUNC.
Ay, we must leave all to the determination of time. Mr. Pamphlet, I'm heartily obliged to you for this visit: I love you better than any man in England. To think the same of the Commonwealth is the truest and best foundation of friendship.

PAMPHLET.

And for my part, Mr. Quidnunc, I love you better than I do England itſelf.

QUIDNUNC.

That's kind, that's kind: there is nothing I would not do, Mr. Pamphlet, to ſerve you.

PAMPHLET.

Mr. Quidnunc, I know you are a man of integrity and honour; I know you are; and now ſince we have opened our hearts, there is a thing, Mr. Quidnunc, in which you can ſerve me. You know, Sir, this is in the fullneſs of our hearts,---you know you have my note for a trifle. Hard dealing with aſſignees,---now, could not you, to ſerve a friend, could not you throw that note into the fire?

QUIDNUNC.

How! but would that be honeſt?

PAMPHLET.

Leave that to me: a refin'd ſtroke of policy: papers have been deſtroyed in all governments.

QUIDNUNC.

So they have: it ſhall be done; it will be political; it will indeed. It will ballance accounts between us. But now that I have mentioned a ballance of accounts, pray, Mr. Pamphlet, what do you take to be the true political ballance of power?

PAMPHLET.

What do I take to be the ballance of power?

QUIDNUNC.

Ay; what do you take to be the ballance of power?

PAMPHLET.

The ballance of power: what do I take to be the ballance of power? The ballance of power (*shuts his eyes*) what do I take to be the ballance of power?

QUIDNUNC.

The ballance of power, I take to be, when the Court of Aldermen sits.

PAMPHLET.

No, no, no such thing: wide of the mark.

QUIDNUNC.

Yes, yes, I am right: the bird in the eye.

PAMPHLET.

No, no: the ballance of power is, when the foundations of government and the superstructures are natural.

QUIDNUNC.

How do you mean natural?

PAMPHLET.

Prithee be quiet man; this is the language. The ballance of power is, when the superstructures are reduced to proper ballances, or when the ballances are not reduced to unnatural superstructures.

QUIDNUNC.

That won't do: I differ; with submission I differ:
I take

I take the ballance of power to be, when the fortifications of *Dunquerque* are demolish'd.

(Both in a passion and walking about.)

PAMPHLET.
But I tell you, Mr. Quidnunc---

QUIDNUNC.
I say, Mr. Pamphlet.---

PAMPHLET.
Hear me, Mr. Quidnunc.

QUIDNUNC.
Give me leave, Mr. Pamphlet.

PAMPHLET.
I must observe, Sir,---

QUIDNUNC.
I am convinc'd Sir, that---

PAMPHLET.
That the ballance of power---

QUIDNUNC.
That the fortifications of *Dunquerque*---

PAMPHLET. *(making towards the door, and* QUIDNUNC *following him)*
Depends upon the ballances and the superstructures---

QUIDNUNC.
Conſtitute the true political equilibrium.

PAMPHLET.
Nor will I converſe with a man---

QUIDNUNC.
And, Sir, I never deſire to ſee your face,---

PAMPHLET.
Of ſuch anti-conſtitutional principles,---

QUIDNUNC.
Nor the face of any man who is ſuch a Frenchman in his heart, and has ſuch notions of the ballance of power. [*Exeunt.*

QUIDNUNC. (*re-entering*)
Ay, I have found him out: ſuch abominable principles! I never deſire to converſe with any man of his notions; no, never while I live. He does not think of the conſtitution as I do: I will have no connection with a man of his character.

Re-enter PAMPHLET.

PAMPHLET.
Mr. Quidnunc, one word, Sir, if you pleaſe.

QUIDNUNC.
Sir, I never deſire to ſee your face.

PAMPHLET.
My property, Mr. Quidnunc: I ſhan't leave my pro-

property in the house of a bankrupt. (*twisting his handkerchief round his arm*) A silly, empty, incomprehensible blockhead!

QUIDNUNC.

Blockhead, Mr. Pamphlet?

PAMPHLET.

A blockhead to use me thus, when I have you so much in my power.

QUIDNUNC.

In your power!

PAMPHLET.

In my power, Sir: it's in my power to hang you.

QUIDNUNC.

To hang me!

PAMPHLET.

Yes, Sir; to hang you. (*drawing on his coat*) Did not you propose, but this moment, did not you desire me to combine and confederate to burn a note, and defraud your creditors?

QUIDNUNC.

I desire it!

PAMPHLET.

Yes, Mr. Quidnunc, but I shall detect you to the world. I'll give your character.---You shall have a sixpenny touch next week.

Flebit et insignis totâ cantabitur urbe.

[*Exit* Pamphlet.

QUID-

Quidnunc.

Mercy on me! there's the effect of his anti-con-
stitutional principles! The spirit of his whole party;
I never desire to exchange another word with him.

Enter Termagant.

Termagant.

Here's a pother indeed!---did you call me?

Quidnunc.

No, you trollop, no.

Termagant.

Will you go to bed?

Quidnunc.

No, no, no, no,---I tell you, no.

Termagant.

Better go to rest, Sir; I heard a doctor of physic
say as how, when a man is past his grand *crime*---
what the deuce makes me forget my word?---his
grand *crime-hysteric*, no, no, that's not it---*clytemnester*
ay, that's it: when a man is past his grand *clytemnester*, nothing is so good to assist nature as rest, and
the *non-naturals*.

Quidnunc.

Hold your prating: I'll not go to bed; I'll step
to my brother Feeble; I want to have some talk with
him, and I'll go to him directly. [*Exit* Quidnunc.

Termagant.

Go thy ways for an old hocus-pocus of a newsmonger

monger---You'll have good luck if you find your daughter here when you come back: Mr. Bellmour will be here in the *intrim*, and if he does not carry her off, why then I shall think him a mere shilly shally *feller*; and by my troth I shall think him as bad a *politishing* as yourself.---Well, as I live and breath, I wonders what the dickens the man sees in these newspapers, to be for ever *toxicated* with them. Let me see one of them, to try if I can *westigate* any thing--- (*takes the newspaper and reads*)

" Yesterday at noon arrived at his lodgings in
" Pall mall, John Stukely, Esq; for the remainder
" of the winter season."

Where the devil has the man been?---who knows him, or cares a minikin pin about him? He may go to Jericho for what I cares.

" The same day Mr. William Tabby, an eminent
" man-milliner, was married to Miss Minikin,
" daughter of Mr. Minikin, a considerable haber-
" dasher in Bearbinder-lane."

What the dickens is this to me? Can't Miss Minikin and her Man-milliner go to bed, and hold their tongues? Why must they kiss and tell?

" By advices from *Violenna*---this is *policies* now--- (*reads to herself*)---" and promises a general peace." ---Why can't that make the old curmudgeon happy?

" By letters from Paris"---this is more *policies*--- (*reads to herself*) " and all seems tending to a ge-
" neral rupture."---What the devil does the *feller* mean?---Did not he tell me this moment there was to be a peace? and now its bloody news again! To go to tell me such an impudent lye to my face!

" At the Academy in Essex-street, Grown People
" are taught to dance."

Grown People are taught to dance! I likes that well enough; I should like to be *betterer* in my dancing. I likes the *figerre* of a *minute* as well as a *figerre* in speech (*dances and sings*); but such *trumpry* as the

Vol. II.   S   news

news is, with Kings, and Cheesemongers, and Bishops, and *Highwarman*, and Ladies Prayer-Books, and Lap-Dogs, and the *Domodary* and *Camomile*, and Ambassadors, and Hair-Cutters, all higgledy piggledy together. As I hope for *marcy*, I'll never read another paper. And I wishes old Quidnunc would do the same. If the man would do as I do, there would be some sense in it. If, instead of his *policies*, he would *manure* his mind like me, and read good *altars*, and improve himself in fine *langidge*, and *bombast*, and *polite accollishments*---

[*Exit singing and dancing.*

Scene *the* STREET.

Enter BELLMOUR, ROVEWELL, *and* BRISK.

BELLMOUR.

Women ever were, and ever will be fantastic beings, vain, capricious, and fond of mischief.

BRISK.

Well argued, master.

ROVEWELL. (*sings*)

Deceit is in every woman,
But none in a bumper can be, my brave boys,
But none in a bumper can be.

BELLMOUR.

To be insulted thus, with such a contemptuous answer to a message of such tender import! she might methinks at least have treated me with good manners, if not with a more grateful return.

ROVEWELL.

Confusion to her manners! let us go and drink t'other bumper to drown sorrow.

BELLMOUR.

I'll shake off her fetters: I will Brisk, this very night I will.

BRISK.

That's right, master, and let her know we have found her out, and as the poet says,
"*She that will not when she may,*
"*When she will, she shall have nay,*" Master.

BELLMOUR.

Very true, Brisk, very true; the ingratitude of it touches to the quick. My dear Rovewell, only come and see me take a final leave.

ROVEWELL.

No, truly, not I: none of your virtuous minxes for me. I'll set you down there, if you've a mind to play the fool. I know she'll melt you with a tear, and make a puppy of you with a smile, and so I'll not be witness to it.

BELLMOUR.

You're quite mistaken, I assure you: you shall see me most manfully upbraid her with her ingratitude, and with more joy than a fugitive galley slave, escape from the oar to which I have been chain'd.

BRISK.

Master, Master, now's our time, for look by the

glimmering of yonder lamp, who comes along by the side of the wall.

BELLMOUR.

Her father, by all that's lucky; my dear Rovewell, let us drive off.

ROVEWELL.

No, I'll speak a good word to him for you.

BELLMOUR.

Not for the world; prithee come along.

[*Exeunt.*

Enter QUIDNUNC, *with a dark lanthorn.*

QUIDNUNC.

If the Grand Turk should actually commence open hostility, and the House-bug Tartars make a diversion upon the frontiers, why then it's my opinion, time will discover to us a great deal more of the matter.

WATCH. *(within)*

Past eleven o'clock, a cloudy night.

QUIDNUNC.

Hey! past eleven o'clock! 'Sbodikins, my brother Feeble will be gone to bed: but he shan't sleep till I have some chat with him. Hark'ye watchman, watchman.

Enter WATCHAN.

WATCH.

Call, master!

Quidnunc.

Ay, ſtep hither, ſtep hither: have you heard any news?

Watch.

News, maſter!

Quidnunc.

Ay, about the Pruſſians or the Ruſſians?

Watch.

Ruſſians, maſter!

Quidnunc.

Yes; or the movements in Pomerania?

Watch.

La, maſter, I know nothing---poor gentleman--- *(pointing to his head)* Good night to you maſter--- Paſt eleven o'clock. [*Exit* Watchman.

Quidnunc.

That man now has a place under the government, and you ſee how guarded he is. The diſcretion of office! His mouth is padlockt. Not a word: he won't ſpeak. But I am loſing time. (*knocks at the door*) Hazy weather (*looking up*); the wind's fix'd in that quarter, and we ſhan't have any mails this week to come. Come about good wind, do, come about.

Enter Betty.

Betty.

La, Sir, is it you?

Quid-

QUIDNUNC.
Is your master at home, Mrs. Betty?

BETTY.
Gone to bed, Sir.

QUIDNUNC.
Well, well, I'll step up to him.

BETTY.
Must not disturb him for the world, Sir.

QUIDNUNC.
Business of the utmost importance.

BETTY.
Pray consider, Sir, my master an't well.

QUIDNUNC.
Prithee be quiet, woman; I must see him.
[*Exeunt.*

Scene a ROOM *in* FEEBLE's HOUSE.

Enter FEEBLE *in his night-gown.*

FEEBLE.
I was just stepping into bed; bless my heart, what can this man want?---I know his voice: I hope no new misfortune brings him at this hour.

QUIDNUNC. (*within*)
Hold your tongue you foolish hussey,---he'll be glad to see me.---Brother Feeble,-- Brother Feeble!

FEEBLE.

Feeble.
What can be the matter?

Enter Quidnunc.

Quidnunc.
Brother Feeble, I give you joy. The Nabob's demolish'd. (*sings*) " Britons strike home, re-" venge," &c.

Feeble.
Lackaday, Mr. Quidnunc, how can you serve me thus?

Quidnunc.
Suraja Dowla is no more.

Feeble.
Poor man! he's stark staring mad.

Quidnunc.
Our men diverted themselves with killing their bullocks and their camels, till they diflodged the enemy from the octagon, and the counterscarp, and the bunglo.

Feeble.
I'll hear the rest to-morrow morning. Oh! I'm ready to die.

Quidnunc.
Odsheart man be of good chear. The new Nabob Jaffier Ally Cawn has acceded to a treaty; and the English Company have got all their rights in the Phirmaud and the Hushbulhoorums.

Feeble

Feeble.

But dear heart, Mr. Quidnunc, why am I to be disturb'd for this?

Quidnunc.

We had but two Seapoys killed, three Chokeys, four Gaul-walls, and two Zemidars. (*sings*) "Bri-
"tons never shall be slaves!"

Feeble.

Would not to-morrow morning do as well for this?

Quidnunc.

Light up your windows, man, light up your windows. Chandernagore is taken.

Feeble.

Well, well, I'm glad of it. Good night. (*going*)

Quidnunc.

Here, here's the Gazette.

Feeble.

Oh, I shall certainly faint. (*sits down*)

Quidnunc.

Ay, ay, sit down: I'll read it to you. (*reads*) nay, don't run away---I've more news to tell you, there's an account from Williamsburgh in America. The Superintendant of Indian affairs---

Feeble.

Dear Sir, dear Sir,---(*avoiding him*)

QUIDNUNC.

Has settled matters with the Cherokees---*(following him)*

FEEBLE.

Enough, enough,---*(avoiding him)*

QUIDNUNC.

In the same manner he did before with the Catabaws. *(after him)*

FEEBLE.

Well, well, your servant.---*(from him)*

QUIDNUNC.

So that the back inhabitants---*(after him)*

FEEBLE.

I wish you would let me be a quiet inhabitant in my own house.

QUIDNUNC.

So that the back inhabitants will now be secured by the Cherokees and the Catabaws.

FEEBLE.

You'd better go home, and think of appearing before the Commissioners.

QUIDNUNC.

Go home! no, no, I'll go and talk the matter over at our coffee-house.

FEEBLE.

FEEBLE.

Do so, do so.

QUIDNUNC. *(returning)*

Mr. Feeble,---I had a dispute about the balance of power.---Pray now can you tell---

FEEBLE.

I know nothing of the matter.

QUIDNUNC.

Well, another time will do for that---I have a great deal to say about that (*going, returns*) right, I had like to have forgot, there's an erratum in the last Gazette.

FEEBLE.

With all my heart.

QUIDNUNC.

Page 3, line 1, col. 1, and 3, for *bombs* read *booms*.

FEEBLE.

Read what you will.

QUIDNUNC.

Nay, but that alters the sense, you know. Well, now your servant. If I hear any more news I'll come and tell you.

FEEBLE.

For Heaven's sake no more.

Quidnunc.

I'll be with you before you're out of your first sleep.

Feeble.

Good-night, good-night. [*Runs off.*

Quidnunc.

I forgot to tell you: the Emperor of *Morocco* is dead. Brother Feeble, do you hear? (*bawls through the key-hole*) The Emperor of *Morocco* is dead. So, now I have made him happy, I'll go to our coffee-house, and make them all happy there. (*sings*) " Rule Britannia, Britannia rule the waves"---
[*Exit.*

Scene a Street: a shabby house in front, with a barber's pole, and the windows lighted up.

Enter Quidnunc.

Quidnunc.

Ha! friend Razor! He is a good subject, a true English heart. He makes a right use of a rejoicing night. Our victories are not thrown away upon him. Who knows but he may have heard more intelligence? (*knocks at the door*)

Razor. (*looking out of the window*)

Razor.

Anan!

Quidnunc.

Friend Razor.

T 2 Razor.

Razor.

My Mafter Quidnunc! I'm rejoicing for the news. Will you partake of a pipe? I'll open the door.

Quidnunc.

Not now, friend Razor.

Razor.

I've fomething to tell you; I'll come down.

Quidnunc.

This may be worth ftaying for: what can he have heard!

Enter Razor, *in a cap, a pipe in his mouth, and a tankard in his hand.*

Razor.

Say, here's to you, Mafter Quidnunc.

Quidnunc.

What have you heard? What have you heard?

Razor.

The Confumers of Oats are to meet next week.

Quidnunc.

Thofe Confumers of Oats have been meeting any time thefe ten years to my knowledge, and I never could find what they are about.

Razor.

Things an't right, I fear: its enough to pull down a body's fpirits--- *(drinks)*

No,

QUIDNUNC.

No, nothing to fear. I can tell you some good news. A certain great Potentate has not heard high mass the Lord knows when.

RAZOR.

That puts a body in spirits again. (*drinks*) Here, drink no wooden shoes.

QUIDNUNC.

With all my heart----(*drinks*) Good liquor this, Master Razor; of a cold night.

RAZOR.

Yes, I put a quartern of British brandy in my beer. Whu!---Do you know what a rebel my wife is?

QUIDNUNC.

A rebel!

RAZOR.

Ay, a rebel---I earned nineteen-pence halfpenny to-day, and she wanted to lay out all that great sum upon the children. Whu---but I bought those candles for the good of my country, to rejoice with as a body may say, a little *Virginy* for my pipe, and this sup of hot. Whu. Bitter cold.

QUIDNUNC.

Ay, you're an honest man, and if every body were like you and me, what a nation we should be!

RAZOR.

Very true! (*shakes his head*)

Quidnunc.

I can give you the Gazette to read.

Razor.

Can you! a thousand thanks. I'll take it home to you when I have done.---(*drinks and staggers*)

Quidnunc.

Friend Razor, you begin to be a little in for't.

Razor.

Yes, I have a whirligigg of a head. But a body shou'd take a cheering glass sometimes for the good of one's country.

Quidnunc.

Well, I shall be at home in half an hour!--- Hark'ye.

Razor.

Anan!

Quidnunc.

I have made a rare discovery. Florida will be able to supply Jamaica with peet for their winters firings. I had it from a deep politician.

Razor.

Ay! I am glad the poor people of Jamaica will have Florida peet to burn. They may now have a little firing in the winter. I don't know what the news is, but I have been rejoicing for the good of my country. I'll go and read the Gazette, to see a little what it's about. After all is said and done, O rare Old England! (*goes into his house*)

QUIDNUNC.

Ay! rare Old England! ſtrong enough ſtill for all our enemies; we ſhan't be a bankrupt nation yet, and that's ſome comfort---I will now go and ſee who is up at our coffee-houſe, and diſcuſs points with our political club. [*Exit.*

Scene the UPHOLSTERER'S HOUSE.

Enter HARRIET *and* BELLMOUR.

HARRIET.

I don't know what to ſay Mr. Bellmour. It is difficult to refuſe you. A heart touched as mine has been, cannot eaſily reſolve to give you a moment's uneaſineſs. And yet your propoſal---

BELLMOUR.

It is a fair and honourable propoſal. It ſprings from eſteem and true affection. You cannot doubt my honour.

HARRIET.

No, Mr. Bellmour: to form an ill opinion of you is impoſſible: but you may judge otherwiſe of me. What will be your ſentiment hereafter, ſhould I now be wanting in that duty, which I owe my father?

BELLMOUR.

You have promiſed me your hand. Your father unreaſonably withholds it. To all his juſt commands you owe obedience: but when the whims and oddities of a wild diſordered imagination have no other tendency than to involve you in the ruin, which has unhappily befallen himſelf, why muſt you

be

be a sacrifice to his humours? And why must I be rendered miserable, Harriet?

Harriet.

But then, to comply with your solicitations, and leave my father in a scene of trouble and misfortune---

Bellmour.

It will be the means of making his misfortunes lighter. In his moments of reflection he will feel with pleasure that his conduct has not prevented your happiness. You will then have the means of behaving to him with gratitude and generosity.

Harriet.

But my uncle Feeble what will he say?

Bellmour.

You may depend upon his approbation. I will be answerable for it: a coach is now waiting at the end of the street to receive you. Harriet, will you refuse me your hand?

Harriet.

Must I give it? I don't know what to say. Why don't you take it?

Enter Termagant.

Termagant.

Undone, undone! Oh! my stars, I am all over in such a tribulation. The old newsmonger is coming.

BELLMOUR.

Diſtraction!---what brings him here ſo ſoon?

TERMAGANT.

Oh! Mr. Bellmour, this overpowers me quite. What can I ſay to him?

TERMAGANT.

The devil is in it: this is ſuch a croſs accident. I am at my wit's end. No; that's not true neither. I have it: I'll tell you what to do. Don't *fruſtrate* yourſelf, ma'am. Away, Mr. Bellmour, into that room. He never will find you out. Away, fly Mr. Bellmour. Do you ſtay, Miſs Harriet, and talk to the old gentleman. When you have ſeen him, and wiſhed him a good night, you may ſlip down ſtairs, and ſo make the beſt of your way to the coach at the end of the ſtreet---I ſhall find ſome nonſenſe news for the old politician, and when I get him to bed, Mr. Bellmour may follow you, madam. Why don't you go, Mr. Bellmour? You are enough to ruin a body.

BELLMOUR.

I am gone, I'll be govern'd by you.   [*Exit.*

HARRIET.

Oh! Termagant, I ſhall never be able to go through this buſineſs: my ſtrength fails me.

TERMAGANT.

Have courage, madam. I hear him coming. Let me ſee: have I nothing in my pocket to amuſe him? Yes, yes; this will do; never fear, Miſs Harriet. Now let the old walking Gazette come as ſoon as he will. I am ready for him, I warrant me.

Enter QUIDNUNC.

QUIDNUNC.

Fy upon it, fy upon it! All the coffee-houses shut up. Harriet, what makes you out of bed at this late hour?

TERMAGANT.

A rejoicing night, Sir: but this love of her country does not agree much with her. She is quite sick for the good of Old England----Speak to him, madam.

HARRIET.

I am frightened out of my wits, Termagant. I shall faint.

QUIDNUNC.

It is well we have not a female Parliament. Late debates would be too much for her spirits. Get to rest, Harriet; get to bed.

HARRIET.

I wish you a good night, Sir. [*Exit.*

TERMAGANT. *(going with her)*
This will do purely, ma'am.

QUIDNUNC.

Where is my *Salmon's Gazetteer*, and my maps of the world? I must see all these places before I sleep. They are in that room, I believe.

(going towards the door)

TERMAGANT. *(returning)*
What is he about now?---Sir, Sir, Sir---Here has been

been Mr.---I forget his name---He that writes letters in the news-papers about paying off the national debt---Mr. Ruin, Sir-- he has been here, and he desires you'll read his new project, and give him your thoughts about it.

Quidnunc.

Give me the paper; let me see it.

Termagant.

The deuce fetch it. Here is something that so catches and hitches in my pocket. There, there it is. (*gives him the paper, and drops a letter*) Had not you better go and read it in bed, Sir? Bed is a pure place for thinking.

Quidnunc.

So it is Termagant. Go and lock the street door, and then---

Termagant.

Yes, Sir. I'll be with you in an instant. And so now I shall get Miss Harriet clear off--- [*Exit.*

Quidnunc.

Po! the foolish jade! this is an old paper. Hey; what have we here? (*takes up a letter*) How, how is this? " *To Miss Harriet Quidnunc.*" Let me see; let me see. (*reads eagerly*)---" *My dearest Harriet---no longer in*
" *suspence---given you every proof---constancy and love*
" *----your happiness---father's obstinacy*"----Here's a
" villain for you----*convey you to a family*"----Will you so?--." *and there you may remain in perfect secu-*
" *rity, till you resign your person to the arms of your*
" *eternal admirer---Bellmour.*"---So, so! This is as good as a state paper: here is Machiavel at work: Why daughter Harriet, where is she? Harriet I say

say *(bawls violently)* A Plot! A Conspiracy! Gunpowder Treason! Robbery! Murder!

Enter TERMAGANT.

TERMAGANT.

Law, Sir, what is the matter now?

QUIDNUNC.

I have found you out, traitress. Here is Mr. Bellmour's letter. Rob me of my daughter! where is Harriet? Search the house; call the watch; alarm the neighbours; I'll go and rouze the whole world. [*Exit.*

TERMAGANT.

I am all over in such a *quandary*. Dear me! what shall I do?

BELLMOUR. *(peeping in)*

Blundering busy-body! you have marr'd all. This is your doing. What possessed you to give him that letter?

TERMAGANT.

I did not do it on purpose; as I hope for mercy, I did not. Don't be angry with me, Sir. *(cries)*

BELLMOUR.

Why do you screem so? Is the woman crazy?

TERMAGANT.

I did not go for to give it him; *(cries)* I would have seen him gibbeted first. I found the letter in my mistress's bed-chamber, and my CURIOSITY did make me peep into it. Says my CURIOSITY, " Now
" Ter-

" Termagant you may gratify yourself by finding
" out the contents of that letter; which you have
" had such a plaguy itching for." My Curiosity
did say so; and then I own my respect for my
mistress did say to me, " Hussey, how dare you to
" meddle with what does not belong to you? Keep
" your distance, and let your mistress's secrets
" alone." And then upon that in comes my unlucky Curiosity again, " Read it, I tell you, Ter-
" magant; a woman of spirit should know every
" thing."---Let it alone, you jade," says my Respect; " its as much as your place is worth."----
" What significations a place with an old bankrup-
" per?" says my Curiosity, " there's more places
" than one; and so read it, I tell you, Termagant"---
And I did so. (*cries bitterly*) I did read it, what
could I do, Heaven help me? I did read it; I don't
go to deny it, I don't, I don't.---

(*cries very bitterly*)

BELLMOUR.
Hush; have you a mind to ruin me?

TERMAGANT.
And after I had read it, thinks me I, I'll give it
safe into Miss Harriet's own hand, and her crazy old
father shan't see it; and so as my ill stars would
have it, as I was giving him a newspaper, I run my
hand full into the lyon's mouth. (*cries*)

A loud rap at the door.

BELLMOUR.
There, there; you have rouzed the neighbourhood, and I shall be detected.

QUID-

QUIDNUNC. *(within)*
Bring him along; bring the villain in.

BELLMOUR.
Death and distraction! our whole scheme is ruin'd.

Enter QUIDNUNC, *leading* HARRIET.

QUIDNUNC.
Walk in, Jezabel; I have caught you. Lead that traitor this way.

TERMAGANT.
Oh! my dear, young mistress. *(taking her by the hand)*

QUIDNUNC.
Let me see the plunderer, that would rob me of my daughter.

WATCHMAN. *(within)*
Ay, ay; this way, Sir.

RAZOR. *(within)*
Rob my master Quidnunc! secure him; knock him down.

Enter RAZOR *and* WATCHMEN, *leading in* ROVEWELL.

WATCHMAN.
We have him fast: now who are you?

RAZOR.

RAZOR.

Ay, who are you? Whence come you?

QUIDNUNC.

Away with him to the round-house. I'll go with him: I may meet a Parliament-man in the round-house to tell me some news. What business have you with my daughter?

ROVEWELL.

Wounds! if your daughter will walk the streets at this late hour, a gentleman has a right to confider her as fair game.

BELLMOUR.

Rovewell, was this well done? What unlucky planet sent you this way?

QUIDNUNC.

How! Bellmour here! the enemy in my very camp.

BELLMOUR.

I am no enemy, Sir. My designs are honourable. You see I scorn to conceal myself.

QUIDNUNC.

I see you do: a bold-faced ruffian! Here, seize 'em both. I charge them both. Away with them.

RAZOR.

Put 'em both in irons; handcuff 'em; secure 'em this moment.

BELL-

BELLMOUR.

Don't frighten the lady: here is my sword: I surrender.

RAZOR. (*strips off his coat*)

Lay hold of that traitor. (*attacking* Rovewell) Seize him; bind him fast.

ROVEWELL.

Dastards! villains! stand off.

RAZOR.

Fall on him neighbours; that's right; now we have him. [Rovewell *is seized.*

ROVEWELL.

Rascals, you have overpower'd me.

RAZOR.

Victory!---I have conquered. (*puts on his coat*) Here, Master Quidnunc, I have brought you back the Gazette.

TERMAGANT.

I believes as sure as any thing that he is a *highwareman*, and as how it was he that robbed the mail.

QUIDNUNC.

Rob the mail, and stop all the news! search him: he may have the letters belonging to the mail in his pocket. Here, here; here's a letter. What is it? (*reads*) "To Mr. Abraham Quidnunc." How! how is this? (*opens and reads*)---" *Your dutiful son, John Quidnunc.*" Quidnunc! is that your name?

ROVEWELL.

Quidnunc is my name, Sir, and Rovewell was but affumed; a travelling title.

QUIDNUNC.

And are you my fon?

RAZOR. *(looking at him)*

Oh! my dear Sir; it is he, (*embraces him, and powders him all over*) it is he fure enough---I remember the mole on his cheek. I fhaved his firft beard.

QUIDNUNC.

What, juft returned from the Weft Indies?

ROVEWELL.

Even fo, and the owner of a rich plantation.

QUIDNUNC.

By being a great politician, I fuppofe.

ROVEWELL.

By marrying a planter's widow. I have now fortune fufficient to afford you, Sir, the comforts and enjoyments of life.

RAZOR.

This is true joy. You'll let Razor fhave you, I hope, mafter.

ROVEWELL.

Honeft Razor, I fhan't forget you. This is a lucky difcovery. I have both ability and inclination, Sir, to convince you that I know and feel the duty I owe to a father. I shall now atone for the irregularities of my youth. Bellmour, give me your hand. He is an honest fellow, Sir, and if you will bestow my sister upon him, you will add to the joy of this unexpected meeting.

Quidnunc.

Why, I think it will make a good paragraph in the papers.

Termagant.

There, Madam, *calcine* your person to him.

Rovewell.

What do you hesitate, Bellmour? Here, take her, man; take her at once. I hope to know her better, and to find that she is worthy of so honest a fellow.

Quidnunc.

Pray now, what are the Spaniards doing in the Bay of Honduras?

Rovewell.

Truce with politicks for the present, if you please, Sir. We will think of our own affairs, before we concern ourselves about the ballance of power.

Razor.

With all my heart: I am pure happy now.

Come, Master Quidnunc, now with news have done,
Bless'd in your wealth, your daughter and your son.
May discord cease; faction no more be seen;
Be *high* and *low* for Country, King, and Queen.

The
Old Maid

THE
OLD MAID;
A
COMEDY,
In TWO ACTS.

Performed at the

THEATRE ROYAL

IN

DRURY-LANE.

Tempus erit, quo tu, quæ nunc excludis amantem,
Frigida Desertâ Nocte jacebis Anus.
Ovid.

Dramatis Personæ.

MEN.

Clerimont,	Mr. Obrien.
Capt. Cape,	Mr. King.
Mr. Harlow,	Mr. Kennedy.
Mr. Heartwell,	Mr. Phillips.
Footman,	Mr. Castle.

WOMEN.

Mrs. Harlow,	Miss Haughton.
Miss Harlow,	Mrs. Kennedy.
Trifle,	Miss Hippisley.

THE
OLD MAID.

ACT the FIRST.

Enter Mrs. HARLOW *and Miſs* HARLOW.

Mrs. HARLOW.

MY dear ſiſter, let me tell you---

Miſs HARLOW.

But, my dear ſiſter, let me tell you it is in vain; you can ſay nothing that will have any effect.

Mrs. HARLOW.

Not if you won't hear me; only hear me.

Miſs HARLOW.

Oh! ma'am, I know you love to hear yourſelf talk, and ſo pleaſe yourſelf; talk on at your uſual rate, if your fancy ſo inclines you; but I have taken my reſolution, and nothing ſhall alter it.

Mrs. HARLOW.

And yet, upon due reflection your mind may change.

Miſs Harlow.
Never, ſiſter, never.

Mrs. Harlow.
You can't be ſure of that, ſiſter; when you have conſidered every thing---

Miſs Harlow.
Upon no conſideration.

Mrs. Harlow.
You don't know how that may be: recollect, ſiſter, that you are no chicken: you are not now in that ſprightly ſeaſon of life, when giddineſs and folly are excuſable, nay becoming. Your age, ſiſter---

Miſs Harlow.
Age, ma'am---

Mrs. Harlow.
Do but hear me, ſiſter; do but hear me. A perſon of your years---

Miſs Harlow.
My years, ſiſter!---Upon my word---

Mrs. Harlow.
Nay, no offence, ſiſter---

Miſs Harlow.
But there is offence, ma'am: I don't underſtand what you mean by it. Always thwarting me with my years; my years, indeed! when perhaps, ma'am, if I was to die of old age, ſome folks might have reaſon to look about them.

Mrs. Harlow.

She feels it, I fee---oh! how I delight in mortifying her---(*afide*)---fifter, if I did not love you, I am fure I fhould not talk to you in this manner. But how can you make fo unkind a return as to alarm me about myfelf?---In fome fixteen or eighteen years after you, to be fure, I own I fhall begin to think of making my will. How could you be fo fevere?---

Mifs Harlow.

Some fixteen or eighteen years, ma'am!---if you you would own the truth, ma'am,---I believe ma'am,---you would not find, ma'am, that the difparity, ma'am, is not fo very great, ma'am---

Mrs. Harlow.

Well! I vow paffion becomes you inordinately: It blends a few rofes with the lillies of your cheek, and---

Mifs Harlow.

And though you are married to my brother, ma'am, I would have you to know, ma'am, that you are not thereby any way authorifed, to take unbecoming liberties with his fifter. I am independent of my brother, ma'am: my fortune is in my own hands, ma'am, and ma'am---

Mrs. Harlow.

Well! do you know when your blood circulates a little, that I think you look mighty well? But you was in the wrong not to marry at my age. Sweet three and twenty! you can't conceive what a deal of
good

good it would have done your temper and your fpirits, if you had married early.

Mifs Harlow.
Infolent! provoking, female malice!

Mrs. Harlow.
But to be waiting till it is almoft too late in the day, and force one's felf to fay ftrange things; with the tongue and heart at variance all the time----" I don't mind the hideous men" " I am very happy as I am."---" I don't defire to change my condition"--- and while thofe words are at your tongue's end, the heart murmurs inwardly, and flutters upon the tenter-hooks of expectation.

Mifs Harlow.
I upon tenter-hooks!

Mrs. Harlow.
And to be at this work of four grapes, till one is turned of three and forty!

Mifs Harlow.
Three and forty, ma'am!---I defire, fifter---I defire, ma'am---three and forty, ma'am!

Mrs. Harlow.
Nay---nay---nay---don't be angry; don't blame me; blame my hufband; he is your own brother, and he knows your age: he told me fo.

Mifs Harlow.
Oh! ma'am, I fee your drift: but you need not give yourfelf thofe airs, ma'am---the men don't fee with your eyes, ma'am---years, indeed!---Three and

and forty, truly!---I'll assure you---upon my word---
very fine!---But I see plainly, ma'am, what you
are at---Mr. Clerimont, madam!---Mr. Clerimont,
sister! that's what frets you. A young husband,
ma'am; younger than your husband, ma'am: Mr.
Clerimont, let me tell you---

Enter TRIFLE.

TRIFLE.

Oh! rare news, ma'am, charming news: we have
got another letter.

Miss HARLOW.

From whom?---from Mr. Clerimont?---where
is it?

TRIFLE.

Yes, ma'am! from Mr. Clerimont, ma'am.

Miss HARLOW.

Let me see it; let me see it; quick; quick;
(reads)
" Madam,
" The honour of a letter from you has so filled
" my mind with joy and gratitude, that I want
" words of force to reach but half my meaning. I
" can only say that you have revived a heart that
" was expiring for you, and now beats for you
" alone"---

There sister, mind that! years indeed!
(reads to herself)

Mrs. HARLOW.

I wish you joy, sister: I wish I had not gone to
Rane-

Ranelagh with her last week. Who could have thought that her faded beauties would have made such an impression? (*aside*)

Miss Harlow.

Mind here again, sister. --- (*reads*) " Ever since I
" had the good fortune of seeing you at Ranelagh,
" your idea has been ever present to me; and
" since you now give me leave, I shall, without
" delay, wait upon your brother. The terms he may
" think proper to demand, I shall readily subscribe to;
" for to be your slave is dearer to me than liberty. I
" have the honour to remain

" The humblest of your admirers,

" Clerimont."

There, sister!

Mrs. Harlow

Well! I wish you joy again: but remember I tell you, take care what you do. He is young, and of course giddy and inconstant.

Miss Harlow.

He is warm, passionate, and tender.

Mrs. Harlow.

But you don't know how long that may last; and here are you going to break off a very suitable match, which all your friends liked and approved, a match with captain Cape, who to be sure---

Miss Harlow.

Don't name captain Cape, I beseech you, don't name him.

Mrs.

Mrs. Harlow.

Captain Cape, let me tell you, is not to be despised. He has acquired by his voyages to India a very pretty fortune: has a charming box of a house upon Hackney-Marsh, and is of an age every way suitable to you.

Miss Harlow.

There again now!---age! age! age! for ever!---years---years---my years! But I tell you once for all, Mr. Clerimont does not see with your eyes. I am determined to hear no more of captain Cape. Odious Hackney-Marsh! ah! sister, you would be glad to see me married in a middling way.

Mrs. Harlow,

I, sister!---I am sure nobody will rejoice more at your preferment. I am resolved never to visit her if Mr. Clerimont marries her. (*aside*)

Miss Harlow.

To cut the matter short, sister, Mr. Clerimont has won my heart: young, handsome, rich, town house, country house, equipage! To him, and only him will I surrender myself. Three and forty, indeed!---ha! ha!---you see, my dear, dear sister, that these features are still regular and blooming; that the love-darting eye has not quite forsook me; and that I have made a conquest which your boasted youth might be vain of.

Mrs. Harlow.

Oh! ma'am, I beg you pardon, if I have taken too much liberty, it has all arisen from affection and regard: your good is all I aim at, sister.

Miss Harlow.

I humbly thank you for your advice, my sweet dear friendly sister; but don't envy me, I beg you won't; don't fret yourself; you can't conceive what a deal of good serenity of mind will do your health. I'll go and write an answer directly to this charming, charming letter. Sister, yours. I shall be glad to see you, sister, at my house in Hill-street, when I am Mrs. Clerimont. And remember what I tell you: some faces retain their bloom and beauty longer than you imagine, my dear sister. Come, Trifle, let me fly this moment. Sister, your servant.

[*Exit with* Trifle.

Mrs. Harlow.

Your servant, my dear!---Well! I am determined to lead the gayest life in nature, if she marries Clerimont.----I'll have a new equipage, that's one thing: and I"l have greater routs than her, that's another: Positively, I must outshine her there; and I'll keep up a polite enmity with her; go and see her, may be once or twice in a winter; Ma'am, I am really so " hurried with such a number of acquaintances, that " I can't possibly find time.". And then to provoke her, " I wish you joy, sister, I hear you are breeding." Ha! ha!---that will so mortify her---" I " wish it may be a boy, sister." Ha! ha!---And then when her husband begins to despise her; " really, sister, I pity you; had you taken my ad- " vice, and married the India captain---your case is " a compassionate one"---Compassion is so insolent when a body feels none at all. Ha! ha! it is the finest way of insulting.

Enter

Enter Mr. HARLOW.

Mr. HARLOW.

So, my dear; how are my sister's affairs going on?

Mrs. HARLOW.

Why, my dear, she has had another letter from Mr. Clerimont. Did you ever hear of such a strange unaccountable thing patched up in a hurry here?

Mr. HARLOW.

Why it is sudden, to be sure.

Mrs. HARLOW.

Upon my word, I think you had better advise her not to break off with captain Cape.

Mr. HARLOW.

No, not I---I wish she may be married to one or other of them. Her temper is really grown so very sour, and there is such eternal wrangling between you both, that I wish to see her in her own house, for the peace and quiet of mine.

Mrs. HARLOW.

Do you know this Mr. Clerimont?

Mr. HARLOW.

No; but I have heard of the family. There is. very fine fortune. I wish he may hold his intention

Mrs. HARLOW.

I wish he may, but I doubt it.

Mr.

Mr. Harlow.

And truly so do I; for between ourselves, I see no charms in my sister.

Mrs. Harlow.

For my part I can't comprehend it. How she could strike his fancy, is to me the most astonishing thing: After this, I shall be surprised at nothing.

Mr. Harlow.

Well! strange things do happen. So she is but married out of the way, I am satisfied. An old maid in a house is the devil.

Enter a Servant.

Servant.

Mr. Clerimont, Sir, to wait on you.

Mr. Harlow.

Shew him in. (*Exit* Servant) How comes this visit, pray?

Mrs. Harlow.

My sister wrote to him to explain himself to you. The affair seems now to grow serious. The gentleman seems in earnest, and in a hurry too. Well, I suppose he wants to talk to you: I'll leave you to yourselves. (*aside as she goes out*) The man must be mad to think of her. He must have a strange taste indeed. [*Exit.*

Enter

Enter CLERIMONT.

Mr. HARLOW.
Your moſt obedient, Sir: be pleaſed to walk in.

CLERIMONT.
I preſume, Sir, you are no ſtranger to the buſineſs that occaſions this viſit.

Mr. HARLOW.
Sir, the honour you do me and my family---

CLERIMONT.
Oh! Sir, to be allied to your family by ſo tender a tie as a marriage with your ſiſter, will at once reflect a credit upon me, and conduce to my happineſs in the moſt eſſential point. I adore your ſiſter, Sir: my ſentiments are not to be expreſſed: ſhe charmed me at the very firſt ſight.

Mr. HARLOW. *(aſide)*
The devil ſhe did!

CLERIMONT.
The ſenſibility of her countenance, the elegance of her figure, the ſweetneſs of her manner---

Mr. HARLOW.
Sir, you are pleaſed to---compliment!

CLERIMONT.
Compliment! I ſpeak the language of the heart. Where merit is ſo apparent, ſo tranſcending all praiſe, he muſt have great ſkill in flattery, who can give an air of compliment to that juſtice, which your ſiſter claims from all.

Mr.

Mr. Harlow.

The sweetness of my sister's manner. (*aside*) Ha! ha!

Clerimont.

I saw her, for the first time, a few nights ago at Ranelagh: though there was a croud of beauties in the room, thronging and pressing all around, yet she shone amongst them with superior lustre. She was walking arm in arm with another lady. No opportunity offered for me to form an acquaintance amidst the hurry and bustle of the place. I enquired their names as they were going into their chariot: I was told they were Mrs. and Miss Harlow. From that moment she won my heart. At one glance I became the willing captive of her beauty.

Mr. Harlow.

A very candid declaration, Sir!---how can this be? The bloom has been off the peach any time these fifteen years, to my knowledge. (*aside*)---You see my sister with a favourable eye, Sir.

Clerimont.

A favourable eye! He must greatly want discernment, who has not a quick perception of her merit.

Mr. Harlow.

You do her a great deal of honour. But this affair---is it not somewhat sudden, Sir?

Clerimont.

I grant it. You may indeed be surprized at it, Sir; nor should I have been hardy enough to make any overtures to you,---at least yet awhile,---if she herself had not condescended to listen to my passion. She

She has authorized me under her own fair hand to apply to her brother for his confent.

Mr. Harlow.

I fhall be very ready, Sir, to give my approbation to my fifter's happinefs.

Clerimont.

No doubt you will. But let me not cherifh an unavailing flame, a flame that already lights up all my tendereft paffions.

Mr. Harlow.

To you, Sir, there can be no exception. I am not altogether a ftranger to your family and fortune. His language is warm, confidering my fifter's age; but I won't hurt her preferment. (*afide*)---You will pardon me, Sir, if I obferve one thing : you are, as one may fay, juft coming into life. Have you left the Univerfity ?

Clerimont.

Left it, Sir?---above a year. I am almoft two and twenty.

Mr. Harlow.

And yet, this is a delicate point : have you confulted your friends ?

Clerimont.

I have : my uncle, Mr. Heartwell, who propofes to leave me a very handfome addition to my fortune, which is confiderable already, he, Sir---

Mr. Harlow.

Well, Sir, if he has no objection, I can have none.

Clerimont.

He has none, Sir; he has given his consent; he desires me to lose no time. I will bring him to pay you a visit. He approves my choice. You shall have it out of his own mouth. Name your hour, and he shall attend you.

Mr. Harlow.

Any time to-day. I shall stay at home on purpose.

Clerimont.

In the evening I will conduct him hither. In the mean time I feel an attachment here: the lady, Sir---

Mr. Harlow.

Oh! you want to see my sister. I will send her to you, Sir, this instant. I beg your pardon for leaving you alone. Ha! ha! who could have thought of her making a conquest at last? [*Exit.*

Clerimont.

Your politeness, Sir, upon this occasion, will lay me under the most lasting obligation.---Now, Clerimont, now your heart may rest content: your doubts and fears may all subside, and joy and rapture take their place. Miss Harlow shall be mine: she receives my vows; she approves my passion. (*sings and dances*) Soft! here she comes---her very appearance controuls my wildest hopes, and hushes my proud heart into respect and silent admiration.

Enter Mrs. Harlow.

Mrs. Harlow.

I beg your pardon, Sir, I intrude, perhaps.

Clerimont.

Madam, (*bows respectfully*) you never can intrude, Madam. You---you must be ever welcome.

Mrs. Harlow.

I thought Mr. Harlow was here, Sir.

Clerimont.

Madam, he is but just gone. How a single glance of that deluding eye overaws and checks each wish that flutters in my heart. (*aside*)

Mrs. Harlow.

I wonder he would leave you alone, Sir. That is not so polite in his own house.

Clerimont.

How her modesty throws a veil over her inclinations!---My tongue faulters!---I can't speak to her.
(*aside*)

Mrs. Harlow.

He seems in confusion. A pretty man too!---That this should be my sister's luck!--- (*aside*)

Clerimont.

Madam!---(*embarrassed*)

Mrs. Harlow.

I imagine you have been talking to him on the subject of the letter you sent this morning.

Clerimont.

Madam, I have presumed to---

Mrs. Harlow.

You are the only person, Sir, that will call it presumption. Mr. Harlow has no objection, I hope.

Clerimont.

She hopes! Heavens bless her for the word---(*aside*)---Madam, he has frankly consented, if his sister will do me that honour.

Mrs. Harlow.

You do his sister a great deal of honour, Sir,---(*aside*) a great deal more than she deserves, if he knew all.

Clerimont.

How her modesty makes her turn aside that lovely countenance!---Mr. Harlow, Madam, encouraged me to entertain a gleam of hope.

Mrs. Harlow.

I think you need not despair, Sir, if I may venture to hazard my sentiment.

Clerimont.

No doubt you may.

Mrs. Harlow.

Then, without doubt---(*turns away*) Her success is too provoking---(*turns to him*) I believe, Sir,---I think you may entertain some degree of hope.

Clerimont.

How coyly she pronounces it!---" Oh! sweet reluctant amorous delay."---Madam, you make me happy.

happy. If any thing could add to the ardour of my affection, you have done it. (*turns from her*) Generous Miss Harlow!

Mrs. Harlow.

A proposal so honourable on your part, claims attention, and cannot easily be rejected; Mr. Harlow has too much regard for his sister; and the whole family hold themselves much obliged to you.

Clerimont.

Madam, this extreme condescension has added rapture to the sentiments I felt before: it shall be the endeavour of my life to prove deserving of the amiable object I have dared to aspire to.

Mrs. Harlow.

Sir, I make no doubt of your sincerity. I have already declared my sentiments. You know Mr. Harlow's; and if my sister gives her approbation, nothing will be wanting to conclude this business. If no difficulties arise from her-----her temper is uncertain---as to my consent, Sir, your air, your manner have commanded it. Sir, your most obedient: I'll send my sister to you. [*Exit.*

Clerimont.

Madam, (*bowing*) I shall endeavour to repay this goodness with excess of gratitude. She is an angel!---and yet, stupid that I am, I could not give vent to the tenderness with which my heart is ready to dissolve. It is ever so with sincere and generous love; it fills the soul with rapture, and then denies the power of uttering what we so exquisitely feel. Generous Miss Harlow! who could thus see thro' my confusion, interpret all appearances favourably, and with a dignity superior to her sex's

little

little arts, forego the idle ceremonies of coquetting, teazing, and tormenting her admirer. I hear somebody. Oh! here comes Miſtreſs Harlow: what a gloom ſits upon her features!---She aſſumes authority here I find. But I'll endeavour by inſinuation and reſpect to make her my friend, or at leaſt to ſoften prejudices, and get the better of that ſour, ill-natured temper.

Enter Miſs HARLOW.

Miſs HARLOW.
My ſiſter has told me, Sir---

CLERIMONT.
Ma'am---(*bowing chearfully*)

Miſs HARLOW.
He is a ſweet figure, (*aſide*)

CLERIMONT.
She rather looks like Miſs Harlow's mother than her ſiſter-in-law---(*aſide*)

Miſs HARLOW.
He ſeems abaſh'd----his reſpect is the cauſe----(*aſide*)---My ſiſter told me, Sir, that you was here. I beg pardon for making you wait ſo long.

CLERIMONT.
Oh, ma'am, (*bows*) the gloom diſappears from her face, but the lines of ill-nature remain. (*aſide*)

Miſs HARLOW.
In his confuſion I ſee the ardour of his paſſion.---He has not recovered himſelf!---I'll cheer him with

affability---(*aside*)---Sir, the letter you was pleased to send, my sister has seen, and---

Clerimont.
And has assured me that she has no objection.

Miss Harlow.
I am glad of that, Sir---I was afraid---

Clerimont.
No objection. And Mr. Harlow---I have seen him too. He has honoured me with his consent. Now, madam, the only doubt remains with you. May I be permitted to hope---

Miss Harlow.
Sir, you appear like a gentleman,---and---

Clerimont.
Madam, believe me, never was love more sincere, more justly founded on esteem, or kindled into higher admiration.

Miss Harlow.
Sir, with the rest of the family I hold myself much obliged to you, and---

Clerimont.
Obliged!---'tis I that am obliged. There is no merit on my side: it is the consequence of impressions made upon my heart; and what heart can resist such beauty, such various graces!

Miss Harlow.
The warmth of your expression, Sir---I wish my sister heard him. (*aside*) I am afraid you are lavish

of your praise; and the short date of your love, Sir---

Clerimont.

It will burn with unabating ardor. The same charms that first inspired it, will for ever cherish, and add new fuel to the flame.---You cannot doubt me, Madam: no, you will not harbour an ungenerous suspicion. You use this stile, to put my sincerity to the proof. That, Madam, I perceive is your aim: but could you read the feelings of my heart, you would not thus cruelly keep me in suspence.

Miss Harlow.

Heavens! if my sister saw my power over him ---(*aside*)---A little suspence cannot be deem'd unreasonable. Marriage is an important affair; an affair for life; and some caution you will allow to be necessary.

Clerimont.

Madam!---(*disconcerted*)---Oh! I dread the sourness of her look! (*aside*)

Miss Harlow.

One thing, Sir, you will permit me to observe. You seem to dwell chiefly on articles of external and superficial merit; whereas the more valuable qualities of the mind, prudence, good sense, a well-regulated conduct---

Clerimont.

Oh! Ma'am, I am not inattentive to those matters: she has a notable household understanding, I warrant her----(*aside*)----But let me intreat you, Madam, to do justice to my principles, and believe that

that never yet a fond, fond heart declared itself with more sincerity.

Miss Harlow.

Sir, I will frankly own that I have been trying you all this time, and from henceforth all doubts are banished.

Clerimont.

Your words recall me to new life. I shall for ever study to merit this goodness. But your fair sister, do you think I can depend upon her consent? May I flatter myself she will not change her mind?

Miss Harlow.

My sister cannot be insensible of your merit, and the honour you do her and the whole family. And, Sir, as far as I can act with propriety in the affair, I will endeavour to keep them all in a disposition to favour your pretensions.

Clerimont.

Madam---*(bows.)*

Miss Harlow.

You have an interest in my breast that will be busy for you.

Clerimont.

I am eternally devoted to you, Madam---*(bows.)*

Miss Harlow.

How modest, and yet how expressive he is!
(Aside.)

Clerimont.

Madam, I shall be for ever sensible of this extreme condescension. I shall think no pains too great to prove the gratitude and esteem I bear you. I beg my compliments to Mr. Harlow. I shall be here with my uncle in the evening; as early as possible I shall come. My respects to your sister, Ma'am---and pray, Madam, keep her in my interest---Madam, your most obedient---I have managed the motherly lady finely, I think (*aside*)
[*Bows, and Exit.*

Miss Harlow.

What will my sister say now? I shall hear no more of her taunts. A malicious thing! I fancy she now sees that your giddy flirts are not always the highest beauties. Set her up, indeed! Had she but heard him, the dear man! what sweet things he said! and what sweet things he looked. Well, I am enchanted with him. I shall love him to distraction.

Enter Mrs. Harlow.

Mrs. Harlow.

Well, sister!---how!---what does he say?

Miss Harlow.

Say, sister!---Every thing that is charming: he is the prettiest man! and so polite, so sensible, so elegant, so every thing that is agreeable!

Mrs. Harlow.

Well! I am glad of it. But all's well that ends well.

Miss Harlow.

Envy, sister! Envy, and downright malice!---Oh! had you heard all the tender things he uttered, and with that extasy too! that tenderness! that delight restrained by modesty!

Mrs. Harlow.

All that is very true: but still I feel, methinks, as if every thing was not right: I can't well explain myself; but there is to me something odd in the whole business.

Miss Harlow.

Oh! I don't doubt but you will say so. You will find, however, that I have beauty enough left to make some noise in the world. The men, sister, are the best judges of female beauty. Don't concern yourself about the affair, sister: the men are the best judges; leave it all to them.

Mrs. Harlow.

But only think of a lover you never saw but once at Ranelagh.

Miss Harlow.

Very true! but even then I saw what work I made in his heart. Don't you remember how he followed us up and down the room? Oh! I am in raptures with him, and he is in raptures with me, and in a few days, sister, Mrs. Clerimont will be glad to see you.

Enter Mr. Harlow.

Mr. Harlow.

So, sister! how stand matters now?

Miss Harlow.

As I could wish. I shall no more be a trouble to you. He has declared himself in the most warm and vehement manner; tho' my sister has her doubts; she is a good friend, she is afraid of my success.

Mrs. Harlow.

Pray, sister, don't think so meanly of me. I understand that sneer, Ma'am.

Miss Harlow.
And I understand you too, Ma'am.

Mr. Harlow.

Come, come, I desire we may have no quarrelling. You two are always wrangling. But when you are separated, it is to be hoped you will then be more amicable. Things are now in a fair way. Tho', sister, let me tell you I am afraid our India friend will think himself ill treated.

Mrs. Harlow.

That's what I fear too: that's my reason for speaking. Captain Cape, in my opinion, will have reason to think himself ill used.

Miss Harlow.

Oh! never throw away a thought on him. Mr. Clerimont has my heart; and now I think I am settled for life, sister---I love to plague her *(aside)* ---I say, sister, whatever doubts you may have, you will see me settled for life, for life, for life, my dear sister.

Enter

Enter SERVANT.

SERVANT.

Dinner is ferved, Sir.

Mr. HARLOW.

Very well! come, fifter, I give you joy. Let us in to dinner.

Mifs HARLOW.

Oh! vulgar!---I can't eat---I muft go and drefs my head over again, and do a thoufand things;---for I am determined I'll look this afternoon as well as ever I can. [*Exit.*

Mrs. HARLOW.

Is not all this amazing, my dear? her head is turned.

Mr. HARLOW.

Well, let it all pafs: don't you mind it: don't you fay any thing. Let her get married if fhe can. I am fure I fhall rejoice at it.

Mrs. HARLOW.

And upon my word, my dear, fo fhall I. If I interfere, it is purely out of friendfhip.

Mr. HARLOW.

Be advifed by me: fay no more to her. If the affair goes on, we fhall fairly get rid of her. Her peevifh humours, and her maiden temper, are become infupportable. Come, let us in to dinner. If Mr. Clerimont marries her, which indeed will be odd enough, we fhall then enjoy a little peace and quiet in our own houfe. [*Exit.*

Mrs.

Mrs. Harlow.

What in the world could the man fee in her? He will repent of his bargain in a week or a fortnight; that I am fure he will. She is gone to drefs now!---ha! ha!---

 Oh! how fhe rolls her pretty eyes in fpite,
 And looks delightfully with all her might!

Ha! ha! delightfully fhe will look indeed!---

End of the FIRST ACT.

ACT the SECOND.

Enter a SERVANT, *and* Capt. CAPE.

SERVANT.

YES, Sir, my master is at home: he has just done dinner, Sir.

Capt. CAPE.

Very well then; tell him I would speak a word with him.

SERVANT.

I beg pardon, Sir; I am but a stranger in the family---who shall I say?

Capt. CAPE,

Capt. Cape, tell him.

SERVANT.

Yes, Sir. [*Exit.*

Capt. CAPE.

I can hardly believe my own eyes. S'death! I am almost inclined to think this letter, signed with Miss Harlow's name, a mere forgery by some enemy, to drive me into an excess of passion, and so injure us both: I don't know what to say to it.

Enter

Enter Mr. HARLOW.

Capt. CAPE.

I have waited on you about an extraordinary affair; I can't comprehend it, Sir. Here is a letter with your ſiſter's name---Look at it, Sir: is that her hand-writing?

Mr. HARLOW.

Yes, Sir; I take it to be her writing.

Capt. CAPE.

And do you know the contents?

Mr. HARLOW.

I can't ſay I have read it; but---

Capt. Cape.

But you know the purport of it?

Mr. HARLOW.

Partly.

Capt. CAPE.

You do?---and is it not baſe treatment, Sir? Is it not unwarrantable? Can you juſtify her?

Mr. HARLOW.

For my part, I leave women to manage their own affairs. I am not fond of intermeddling.

Capt. CAPE.

But, Sir, let me aſk you: Was not every thing agreed upon? Are not the writings now in the lawyers hands? Was not next week fixed for our wedding?

Mr.

Mr. HARLOW.

I underſtood it ſo.

Capt. CAPE.

Very well then: you ſee how ſhe treats me. She writes me here in a contemptuous ſtile, that ſhe recalls her promiſe; it was raſhly given; ſhe has thought better of it; ſhe will liſten to me no more; ſhe is going to diſpoſe of herſelf to a gentleman with whom ſhe can be happy for life. There, that's free and eaſy, is not it? What do you ſay to that?

Mr. HARLOW.

Why really, Sir, it is not my affair. I have nothing to ſay to it.

Capt. CAPE.

Nothing to ſay to it!---Sir, I imagined I was dealing with people of honour.

Mr. HARLOW.

You have been dealing with a woman, and you know---

Capt. CAPE.

Yes, I know; I know the treachery of the ſex. Who is this gentleman, pray?

Mr. HARLOW.

His name is Clerimont. They have fixed the affair among themſelves, and amongſt them be it for me.

Capt. CAPE.

Very fine! mighty fine!---is Miſs Harlow at home, Sir?

Mr. Harlow.

She is; and here she comes this way.

Capt. Cape.

Very well!---let me hear it from herself, that's all: I desire to hear her speak for herself.

Mr. Harlow.

With all my heart. I'll leave you together: you know, Captain, I was never fond of being concerned in these affairs. [*Exit.*

Enter Miss Harlow.

Miss Harlow.

Capt. Cape, this is mighty odd: I thought my letter informed you---

Capt. Cape.

Madam, I acknowledge the receipt of your letter, and, Madam, the usage is so extraordinary, that I hold myself excusable, if I refuse to comply with the terms you impose upon me.

Miss Harlow.

Not comply? I don't understand you.

Capt. Cape.

Mistake me not; I am not come to whimper or to whine, and to make a puppy of myself again. That, Madam, is all blown over.

Miss Harlow.

Well, there is no harm done, and you will survive this I hope.

Capt.

Capt. Cape.

Survive it!

Miss Harlow.

Yes;---you wont't grow desperate: suppose you were to order somebody to take care of you, because you know fits of despair are sudden, and you may rashly do yourself a mischief. Don't do any such thing, I beg you won't.

Capt. Cape.

This insult, Madam!---Do myself a mischief! Don't flatter yourself that it is in your power to make me unhappy. It is not vexation brings me hither, that let me assure you.

Miss Harlow.

Then let vexation take you away. We were never designed for one another.

Capt. Cape.

My amazement brings me hither; amazement that any woman can behave---but I don't want to upbraid---I only come to ask---for I can hardly as yet believe it---I only come to ask if I am to credit this pretty epistle?

Miss Harlow.

Every syllable: therefore take your answer, Sir, and truce with your importunity.

Capt. Cape.

Very well, Ma'am, very well---your humble servant, Madam---I promise you, Ma'am, I can repay this scorn with scorn; with tenfold scorn, Madam, such as this treatment deserves; that's all;

all: I fay no more---your fervant Ma'am---but let me afk you---is this a juft return for all the attendance I have paid you thefe three years paft?

Mifs Harlow.

Perfectly juft, Sir; three years!---how could you be a dangler fo long? I told you what it would come to: can you think that raifing a woman's expectation, and tiring her out of all patience, is the way to make fure of her at laft? you ought to have been a brifker lover, you ought indeed, Sir. I am now contracted to another, and fo there is an end of every thing between us.

Capt. Cape.

Very well, Madam,---and yet I can't bear to be defpifed by her---and can you, Mifs Harlow, can you find it in your heart to treat me with this difdain? have you no compaffion?

Mifs Harlow.

No, pofitively none, Sir, none; none.

Capt. Cape.

Your own Capt. Cape, whom you------

Mifs Harlow.

Whom I defpife.

Capt. Cape.

Whom you have fo often encouraged to adore you.

Mifs Harlow.

Pray Sir, don't touch my hand: it is now the property of another.

Capt.

Capt. CAPE.

Can't you still break off with him?

Miss HARLOW.

No Sir, I can't; I won't; I love him, and if you are a man of honour, you will speak to me no more; desist, Sir, for if you don't, my brother shall tell you of it, and to-morrow Mr. Clerimont shall tell you of it.

Capt. CAPE.

Mr. Clerimont, Madam, shall fight me for daring------

Miss HARLOW.

And must I fight you too most noble, valiant Captain?

Capt. CAPE.

Laughed at too!

Miss HARLOW.

What a passion you are in!---I can't bear to see a man in such a passion. Oh! I have a happy riddance of you: the violence of your temper is dreadful. I won't stay a moment longer with you; you frighten me: you have your answer,---and so your servant Sir. *Exit.*

Capt. CAPE.

Ay! she is gone off like a fury, and the furies catch her, say I. I will never put up with this: I will find out this Mr. Clerimont: he shall be accountable to me; Mr. Harlow too shall be accountable; and---

Enter

Enter Mr. *and* Mrs. HARLOW.

Mr. Harlow, I am used very ill here, by all of you, and Sir, let me tell you---

Mr. HARLOW.

Nay; don't be angry with me. I was not to marry you.

Capt. CAPE.

But Sir, I can't help being angry. I must be angry: and let me tell you, you don't behave like a gentleman.

Mrs. HARLOW.

How can Mr. Harlow help it, Sir, if my sister---

Mr. HARLOW.

You are too warm; you are indeed. Let us talk this matter over a bottle.

Capt. CAPE.

No, Sir: no bottle: over a cannon, if you will.

Mrs. HARLOW.

Mercy on me! I beg you won't talk in that terrible manner: you frighten me out of my wits.

Mr. HARLOW.

Be you quiet, my dear. Capt. Cape, I beg you will just step into that room with me; and if, in the dispatching of one bottle, I don't acquit myself of all sinister dealing, why then---come, come, be a little moderate: you shall step with me: I'll take it as a favour. Come, come, you must.

Capt.

Capt. Cape.

I always found you a gentleman, Mr. Harlow, and so with all my heart, I don't care if I do talk the matter over.

Miss Harlow.

That's fair, and I am obliged to you. Come, I'll shew you the way. [*Exeunt.*

Mrs. Harlow.

Just as I foresaw: my sister was sure of him, and now is she going to break off for a young man, who will despise her in a little time. I wish she would have Capt. Cape.

Enter Miss. Harlow.

Miss Harlow.

Is he gone, sister?

Mrs. Harlow.

No; and here is the deuce and all to do. He is for fighting every body: upon my word you are wrong: you don't behave genteelly in the affair.

Miss Harlow.

Genteelly! I like that notion prodigiously: an't I going to marry genteelly?

Mrs. Harlow.

Well, follow your own inclinations. I won't intermeddle any more, I promise you. I'll step into the parlour, and see what they are about. [*Exit.*

Miss Harlow.

As you please, Ma'am. I see plainly the ill-natured thing can't bear my success. Heavens! here comes Mr. Clerimont.

Enter Mr. Clerimont.

Miss Harlow.

You are earlier than I expected, Sir.

Clerimont.

I have flown, Madam, upon the wings of love. I have seen my uncle: he will be here within this half hour. Every thing succeeds to my wishes. I hope there is no alteration here since I saw you.

Miss Harlow.

Nothing of moment, Sir.

Clerimont.

You alarm me: Mr. Harlow has not changed his mind, I hope.

Miss Harlow.

No, he continues in the same opinion.

Clerimont.

And your sister---I tremble with doubt and fear---she does not surely recede from the sentiments she flattered me with.

Miss Harlow.

Why there, indeed, I can't say much. She seems to---

CLERIMONT.
How!

MISS HARLOW.
She---I don't know what to make of her.

CLERIMONT.
I am on the rack: in pity, do not torture me.

MISS HARLOW.
How tremblingly solicitous he is---Oh! I have made a sure conquest. (*aside*)---Why, she, Sir---

CLERIMONT.
I am all attention, Madam. (*disconcerted*)

MISS HARLOW.
She does not seem entirely to approve.

CLERIMONT.
You kill me with despair.

MISS HARLOW.
Oh! he is deeply smitten. (*aside*)---She thinks another match would suit better.

CLERIMONT.
Another match!

MISS HARLOW.
Yes, another; an India captain, who has made his proposals; but I shall take care to see him dismissed.

CLERIMONT.

Will you?

Miss HARLOW.

I promise you I will. Though he runs much in my sister's head, and she has taken great pains to bring the family over to her opinion.

CLERIMONT.

How cruel! I could not have expected that from her. But has she fixed her heart upon a match with this other gentleman?

Miss HARLOW.

Why, truly I think she has: but my will in this affair ought, and shall be consulted.

CLERIMONT.

It is highly proper, Madam. Your long acquaintance with the world---

Mrs. HARLOW.

Long acquaintance, Sir! I have a few years experience only.

CLERIMONT.

That is, your good sense, ma'am---Oh! confound my tongue! how that slipt from me. (*aside*)---Your good sense,---your early good sense,---and---and---inclination should be consulted.

Mrs. HARLOW.

And they shall, Sir. Hark! I hear her coming. I'll leave you this opportunity to speak to her once more,

more, and try to win her over by perfuafion. It will make things eafy if you can. I am gone, Sir.
[*Curtfies affectedly and Exit.*

CLERIMONT.

The happinefs of my life will be owing to you, Madam. The woman is really better-natured than I thought. She comes, the lovely tyrant comes.

Enter Mrs. HARLOW.

CLERIMONT.

She triumphs in her cruelty, and I am ruined.
(*Afide*)

Mrs. HARLOW.

You feem uneafy, Sir. I hope no misfortune---

CLERIMONT.

The fevereft misfortune !---you have broke my heart.

Mrs. HARLOW.

I break your heart, Sir?

CLERIMONT.

Yes, cruel fair, you---you have undone me.

Mrs. HARLOW.

How can that be, Sir?

CLERIMONT.

And you feem unconfcious of the mifchief you have made.

Mrs. HARLOW

Pray unriddle.

CLERIMONT.

Your sister has told me all.

Mrs. HARLOW.

Ha! ha! what has she told you, Sir?

CLERIMONT.

It may be sport to you, but to me 'tis death.

Mrs. HARLOW.

What is death?

CLERIMONT.

The gentleman from India, Madam----I have heard it all---you can give him a preference; you can blast my hopes, my fond delighted hopes, which you yourself had cherished.

Mrs. HARLOW.

The gentleman is a very good sort of a man.

CLERIMONT.

She loves him, I see---(*aside*)---Madam, I perceive my doom is fixed, and fixed by you.

Mrs. HARLOW.

How have I fixed your doom?---If I speak favourably of Captain Cape, it is no more than he deserves.

CLE-

Clerimont.
Diſtraction! I cannot bear this---*(aſide)*

Mrs. Harlow.
I believe there is nobody that knows the gentleman, but will give him his due praiſe.

Clerimont.
Love! love! love! *(aſide)*

Mrs. Harlow.
And beſides, his claim is in fact prior to yours.

Clerimont.
And muſt love be governed, like the buſineſs of mechanics, by thy laws of tyrant cuſtom? Can you think ſo, Madam?

Mrs. Harlow.
Why, Sir, you know I am not in love.

Clerimont.
Confuſion!---No, Madam, I ſee you are not.

Mrs. Harlow.
And really, Sir, reaſonably ſpeaking, my ſiſter is for treating Capt. Cape very ill. He has been dancing attendance here theſe three years.

Clerimgnt.
Yet that you knew, when you were pleaſed to fan the riſing flame that matchleſs beauty had kindled in my heart.

Mrs.

Mrs. Harlow.

Matchlefs beauty!----ha! ha!----I cannot but laugh at that. (*afide*)

Clerimont.

Laugh, Madam, if you will at the pangs you yourfelf occafion: yes, triumph, if you will: I am refigned to my fate, fince you will have it fo.

Mrs. Harlow.

I have it fo!---you seem to frighten yourfelf without caufe. If I fpeak favourably of any body elfe, what then? I am not to marry him, you know.

Clerimont.

An't you?

Mrs. Harlow.

I!---No, truly; thank Heaven!

Clerimont.

She revives me. (*afide*)

Mrs. Harlow.

That muft be as my fifter pleafes.

Clerimont.

Muft it?

Mrs. Harlow.

Muft it! To be fure it muft.

Clerimont.

And may I hope fome intereft in your heart?

Mrs. Harlow.

My heart, Sir!

Clerimont.

While it is divided, while another has poſſeſſion of but part of it---

Mrs. Harlow.

I don't underſtand him! Why, it has been given away long ago.

Clerimont.

I pray you do not tyrannize me thus with alternate doubts and fears. If you will but bleſs me with the leaſt kind return---

Mrs. Harlow.

Kind return! what, would you have me fall in love with you?

Clerimont.

It will be generous to him who adores you.

Mrs. Harlow.

Adore me!

Clerimont.

Even to idolatry.

Mrs. Harlow.

What can he mean? I thought my ſiſter was the object of your adoration.

Clerimont.

Your ſiſter, Ma'am! I ſhall ever reſpect her as
my

my friend on this occasion, but love---no--no---she is no object for that.

Mrs. Harlow.
No!

Clerimont.
She may have been handsome in her time, but that has been all over long ago.

Mrs. Harlow.
Well! this is charming---I wish she heard him now, with her new-fangled airs. (*aside*) But let me understand you, Sir: adore me?

Clerimont.
You!---you! and only you! by this fair hand---
(*kisses it*)

Mrs. Harlow.
Hold, hold. This is going too far. But pray, Sir, have you really conceived a passion for me?

Clerimont.
You know I have; a passion of the tenderest nature.

Mrs. Harlow.
And was that your drift in coming hither?

Clerimont.
What else could induce me?

Mrs. Harlow.
And introduced yourself here to have an opportunity of speaking to me?
Cle-

CLERIMONT.
My angel! don't torment me thus.

Mrs. HARLOW.
Angel! and what do you suppose Mr. Harlow will say to this?

CLERIMONT.
Oh! Ma'am---he! he approves my passion.

Mrs. HARLOW.
Does he really? I must speak to him about that.

CLERIMONT.
Do so, Ma'am, you will find me a man of more honour than to deceive you.

Miss HARLOW.
Well! it will be whimsical enough if he does. And my sister too, this will be a charming discovery for her. *(aside)*---Ha! ha! well! really, Sir, this is mighty odd. I'll speak to Mr. Harlow about this matter, and you shall know his answer. *(going.)*

CLERIMONT.
And may I then flatter myself?

Mrs. HARLOW.
Oh! to be sure: such an honourable project! I'll step to him this moment; and then, sister, I shall make such a piece of work for you. *Exit.*

CLERIMONT.
Very well, Ma'am, see Mr. Harlow: he will confirm it all. While there is life there is hope. To lose

that matchless beauty, were the worst misery in the power of fortune to heap upon me.

Enter Miss HARLOW.

MISS HARLOW.
I beg pardon for leaving you all this time---Well, Sir, what says my sister?

CLERIMONT.
She has given me some glimmering hopes.

MISS HARLOW.
Don't be uneasy about her; it shall be as I please---

CLERIMONT.
But with her own free consent it would be better: however, to you I am bound by every tie, and thus let me seal a vow---*(kisses her hand.)*

MISS HARLOW.
He certainly is a very passionate lover. He is ready to eat my hand up with kisses. I wish my sister saw this. *(aside.)* Hush! I hear Captain Cape's voice. The hideous Sea-monster! he is coming this way. I would not see him again for the world. I'll withdraw for a moment, Sir. You'll excuse me: *(kisses her hand and curtsies very low)* your most obedient---Oh! he is a charming man.
[*Curtseys and Exit.*

Enter Capt. CAPE.

Capt. CAPE.
There she goes, the perfidious! Sir, I understand your name is Clerimont.

CLERIMONT.

CLERIMONT.
At your service, Sir.

Capt. CAPE.
Then, draw this moment.

CLERIMONT.
Draw, Sir! for what?

Capt. CAPE.
No evasion, Sir.

CLERIMONT.
Explain the cause.

Capt. CAPE.
The cause is too plain: your making love to that lady, who went out there this moment.

CLERIMONT.
That lady! not I upon my honour, Sir.

Capt. CAPE.
No shuffling, Sir, draw.

CLERIMONT.
Sir, I can repel an Injury like this: but your quarrel is groundless. And, Sir, if ever I made love to that lady, I will lay my bosom naked to your sword. That lady!---I resign all manner of pretension to her.

Capt. CAPE.
You resign her?

CLERIMONT.

Clerimont.

Entirely.

Capt. Cape.

Then I am pacified. (*puts up his sword.*)

Clerimont.

Upon my word, Sir, I never so much as thought of the lady.

Enter Mr. Harlow.

Mr. Harlow.

So, Sir, fine doings you have been carrying on here!

Clerimont.

Sir!

Mr. Harlow.

You have been attempting my wife, I find.

Clerimont.

Upon my word, Mr. Harlow---

Mr. Harlow.

You have behaved in a very base manner, and I insist upon satisfaction. (*draws his sword*)

Clerimont.

This is the strangest accident! I assure you, Sir, ---only give me leave.

Mr.

Mr. Harlow.

I will not give you leave---I infift---

Capt. Cape.

Nay, Mr. Harlow. This is neither time or place: and befides, hear the gentleman; I have been over-hafty, and he has fatisfied me: only hear him.

Mr. Harlow.

Sir, I will believe my own wife. Come on, Sir.

Clerimont.

Without caufe I cannot: I have no quarrel, Sir. You may believe me, Mr. Harlow, when I affure you, that I came into this houfe upon honourable principles: induced, Sir, by my regard for Mifs Harlow.

Capt. Cape.

For Mifs Harlow!---wounds! draw this moment.

Clerimont.

Again! this is downright madnefs: two upon me at once! you will murder me between you.

Mr. Harlow.

There is one too many upon him fure enough: and fo, captain, put up your fword.

Capt. Cape.

Refign your pretenfions to Mifs Harlow.

Clerimont.

CLERIMONT.

Refign Miſs Harlow!---not for the univerſe: in her cauſe, I can be as ready as any bravo of ye all. (*draws his ſword.*)

Mr. HARLOW.

For heaven's ſake, Captain Cape, moderate your anger; this is neither time nor place. I have been too raſh myſelf: I beg you will be pacified. (*He puts up.*)---Mr. Clerimont ſheath your ſword.

CLERIMONT.

I obey, Sir.

Mr. HARLOW.

Captain Cape, how can you? you promiſed me you would let things take their courſe? if my ſiſter will marry the gentleman, how is he to blame?

Capt. CAPE.

Well argued, Sir: I have done:---ſhe is a worthleſs woman, that's all.

CLERIMONT.

A worthleſs woman, Sir!

Capt. CAPE.

Ay! worthleſs.

CLERIMONT.

Damnation!---Draw, Sir!

Mr. HARLOW.

Nay, now, Mr. Clerimont, you are too warm; and

and there's a gentleman coming---this is your uncle, I suppose.

Clerimont.

It is, and he comes opportunely.

Enter Mr. Heartwell.

Mr. Harlow. (*aside.*)

I'll wave all disputes now, that I may conclude my sister's marriage.

Heartwell.

My nephew has informed me, Sir, of the honor you have done him, and I am come to ratify the treaty by my consent.

Mr. Harlow.

I thought it necessary to have the advice of Mr. Clerimont's Friends, as he is very young, and my sister not very handsome.

She is an angel, Sir.

Heartwell.

Patience, Charles, patience. My nephew's estate will provide for his eldest born, and upon the younger branches of his marriage, I mean to settle my fortune.

Mr. Harlow.

Generously spoken, Sir, and after that declaration, there is no occasion for delay. Who waits there? ---tell the ladies they are wanted.

Heartwell.

Heartwell.

I have ever loved my nephew, and since he tells me he has made a good choice, I shall be glad to see him happy.

Capt. Cape.

But, Sir, let me tell you, that your nephew has used me basely, and Sir---

Mr. Harlow.

Po! Captain Cape, now you are wrong again: every thing was settled between us in the other room: recollect yourself; I beg you will---Oh! here come the ladies.

Enter Mrs. Harlow and Miss Harlow.

Miss Harlow.

Now, sister, you shall see that I have completed my conquest.

Clerimont.

At length, I am happy indeed! my lovely, charming bride! thus let me snatch thee to my heart, and thus, and thus---(*embraces Mrs. Harlow.*)

Mr. Harlow.

Death and distraction! before my face---
(pushing him away)

Clerimont.

Prithee indulge my transport: my life, my angel!

A COMEDY.

Mr. HARLOW.

I defire you will defift, Sir: thefe liberties may provoke me too far.

CLERIMONT.

Nay, nay, prithee be quiet: my charming, charming wife!

Mr. HARLOW.

That lady is not your wife.

CLERIMONT.

How my wife, not my wife!---extafy and blifs!

Mr. HARLOW.

Come, come, Sir, this is too much: I defire---

CLERIMONT.

Ha! ha! you are very pleafant, Sir.

Mr. HARLOW.

This is downright madnefs, but it fhall not excufe you: that lady is my wife.

CLERIMONT.

Sir!

Mr. HARLOW.

I fay, Sir, that lady is my wife.

Capt. CAPE.

Ha! ha! I fee through this: it is a comedy of errors, I believe. (*fings*)

HEARTWELL.

What does all this mean?

CLERIMONT.

Your wife, Sir!

Mr. HARLOW.

Yes, my wife: and there is my sister, if you please to take her.

CLERIMONT.

Sir!

Mr. HARLOW.

Sir, this is the lady whom you have desired in marriage.

CLERIMONT.

Who I, Sir? I beg your pardon: that lady I took to be your wife (*pointing to Miss Harlow.*)---and that lady (*pointing to Mrs. Harlow.*) I took to be your sister.

Capt. CAPE *and* Mrs. HARLOW.

Ha! ha! ha!---

Miss HARLOW.

How! how is this? have I been made a fool of all this time? furies! torture! madness!

Capt. CAPE.

Ha! ha!---my lady fair is taken in, I think.

Mrs. HARLOW.

Sister, the men don't see with my eyes---ha! ha!

Capt. CAPE.

Ha! ha! the gentleman is no dangler, Ma'am.

Mrs. Harlow.

This is a complete conqueſt my ſiſter has made.

Miſs Harlow.

I can't bear this---Sir, I deſire I may not be made a jeſt of----did not you ſolicit me? importune me?

Clerimont.

For your intereſt in that lady, whom I took for Miſs Harlow. I beg your pardon if I am miſtaken: I hope there it no harm done.

Miſs Harlow.

Yes, Sir, but there is harm done. I am made ſport of; expoſed to deriſion---Oh! I cannot bear this---I cannot bear it---*(cries)*

Mrs. Harlow.

Don't cry, ſiſter: ſome faces preſerve their bloom longer than others you know---ha! ha!

Capt. Cape.

Loll toll loll---

Heartwell.

This is all a riddle to me: is that lady your wife, Sir?

Mr. Harlow.

She is, Sir.

Heartwell.

And pray nephew; you took that lady for Mr. Harlow's ſiſter, I ſuppoſe.

CLERIMONT.

I did, Sir. I beg pardon for the trouble I have given---I am in such confusion, I can hardly---

HEARTWELL.

Well, well! the thing is cleared up, and you have been proceeding upon a mistake. But you should have known what ground you went upon---ha! ha! I can't help laughing neither.

Mr. HARLOW.

Why faith, nor I---ha! ha!

CLERIMONT.

Since matters have turned out so unexpectedly, I beg pardon for my mistake, and Sir, I take my leave---*(going)*

Miss HARLOW.

And will you treat me in this manner, Sir? Will you draw me into such a scrape, and not---

CLERIMONT.

Madam, that gentleman would cut my throat: his claim is prior to mine; and I dare say, he will be very glad to be reconciled.

Miss HARLOW.

You are a base man then, and I reject you. Captain Cape I see my error, and I resign myself to you.

Capt. CAPE.

No, Madam, I beg to be excused. I have been a dangler too long. I ought to have been a brisker lover. I shall endeavour to survive it, Madam; I

won't

won't do myself a mischief: I have my answer, and I am off, Madam. Loll toll loll---

Mrs. Harlow.
Ha! ha! I told you this my dear sister.

Clerimont.
Madam, I dare say the gentleman will think better of it. Mr. Harlow, I am sorry for all this confusion, and I beg pardon of the whole company for my mistake. Mrs. Harlow, I wish you all happiness, Ma'am---Angelic creature! what a misfortune to lose her! [*Bows and Exit.*

Capt. Cape.
And I will follow his example---Miss Harlow I wish you all happiness. Angelic creature! what a misfortune to lose her!---Upon my soul I think you a most admirable jilt, and so now you may go, and bewail your virginity in the mountains---loll toll loll--- [*Exit.*

Miss Harlow.
Oh! oh! I can't bear to be thus disgraced. I'll go and hide myself from the world for ever. The men are all savages, barbarians, monsters, and I hate the whole sex. [*Exit.*

Mrs. Harlow.
My dear sister, with her beauty and her conquests, ha! ha!

Mr. Harlow.
Ha! ha! whimsical and ridiculous!

Heartwell.

Sir, my nephew is young: I am sorry for this scene of errors, and I hope you'll ascribe the whole to his inexperience.

Mr. Harlow.

I certainly shall, Sir.

Mrs. Harlow.

I cautioned my sister sufficiently about this matter, but vanity got the better of her, and leaves her now a whimsical instance of folly and affectation.

In vain the FADED TOAST her mirror tries,
And counts the cruel murders of her eyes;
For Ridicule, sly-peeping o'er her head,
Will point the roses and the lillies dead;
And while, fond soul! she weaves her myrtle chain,
She proves a subject of the comic strain.

The
Citizen

THE
CITIZEN:
A
COMEDY,

IN TWO ACTS.

Performed at the

THEATRE ROYAL

IN

COVENT-GARDEN.

Æque neglectum pueris senibusque nocebit.

HOR.

Dramatis Personæ.

MEN.

OLD PHILPOT,	Mr. SHUTER.
GEORGE, his Son,	Mr. WOODWARD.
Sir JASPER WILDING,	Mr. DUNSTALL.
YOUNG WILDING,	Mr. DYER.
BEAUFORT,	Mr. BAKER.
DAPPER,	Mr. COSTOLLO.
QUILDRIVE,	Mr. PERRY.

WOMEN.

MARIA,	Miss ELLIOT.
CORINNA,	Miss COCKAYNE.

SERVANTS, &c.

THE

CITIZEN.

ACT the FIRST.

Young Wilding, Beaufort, *and* Will *following*.

Wilding.

HA, ha, my dear Beaufort! a fiery young fellow like you, melted down into a sighing, love-sick dangler after a high heel, a well-turned ancle, and a short petticoat!

Beaufort.

Pr'ythee, my dear Wilding, spare your raillery. Maria's charms---

Wilding.

Maria's charms! And so now you would fain grow wanton in her praise, and make me listen to your raptures about my own sister! Ha! ha, poor Beaufort! Is my sister at home, Will?

Will.

She is, Sir.

Wilding.

How long has my father been gone out?

Will.

WILL.

This hour, Sir.

WILDING.

Very well. Pray give Mr. Beaufort's compliments to my sister. If she is visible this morning, he will wait upon her. (*Exit* WILL.) You will be glad to see her I suppose, Charles.

BEAUFORT.

I live but in her presence.

WILDING.

Live but in her presence! How the devil could the young baggage raise this riot in your heart? 'Tis more than her brother could ever do with any of her sex.

BEAUFORT.

Nay, you have no reason to complain. You are come up to town, post-haste, to marry a wealthy citizen's daughter, who only saw you last season at Tunbridge, and has been languishing for you ever since.

WILDING.

That's more than I do for her; and, to tell you the truth, more than I believe she does for me. This is a match of prudence, man! bargain and sale! My reverend dad and the old put of a citizen finished the business at Lloyd's coffee-house by inch of candle: a mere transfer of property!---" Give your son to " my daughter, and I will give my daughter to your " son." That's the whole affair, and so I am just arrived to consummate the nuptials.

BEAU-

BEAUFORT.

Thou art the happiest fellow

WILDING.

Happy! so I am. What should I be otherwise for? If Miss Sally---upon my soul I forget her name.

BEAUFORT.

Well! that is so like you---Miss Sally Philpot.

WILDING.

Ay! very true: Miss Sally Philpot. She will bring fortune sufficient to pay off an old incumbrance upon the family-estate, and my father is to settle handsomely upon me. I have reason to be contented have not I?

BEAUFORT.

And are you willing to marry her without one spark of love for her?

WILDING.

Love! Why I make myself ridiculous enough by marrying, don't I, without being in love into the bargain? What! am I to pine for a girl that is willing to go to bed to me? Love of all things! My dear Beaufort, one sees so many people breathing raptures about each other before marriage, and dinning their insipidity into the ears of all their acquaintance; " My dear Ma'am, don't you think " him a sweet man? a charminger creature never " was." Then he, on his side---" My life, my an- " gel, oh! she's a paradise of ever blooming sweets!" And then in a month's time, " He's a perfidious " wretch!

"wretch! I wish I had never seen his face: the devil
"was in me when I had any thing to say to him."
"A plague go with her for an inanimate piece; I
"wish she had poisoned herself with all my heart."
That is ever the way; and so you see love is all nonsense; well enough to furnish romances for boys and
girls at circulating libraries; that is all, take my
word for it.

BEAUFORT.

Pho! this is all idle talk; and, in the mean time,
I am ruin'd.

WILDING.

How so?

BEAUFORT.

Why, you know the old couple have bargain'd for
your sister.

WILDING.

Bargain'd for her! And will you pretend you are
in love? Can you look tamely on and see her bar-
tered away at Garraway's, like cochineal, or indigo?
Marry her privately, man, and keep it a secret till
my affair is over.

BEAUFORT.

My dear Wilding, will you propose it to her?

WILDING.

With all my heart. She is very long a coming.
I'll tell you what, if she has a fancy for you, carry
her off at once. But, perhaps, she has a mind to this
cub of a citizen, Miss Sally's brother.

BEAU-

Beaufort.

Oh, no! he's her averſion.

Wilding.

I have never ſeen any of the family but my wife that is to be: my father-in-law, and my brother-in-law, I know nothing of them. What ſort of a fellow is the ſon?

Beaufort.

Oh! a diamond of the firſt water; a buck, Sir, a blood! every night at this end of the town; at twelve next day he ſneaks about the 'Change, in a little bit of a frock and a bob-wig, and looks like a ſedate book-keeper in the eyes of all who behold him.

Wilding.

Upon my word, a gentleman of ſpirit.

Beaufort.

Spirit! He drives a phaeton two ſtory high, keeps his girl at this end of the town, and is the gay George Philpot all round Covent-Garden.

Wilding.

Oh, brave!---and the father?

Beaufort.

The father, Sir---But here comes Maria; take his picture from her. (*ſhe ſings within*)

Wilding.

Hey! ſhe is muſical this morning; ſhe holds her uſual ſpirits, I find.

BEAUFORT.

Yes, the spirit of eighteen, with the idea of a lover in her head.

WILDING.

Ay! and such a lover as you too! Though still in her teens, she can play upon all your foibles, and treat you as she does her monkey, tickle you, torment you, enrage you, sooth you, exalt you, depress you, pity you, laugh at you---*Ecce signum!*

Enter MARIA. (*singing*)

WILDING.

The same giddy girl! Come, my dear sister, have done with your fooling.

MARIA.

Be quiet, brother; let me have my own way; I will go through my song. (*sings*)

WILDING.

I have not seen you this age; ask me how I do?

MARIA.

I won't ask you how I do: I won't take any notice of you, I don't know you.

WILDING.

Do you know this gentleman then? Will you speak to him?

MARIA.

No, I won't speak to him; I'll sing to him; it's my humour to sing. (*sings*)

Beaufort.

Be serious but for a moment, Maria; my all depends upon it.

Maria.

Oh! sweet Sir, you are dying, are you? Then positively I will sing the song; for it is a description of yourself. (*She sings a little*) Brother, how do you do? (*kisses him*) Say nothing, don't interrupt me.
(*sings*)

Wilding.

Have you seen your city lover yet?

Maria.

No; but I long to see him; I fancy he is a curiosity.

Beaufort.

Long to see him, Maria!

Maria.

Yes, long to see him---(Beaufort *fiddles with his lip, and looks thoughtful*) Brother, brother! (*goes to him softly, beckons him to look at* Beaufort) do you see that? (*mimicks him*) Mind him; ha, ha.

Beaufort.

Make me ridiculous if you will, Maria; so do you don't make me unhappy, by marrying this citizen.

Maria.

And would not you have me marry, Sir? What, I must lead a single life to please you, must I? Upon on my word you are a pretty gentleman to make laws for me. *(sings)*

Can it be, or by law, or by equity said,
That a comely young girl ought to die an old maid?

WILDING.

Come, come, Miss Pert, compose yourself a little: this will never do.

MARIA.

My cross, ill-natured brother! But it will do. Lord! what do you both call me hither to plague me? I won't stay among ye---*à l'honeur, à l'honeur ---(running away) à l'honeur.*

WILDING.

Hey, hey, Miss Notable! come back; you must stay. *(forces her back)*

MARIA.

Well, well; what do you want?

WILDING.

Come, truce with your frolicks, Miss Hoyden, and behave like a sensible girl; we have serious business with you.

MARIA.

Have you? Well, come, I will be sensible. There, I blow all my folly away: 'tis gone, gone, and now I'll talk sense. Is that a sensible face?

WILDING.

Po, be quiet, and hear what we have to say to you.

MARIA.

Maria.

I will, I am quiet. It is charming weather; it will be good for the country, this will.

Wilding.

Ridiculous! how can you be so silly?

Maria.

Bless me! I never saw any thing like you. There is no such thing as satisfying you. I am sure it was very good sense, what I said. Papa talks in that manner. Well! I'll be silent then: I won't speak at all; will that satisfy you? *(looks sullen)*

Wilding.

Absurd! no more of this folly, but mind what is said to you. You have not seen your city lover, you say?
 (Maria shrugs her shoulders, and shakes her head)

Wilding.

Why don't you answer?

Beaufort.

My dear Maria, put me out of pain.
 (Maria shrugs her shoulders again)

Wilding.

I'll pinch a piece out of your arm, if you don't answer.

Maria.

Why, no, then; no, no, no, no, no, no; I tell you no.

WILDING.

Ridiculous! Don't be a girl always.

MARIA.

Why don't I tell you I have not seen him? But I am to see him this very day.

BEAUFORT.

To see him this day, Maria?

MARIA.

Ha, ha!---look there, brother; he is beginning again. But don't frighten yourself, and I'll tell you all about it. My papa comes to me this morning---by the by, he makes a fright of himself with this strange dress---Why does he not dress as other gentlemen do, brother?

WILDING.

He dresses like his brother fox-hunters in Wiltshire.

MARIA.

But when he comes to town, I wish he would do as other gentlemen do here. I am almost ashamed of him. But he comes to me this morning---" Hoic!
" hoic! our Moll---Where is the sly pufs? Tally
" ho!"---Did you want me papa?---" Come hither,
" Moll, I'll *gee* you a husband, my girl; one that
" has mettle enow; he'll take cover, I warrant un;
" blood to the bone."

BEAUFORT.

There now, Wilding, did not I tell you this?

WILDING.

Where are you to see the young citizen?

MARIA.

Wy, papa will be at home in an hour, and then he intends to drag me into the city with him, and there the sweet creature is to be introduced to me. The old gentleman, his father, is delighted with me: but I hate him, an old ugly thing.

WILDING.

I never saw him: what sort of a being is he?

MARIA.

Why, he looks like the picture of Avarice, sitting with pleasure upon a bag of money, and trembling for fear any body should come and take it away. He has got square-toed shoes, and little tiny buckles, a brown coat, with small round brass buttons, that looks as if they were new in my great-grandmother's time, and his face all shrivelled and pinched with care, and he shakes his head like a Mandarine upon a chimney-piece---" Ay, ay, Sir Jasper, you are
" right---and then he grins at me---I profess she is
" a very pretty bale of goods. Ay, ay, and my son
" Bob is a very sensible lad---ay, ay! I will under-
" write their happiness for one and a half per
" cent."

WILDING.

Thank you, my dear girl; thank you for this account of my relations.

BEAUFORT.

Destruction to my hopes! Surely, my dear angel, if you have any regard for me---

Maria.

There, there, there he is frightened again.
(*sings* Dearest creature, &c.)

Wilding.

No more of these airs: listen to me, and I'll instruct you how to manage them all.

Maria.

Oh! my dear brother, you are very good. But don't mistake yourself; though just come from a boarding-school, give me leave to manage for myself. There is in this case a man I like, and a man I don't like---It is not you I like (*to* Beaufort) No---I hate you----But let this little head alone; I I know what to do: I shall know how to prefer one, and get rid of the other.

Beaufort.

What will you do, Maria?

Maria.

Ho! ho! that face is enough to make me die with laughing. (*sings*)

Do not grieve me,
Oh! relieve me, &c.

Wilding.

Come, come, you shall listen to me. The old cit, you say, admires you for your understanding; and his son would not marry you, unless he found you a girl of sense and spirit?

Maria.

Maria.

Even so: that is the character of your giddy sister.

Wilding.

Why then I'll tell you. You shall make him hate you for a fool, and so let the refusal come from himself.

Maria.

But how---how, my dear brother? Tell me how?

Wilding.

Why you have seen a play with me, where a man pretends to be a downright country oaf, in order to rule a wife and have a wife.

Maria.

Very well---what then?---what then?---Oh! I have it; I understand you; say no more; 'tis charming; I like it of all things; I'll do it, I will; and I will so plague him, that he shan't know what to make of me. He shall be a very toad-eater to me; the sour, the sweet, the bitter, he shall swallow all, and all shall work upon him alike for my diversion. Say nothing of it: it's all among ourselves; but I won't be cruel. I hate ill-nature, and then who knows but I may take a fancy to him?

Beaufort.

Why will you alarm me thus?

Maria.

Oh! now you are beginning again.
[*Sings*, Voi Amanti, &c. *and Exit.*

Beaufort.

'Sdeath, Wilding, I shall never be your brother-in-law at this rate.

Wilding.

Pshaw, follow me; don't be apprehensive. I'll give her further instructions, and she will execute them I warrant you. The old fellow's daughter shall be mine, and the son may go shift for himself elsewhere. [*Exeunt.*

SCENE II. Old Philpot's House.

Enter Old Philpot, Dapper, *and* Quilldrive.

Old Philpot.

Quilldrive, have those dollars been sent to the Bank, as I ordered?

Quilldrive.

They have, Sir.

Old Philpot.

Very well!---Mr. Dapper, I am not fond of writing any thing of late; but at your request---

Dapper.

You know I would not offer you a bad policy.

Old Philpot.

I believe it. Well, step with me to my closet, and I will look at your policy. How much do you want upon it?

Dap-

DAPPER.

Three thoufand; you had better take that fum; there are very good names upon it.

OLD PHILPOT.

Well, well, ftep with me, and I'll talk to you. Quildrive, run with thofe bills for acceptance. This way, Mr. Dapper, this way. [*Exeunt.*

QUILLDRIVE *folus.*

QUILLDRIVE.

A miferly old curmudgeon! digging, digging money out of the very hearts of mankind; conftantly fcraping together, and yet trembling with anxiety for fear of coming to want. A canting old hypocrite! and yet under his veil of fanctity, he has a liquorifh tooth left; running to the other end of the town flily every evening, and there he has his folitary pleafures in holes and corners.

GEORGE *peeping in.*

GEORGE PHILPOT.

Hift, hift!---Quilldrive!

QUILLDRIVE.

Ha, Mafter George!

GEORGE.

Is Square-toes at home?

QUILLDRIVE.

He is.

GEORGE.

George.
Has he asked for me?

Quilldrive.
He has.

George. *(walks in on tip-toe)*
Does he know I did not lie at home?

Quilldrive.
No; I funk that upon him.

George.
Well done; I'll give you a choice gelding to carry you to Dulwich of a Sunday. Damnation! up all night; stripped of nine hundred pounds; pretty well for one night!---Picqued, repicqued, flamm'd, and capotted every deal!---Old Dry-beard shall pay all. Is forty-seven good? No---Fifty good? No! no, no, no---to the end of the chapter.---Cruel luck! Damn me, its life tho'---this is life---'sdeath! I hear him coming *(runs off and peeps)*---no, all's safe---I must not be caught in these cloaths, Quilldrive.

Quilldrive.
How come you did not leave them at Madam Corinna's, as you generally do?

George.
I was afraid of being too late for old Square-toes, and so I whipt into a hackney-coach, and drove with the windows up, as if I was afraid of a bum-bailey. ---Pretty cloaths, an't they?

Quilldrive.

Ah! Sir---

George.

Reach me one of my mechanic city frocks. No ---stay---it's in the next room, an't it?

Quilldrive.

Yes, Sir.

George.

I'll run and slip it on in a twinkle.   [*Exit.*

Quilldrive *solus.*

Quilldrive.

Mercy on us! what a life does he lead? Old Cojer within here will scrape together for him, and the moment young master comes to possession, "Ill "got, ill gone," I warrant me. A hard card I have to play between 'em both: drudging for the old man, and pimping for the young one. The father is a reservoir of riches, and the son a fountain to play it all away in vanity, vice, and folly.

Re-enter George.

George.

Now I'm equipp'd for the city. Damn the city: I wish the Papishes would set fire to it again. I hate to be beating the hoof here among them. Here comes father---no;---it's Dapper---Quildrive, I'll give you the gelding.

QUILLDRIVE.

Thank you, Sir. [*Exit*.

Enter DAPPER.

DAPPER.

Why you look like a devil, George.

GEORGE.

Yes, I have been up all night; loft all my money, and I am afraid I muft fmafh for it.

DAPPER.

Smafh for it! What have I let you into the fecret for? Have not I advifed you trade upon your own account? and you feel the fweets of it. How much do you owe in the city?

GEORGE.

At leaft twenty thoufand.

DAPPER.

Poh, that's nothing! Bring it up to fifty or fixty thoufand, and then give 'em a good blow up at once. I have enfured the fhip for you.

GEORGE.

Have you?

DAPPER.

The policy's full; I have juft touched your father for the laft three thoufand.

GEORGE.

Excellent! Are the goods re-landed?

DAP-

Dapper.

Every bale. I have had them up to town, and fold them all to a packer for you.

George.

Bravo!---and the ship is loaded with rubbish, I suppose.

Dapper.

Yes; and is now proceeding on her voyage.

George.

And to-morrow, or next day, we shall hear of her being lost on the Goodwin Sands, or sunk between the Needles.

Dapper.

Certainly.

George.

Admirable! and then we shall come upon the Underwriters.

Dapper.

Directly.

George.

My dear Dapper! *(embraces him)*

Dapper.

Yes; I do a dozen every year. How do you think I can live as I do, otherwise?

George.

Very true; shall you be at the club after 'Change?

Dapper.
Without fail.

George.
That's right; it will be a full meeting: we shall have Nat Pig-tail, the dry-salter, there; and Bob Reptile, the 'Change-broker; and Sobersides, the banker. We shall all be there. We shall have deep doings.

Dapper.
Yes, yes; well, a good morning; I must go now, and fill up a policy for a ship that has been lost these three days.

George.
My dear Dapper, thou art the best of friends.

Dapper.
Ay, I'll stand by you. It will be time enough for you to break, when you see your father near his end; then give 'em a tumble; put yourself at the head of his fortune, and begin the world again---Good morning. [*Exit.*

George, *solus.*
Dapper, adieu---Who now in my situation would envy any of your great folks at the court-end! A Lord has nothing to depend upon but his estate: he can't spend you a hundred thousand pounds of other people's money. No---no. I had rather be a little bob-wig citizen, in good credit, than a commissioner of the customs. Commissioner! The King has not so good a thing in his gift, as a commission of bankruptcy. Don't we see them all with
their

their country seats at Hogsden, and Kentish-town, and Newington-butts, and Islington; with their flying Mercuries tipt on the top of the house, their Apollos, their Venus's and their leaden Hercules's in the garden; and themselves sitting before the door, with pipes in their mouths, waiting for a good digestion? Wounds! here comes old Muckworm! Now for a few dry maxims of left-handed wisdom, to prove myself a scoundrel in sentiment, and pass in his eyes for a hopeful young man likely to do well in the world.

Enter OLD PHILPOT.

OLD PHILPOT.
Twelve times twelve is a hundred and forty-four.

GEORGE.
I'll attack him in his own way---Commission at two and a half per cent---

OLD PHILPOT.
There he is, intent upon business! What, plodding, George?

GEORGE.
Thinking a little of the main chance, Sir.

OLD PHILPOT.
That's right; it is a wide world, George.

GEORGE.
Yes, Sir, but you instructed me early in the rudiments of trade.

OLD

OLD PHILPOT.

Ay, ay! I inftilled good principles into thee.

GEORGE.

So you did, Sir. Principal and intereft is all I ever heard from him. (*afide*) I fhall never forget the ftory you recommended to my earlieft notice, Sir.

OLD PHILPOT.

What was that, George? It is quite out of my head.

GEORGE.

It item'd how Mr. Thomas Inkle, of London, merchant, was caft away, and was afterwards protected by a young lady, who grew in love with him, and how he afterwards bargained with a planter to fell her for a flave.

OLD PHILPOT.

Ay, ay, (*laughs*) I recollect it now.

GEORGE.

And when fhe pleaded being with child by him, he was no otherwife moved than to raife his price, and make her turn to better account.

OLD PHILPOT. (*burfts into a laugh*)

I remember it. Ha, ha!---there was the very fpirit of trade! ay---ay---ha, ha!

GEORGE.

There was calculation for you---

OLD

Old Philpot.

Ay, ay.

George.

The Rule of Three---If one gives me so much; what will two give me?

Old Philpot.

Ay, ay. (*laughs*)

George.

That was a hit, Sir.

Old Philpot.

Ay, ay.

George.

That was having his wits about him.

Old Philpot.

Ay, ay! It is a lesson for all young men. It was a hit indeed, ha! ha! (*both laugh*)

George.

What an old negro it is. (*aside*)

Old Philpot.

Thou art a son after my own heart, George.

George.

Trade must be minded. A penny saved, is a penny got.

OLD PHILPOT.

Ay, ay! *(shakes his head, and looks cunning)*

GEORGE.

He that hath money in his purse, won't want a head on his shoulders.

OLD PHILPOT.

Ay, ay.

GEORGE.

Rome was not built in a day. Fortunes are made by degrees. Pains to get, care to keep, and fear to lose.

OLD PHILPOT.

Ay, ay.

GEORGE.

He that lies in bed, his estate feels it.

OLD PHILPOT.

Ay, ay, the good boy.

GEORGE.

The old Curmudgeon! *(aside)* think nothing mean that brings in an honest penny.

OLD PHILPOT.

The good boy! George, I have great hopes of thee.

GEORGE.

Thanks to your example; you have taught me to
be

be cautious in this wide world. Love your neighbour, but don't pull down your hedge.

Old Philpot.

I profess it is a wise saying---I never heard it before; it is a wise saying; and shews how cautious we should be of too much confidence in friendship.

George.

Very true.

Old Philpot.

Friendship has nothing to do with trade.

George.

No---It only draws a man in to lend money.

Old Philpot.

Ay, ay.

George.

There was your neighbour's son, Dick Worthy, who was always cramming his head with Greek and Latin at school; he wanted to borrow of me the other day, but I was too cunning.

Old Philpot.

Ay, ay---let him draw bills of exchange in Greek and Latin, and see where he will get a pound sterling for them.

George.

So I told him. I went to his garret in the Minories; and there I found him in all his misery! and a fine scene it was. There was his wife in a corner of the room, at a washing-tub, up to the elbows in suds; a solitary pork-stake was dangling by a bit of pack-thread, before a melancholy fire; himself seated at a three-legged table, writing a pamphlet against the German war; a child upon his left knee, his right leg employed in rocking a cradle with a brattling in it. And so there was business enough for them all. His wife rubbing away, *(mimicks a washerwoman)* and he writing on, "The King of "Prussia shall have no more subsidies; Saxony shall "be indemnified---He shan't have a foot in Silesia." There's a sweet little baby! (*to the child on his knee*) then he rock'd the cradle, hush ho! hush ho! ---then twisted the griskin, *(snaps his fingers)* hush ho! " The Russians shall have Prussia." (*writes*) Hush ho! hush ho! --- round goes the griskin again, *(snaps his finger---writes)*---and so you have a picture of the whole family.

Old Philpot.

Ha! ha! what becomes of his Greek and Latin now? Fine words butter no parsnips. He had no money from you, I suppose, George?

George.

Oh! no; charity begins at home, says I.

Old Philpot.

And it was wisely said. I have an excellent saying when any man wants to borrow of me. I am ready with my joke---" A fool and his money are " soon parted"---ha, ha, ha!

George.

Ha, ha! A wittier saying there never was.

Old

Old Philpot.

No; that's the truth of wit. A fool and his money are foon parted---ha, ha, ha!

George.

Now if I can wring a handfome fum out of him, it will prove the truth of what he fays. (*afide*) And yet trade has its inconveniencies. Great houfes ftopping payment!

Old Philpot.

Hey---what! you look chagrin'd!---Nothing of that fort has happened to thee, I hope?

George.

A great houfe at Cadiz---Don John de Alvarada ---The Spanifh Galleons not making quick returns ---and fo my bills are come back.

Old Philpot.

Ay!---(*fhakes his head*)

George.

I have indeed a remittance from Meffina. That voyage yields thirty per cent. profit: but this blow coming upon me---

Old Philpot.

Why this is unlucky: how much money?

George.

Three and twenty hundred.

Old Philpot.

George, too many eggs in one bafket. I tell thee, George,

George, I expect Sir Jasper Wilding here presently to conclude the treaty of marriage I have on foot for thee: hush this up, say nothing of it, and in a day or two you may pay these bills with his daughter's portion.

George.

The old rogue! (*aside*) That will never do, I shall be blown upon 'Change: Alvarada will pay in time: he has opened his affairs; he appears a good man.

Old Philpot.

Does he?

George.

A great fortune left; will begin to pay in six monhts; but I must crack before that.

Old Philpot.

It is unlucky! A good man you say he is?

George.

Nobody better.

Old Philpot.

Let me see: suppose I lend this money.

George.

Ah, Sir.

Old Philpot.

How much is your remittance from Messina?

George.

George.

Seven hundred and fifty.

Old Philpot.

Then you want fifteen hundred and fifty.

George.

Exactly.

Old Philpot.

Don Alvarada is a good man you say?

George.

Perfectly good.

Old Philpot.

I will venture to lend the money. You must allow me commission upon those bills for taking them up for honour of the drawer.

George.

Agreed.

Old Philpot.

Lawful interest, while I am out of my money.

George.

I subscribe.

Old Philpot.

A power of attorney to receive the money from Alvarada, when he makes a payment.

Philpot.
You shall have it.

Old Philpot.
Your own bond.

George.
To be sure.

Old Philpot.
Go and get me a check. You shall have a draught on the bank.

George.
Yes, Sir. (*going*)

Old Philpot.
But stay. I had forgot: I must sell out for this. Stocks are under *par*. You must pay the difference.

George.
Was ever such a leech! (*aside*) By all means, Sir.

Old Philpot.
Step and get me a check.

George.
A fool and his money are soon parted. (*aside*.)
[*Exit.*

Old Philpot, *solus*.
What with commission, lawful interest, and his pay-

paying the difference of the stocks, which are higher now than when I bought in, this will be no bad morning's work; and then in the evening, I shall be in the rarest spirits for this new adventure I am re-recommended to. Let me see what is the lady's name. (*takes a letter out*) Corinna! Ay, ay, by the description she is a bale of goods. I shall be in rare spirits. Ay, this is the way, to indulge one's passions and yet conceal them, and to mind one's business in the oity, as if one had no passions at all. I long for the evening methinks. Body o'me---I am a young man still.

Enter QUILLDRIVE.

QUILLDRIVE.
Sir Jasper Wilding, Sir, and his daughter.

OLD PHILPOT.
I am at home.

Enter SIR JASPER *and* MARIA.
(SIR JASPER *dressed as a fox-hunter, and singing*)

OLD PHILPOT.
Sir Jasper, your very humble servant.

SIR JASPER.
Master Philpot, I be glad to zee ye, I be indeed.

OLD PHILPOT.
The like compliment to you, Sir Jasper. Miss Maria, I kiss your fair hand.

MARIA.
Sir, your most obedient.

Sir Jasper.

Ay, ay, I ha brought un to zee you. There's my girl: I ben't afhamed of my girl.

Maria.

That's more than I can fay of my father. Luckily thefe people are as much ftrangers to decorum as my old gentleman, otherwife this vifit from a lady to meet her lover would have an odd appearance. Though fo lately a boarding-fchool girl, I know enough of the world for that. (*afide*)

Old Philpot.

Truly fhe is a blooming young lady, Sir Jafper, and I verily fhall like to take an intereft in her.

Sir Jasper.

I ha brought her to zee ye, and zo your zon may ha' her as foon as he will.

Old Philpot.

Why fhe looks three and a half per cent. better than when I faw her laft.

Maria.

Then there is hopes that in a little time I fhall be above *par*. He rates me like a lottery-ticket.

(*Afide*)

Old Philpot.

Ay, ay, I like her, Sir Jafper: Mifs has the appearance of a very fenfible, difcreet young lady; and to deal freely, without that, fhe would not do for my fon. George is a fhrewd one; I have often heard him declare, no confideration fhould ever prevail on him to marry a fool.

Maria.

Maria.

Ay, you have told me so before, old gentleman, but I have my cue from my brother; and if I don't soon give Master George a surfeit of me, why then I am not a notable girl. (*aside*)

Enter George.

George.

A good clever old cuff this; after my own heart. I think I'll have his daughter, if it is only for the pleasure of hunting with him.

Sir Jasper.

Zon-in-law, gee us your hand. What zay you? Are you ready for my girl?

George.

Say grace as soon as you will, Sir, I'll fall to.

Sir Jasper.

Well zaid. I like you. I like un Master Philpot. I'll tell you what, let un talk to her now.

Old Philpot.

And so he shall. George, she is a bale of goods; speak her fair now, and then you'll be in cash. (*aside*)

George.

I think I had rather not speak to her now. I hate speaking to your modest women. Sir,---Sir, a word in your ear; had not I better break my mind, by advertising for her in a newspaper?

Old Philpot.

Talk fenfe to her, George; fhe is a notable girl. I'll give you a draft upon the bank prefently.

Sir Jasper.

Come along, Mafter Philpot, come along; I ben't afraid of my girl: come along.
[*Exeunt* Sir Jafper *and* Old Philpot.

Maria.

A pretty fort of a lover they have found for me.
(*afide*)

George.

How fhall I fpeak my mind to her? She is almoft a ftranger to me. (*afide*)

Maria.

Now I'll make the hideous thing hate me if I can.
(*afide*)

George.

Ay, fhe is as fharp as a needle, I warrant her.
(*afide*)

Maria.

When will he begin?---Ah, you fright! You rival Mr. Beaufort! I'll give him an averfion to me, that's what I will; and fo let him have the trouble of breaking off the match himfelf: not a word yet? He is in fine confufion. (*looks foolifh*) I think I may as well fit down, Sir.

George.

Ma'am---I---I---I---(*frighted*)---I'll hand you a chair, Ma'am---there, Ma'am. (*bows awkwardly*)

Maria.

A COMEDY.

Maria.
Many thanks to you, Sir.

George.
I'll sit down too. (*in confusion*)

Maria.
Heigho!

George.
Ma'am!

Maria.
Sir!

George.
I thought---I---I---did not you say something, Ma'am?

Maria.
No, Sir; nothing.

George.
I beg your pardon, Ma'am.

Maria.
Oh! you are a sweet creature. (*aside*)

George.
The ice is broke now; I have begun, and so I'll go on.
(*sits silent, looks foolish, and steals a look at her*)

Maria.

MARIA.
An agreeable interview this!

GEORGE.
Pray, Ma'am, do you ever go to concerts?

MARIA.
Concerts! what's that, Sir?

GEORGE.
A mufic meeting.

MARIA.
I have been at a quaker's meeting, but never at a mufick meeting.

GEORGE.
Lord, Ma'am, all the gay world goes to concerts. She notable! I'll take courage, fhe's nobody. Will you give me leave to prefent you a ticket for the Crown and Anchor, Ma'am?

MARIA. (*looking fimple and awkward*)
A ticket! what's a ticket?.

GEORGE.
There, Ma'am, at your fervice.

MARIA. (*curtfys awkwardly*)
I long to fee what a ticket is.

GEORGE.
What a curtfy there is for the St. James's end of
the

the town! I hate her; she seems to be an ideot. (*aside*)

Maria.

Here's a charming ticket he has given me. (*aside*) And is this a ticket, Sir?

George.

Yes, Ma'am---And is this a ticket, Sir?
(*mimicks her aside*)

Maria. (*reads*)

For sale by the candle, the following goods---thirty chests straw hats; fifty tubs chip hats; pepper, sago, borax---ha---ha! such a ticket!

George.

I---I---I have made a mistake Ma'am. Here, here is the right one.

Maria.

You need not mind it, Sir: I never go to such places.

George.

No, Ma'am? I don't know what to make of her. Was you ever at the White-Conduit house?

Maria.

There's a question! (*aside*) Is that a nobleman's seat?

George. (*laughs*)

Simpleton!---No Miss---it is not a nobleman's seat---Lord! it's at Islington.

Maria.

MARIA.
Lord Iflington!---I don't know he.

GEORGE.
The town of Iflington.

MARIA.
I have not the honour of knowing his Lordſhip.

GEORGE.
Iflington is a town, Ma'am.

MARIA.
Oh! it's a town?

GEORGE.
Yes, Ma'am.

MARIA.
I am glad of it. (*laughs*)

GEORGE.
What is ſhe glad of?

MARIA.
A pretty huſband my papa has choſe for me.
(*aſide*)

GEORGE.
What ſhall I ſay to her next? Have you been at the burletta, Ma'am?

MARIA.
Where?

GEORGE.

George.
The burletta?

Maria.
Sir, I would have you to know that I am no such a person. I go to burlettas! I am not what you take me for.

George.
Ma'am?

Maria.
I'm come of good people, Sir; and have been properly educated as a young girl ought to be.

George.
What a damn'd fool she is. *(aside)*---The burletta is an opera, Ma'am.

Maria.
Opera, Sir! I don't know what you mean by this usage; to affront me in this manner!

George.
Affront! I mean quite the reverse, Ma'am; I took you for a connoisseur.

Maria.
Who me a connoisseur, Sir! I desire you won't call me names; I'm sure I never so much as thought of such a thing. Sir, I won't be called a connoisseur ---I won't---I won't---I won't.
(bursts out a crying)

George.

George.

Ma'am, I meant no offence. A connoisseur is a virtuoso.

Maria.

Don't virtuoso me! I am no virtuoso, Sir, I would have you to know it. I am as virtuous a girl as any in England, and I never will be a virtuoso.

(cries bitterly)

George.

But, Ma'am, you mistake me quite.

Maria.

(*In a passion, choaking her tears and sobbing*)

Sir, I am come of as virtuous people as any in England. My family was always remarkable for virtue. My mamma (*bursts out*) was as good a woman as ever was born, and my aunt Bridget (*sobbing*) was a virtuous woman too; and there's my sister Sophy makes as good and virtuous wife as any at all. And so, Sir, don't call me a virtuoso. I won't be brought here to be treated in this manner, I won't---I won't---I won't. (*cries bitterly*)

George.

The girl's a natural. So much the better. I'll marry her, and lock her up. Ma'am, upon my word you misunderstand me.

Maria.

Sir, (*drying her tears*) I won't be called connoisseur by you nor any body. I am no virtuoso, and I'd have you to know it.

George.

GEORGE.

Ma'am, connoisseur and virtuoso are words for a person of taste

MARIA.

Taste! *(sobbing)*

GEORGE.

Yes, Ma'am.

MARIA.

And did you mean to say as how I am a person of taste?

GEORGE.

Undoubtedly.

MARIA.

Sir, your most obedient humble servant; Oh! that's another thing. I have a taste to be sure.

GEORGE.

I know you have, Ma'am. O you're a cursed ninny. *(aside.)*

MARIA.

Yes, I know I have. I can read tolerably; and I begin to write a little.

GEORGE.

Upon my word, you have made a great progress; What could old Square-Toes mean by passing her upon me for a sensible girl? And what a fool I was to be afraid to speak to her? I'll talk to her openly at at once. Come fit down, Mifs. Pray are you inclined to matrimony?

MARIA.

Yes, Sir. (*fmiling*)

GEORGE.

Are you in love?

MARIA.

Yes, Sir.

GEORGE.

Your naturals are always amorous. (*afide*) How fhould you like me?

MARIA.

Of all things. (*fmiling at him*)

GEORGE.

A girl without ceremony. (*afide*) Do you love me?

MARIA.

Yes, Sir.

GEORGE.

But you don't love any body elfe?

MARIA.

Yes, Sir. (*fmiling at him*)

GEORGE.

Frank and free. (*afide*) But not fo well as me?

MARIA.

MARIA.

Yes, Sir.

GEORGE.

Better may hap?

MARIA.

Yes, Sir.

GEORGE.

The devil you do! (*aside*) And, perhaps, if I fhould marry you, I fhould have a chance to be made a---

MARIA.

Yes, Sir. (*looks at him and laughs*)

GEORGE.

The cafe is clear; Mifs Maria, your very humble fervant; you are not for my money I promife you.

MARIA.

Sir.

GEORGE.

I have done, Ma'am, that's all, and I take my leave.

MARIA.

But you'll marry me?

GEORGE.

No, Ma'am, no; no fuch thing. You may provide yourfelf a hufband elfewhere, I am your humble fervant.

MARIA.

Maria.

Not marry me, Mr. Philpot? But you muſt: my papa ſaid you muſt; and I will have you.

George.

There's another proof of her nonſenſe. (*aſide*) Make yourſelf eaſy, for I ſhall have nothing to do with you.

Maria.

Not marry me, Mr. Philpot? (*burſts out in tears*) but I ſay you ſhall, and I will have a huſband, or I'll know the reaſon why. You ſhall, you ſhall---

George.

A pretty ſort of wife they intend for me here!

Maria.

I wonder you an't aſhamed of yourſelf to affront a young girl in this manner. I'll go and tell my papa ---I will---I will---I will. (*crying bitterly*)

George.

And ſo you may. I have no more to ſay to you; and ſo your ſervant, Miſs; your ſervant.

Maria.

A vile barbarous man! (*cries very bitterly*) Ay! and, by goles! my brother Bob ſhall fight you.

George.

What care I for your brother Bob? (*going*)

MARIA.

How can you be so cruel, Mr. Philpot? How can you----Oh---(*cries and struggles with him. Exit* George) (*bursts into a laugh*) I have carried my brother's scheme into execution charmingly. Ho! ho! he will break off the match now of his own accotd---Ha! ha! this is charming; this is fine; this is like a girl of spirit.

End of the FIRST ACT.

ACT the SECOND.

Enter CORINNA, TOM *following her.*

CORINNA.

An elderly gentleman did you say?

TOM.

Yes; that says he has got a letter for you, Ma'am.

CORINNA.

Desire the gentleman to walk up stairs. [*Exit* Tom.] These old fellows will be coming after a body. But they pay well, and so---Servant, Sir.

Enter OLD PHILPOT.

OLD PHILPOT.

Fair lady, your very humble servant. Truly a blooming young girl! Madam, I have a letter here for you from Bob Poacher, whom, I presume, you know.

CORINNA.

Yes, Sir, I know Bob Poacher. He is a very good friend of mine; (*reads to herself*) he speaks so handsomely of you, Sir, and says you are so much of the gentleman, that, to be sure, Sir, I shall endeavour to be agreeable.

Old Philpot.

Really you are very agreeable. You see I am punctual to my hour. (*looks at his watch*)

Corinna.

That is a mighty pretty watch, Sir.

Old Philpot.

Yes, Madam, it is a repeater; it has been in our family for a long time. This is a mighty pretty lodging. I have twenty guineas here in a purse, here they are; (*turns them out upon the table*) as pretty golden rogues as ever fair fingers played with.

Corinna.

I am always agreeable to any thing from a gentleman.

Old Philpot.

There are (*aside*) some light guineas among them. I always put off my light guineas in this way. You are exceedingly welcome, Madam. Your fair hand looks so tempting, I must kiss it. Oh! I could eat it up. Fair lady, your lips look so cherry, they actually invite the touch; (*kisses*) really it makes the difference of cent. per cent. in one's constitution. You have really a mighty pretty foot. Oh, you little rogue! I could smother you with kisses. You little delicate, charming---(*kisses her*)

George *within*.

George.

Gee-houp!---Awhi!---Awhi! Gallows! Awhi!

OLD PHILPOT.

Hey---what is all that? Somebody coming!

CORINNA.

Some young rake, I fancy, coming in whether my fervants will or no.

OLD PHILPOT.

What fhall I do? I would not be feen for the world. Can't you hide me in that room?

CORINNA.

Dear heart! no, Sir: thefe wild young fellows take fuch liberties. He may take it into his head to go in there, and then you will be detected. Get under the table: he fhan't remain long, whoever he is. Here, here, Sir, get under here.

OLD PHILPOT.

Ay, ay; that will do. Don't let him ftay long Give me another bufs. Wounds! I could---

CORINNA.

Hufh! Make hafte.

OLD PHILPOT.

Ay, ay; I will, fair lady. (*creeps under the table and peeps out*) Don't let him ftay long.

CORINNA.

Hufh! filence! you will ruin all elfe.

GEORGE.

Enter GEORGE, *dressed out.*

GEORGE.

Sharper do your work---Awhi! Awhi! So my girl; how doſt do?

CORINNA.

I did not expect to see you ſo ſoon. I thought you was to be at the club. The ſervants told me you came back from the city at two o'clock to dreſs, and ſo I concluded you would have ſtaid all night as uſual.

GEORGE.

No; the run was againſt me again, and I did not care to purſue ill-fortune. But I am ſtrong in caſh, my girl.

CORINNA.

Are you?

GEORGE.

Yes, yes; caſh in plenty.

OLD PHILPOT. *(peeping)*

Ah the ungracious! Theſe are your haunts, are they?

GEORGE.

Yes, yes; I am ſtrong in caſh. I have taken in old curmudgeon ſince I ſaw you.

CORINNA.

As how, pray?

OLD PHILPOT. *(peeping out)*
Ay, as how; let us hear, pray.

GEORGE.
Why, I'll tell you.

OLD PHILPOT. *(peeping)*
Ay! let us hear.

GEORGE.
I talked a world of wisdom to him.

OLD PHILPOT.
Ay!

GEORGE.
Tipt him a few rascally sentiments of a scoundrelly kind of prudence.

OLD PHILPOT.
Ay!

GEORGE.
The old curmudgeon chuckled at it.

OLD PHILPOT.
Ay, ay; the old curmudgeon! ay, ay.

GEORGE.
He is a sad old fellow!

OLD PHILPOT.
Ay! go on.

GEORGE.

George.

And so I appeared to him as deserving of the gallows as he is himself.

Old Philpot.

Well said boy, well said; go on.

George.

And then he took a liking to me. Ay, ay, says he, ay, friendship has nothing to do with trade. George, thou art a son after my own heart; and then as I dealt out little maxims of penury, he grinn'd like a Jew broker, when he has cheated his principal of an eighth per cent. Ay, ay, that is the very spirit of trade. A fool and his money are soon parted. (*mimicking him*) And so, on he went, like Harlequin in a French comedy, tickling himself into a good humour, till, at last, I tickled him out of fifteen hundred and odd pounds.

Old Philpot.

I have a mind to rise and break his bones. But then I discover myself. Lie still, Isaac, lie still.

George.

I understand trap. I talked of a great house stopping payment. The thing was true enough, but I had no dealing with them.

Old Philpot.

Ay, ay.

George.

And so, for fear of breaking off a match with an ideot

ideot he wants me to marry, he lent me the money, and cheated me into the bargain.

Old Philpot.

Ay, you have found it out; have ye?

George.

No old usurer in England, grown hard-hearted in his trade, could have dealt worse with me. I must have commission upon these bills for taking them up for honour of the drawer; your bond; lawful interest, while I am out of my money; and the difference for selling out of the stocks. An old miserly good for nothing skin-flint.

Old Philpot.

My blood boils to be at him. Go on, can you tell us a little more?

George.

Po! he is an old worthless miser, and so I will talk no more about him. Come give me a kiss.
(they kiss)

Old Philpot.

The young dog, how he fastens his lips to her!

George.

You shall go with me to Epsom next Sunday.

Corinna.

Shall I? That's charming.

George.

You shall: in my chariot; I drive.

CORINNA.

But I don't like to fee you drive.

GEORGE.

But I like it. I am as good a coachman as any in England. There was my lord---What d'ye call him---He kept a ſtage-coach for his own driving, but, Lord! he was nothing to me.

CORINNA.

No!

GEORGE.

Oh! no; I know my road-work, my girl, when I have my coachman's hat on---Is my hat come home?

CORINNA.

It hangs up yonder! but I don't like it.

GEORGE.

Let me fee it. Ay! the very thing. Mind me when I go to work: throw my eyes about a few; handle the braces; take the off-leader by the jaw; here you, how have you curbed this horfe up? Let him out a link, do you blood of a---whoo eh!---Jewel---Button!---whoo eh! Come here, you Sir, how have you coupled Gallows? You know he'll take the bar of Sharper. Take him in two holes, do. There's four pretty little knots as any in England---Whoo eh!

CORINNA.

But can't you let your coachman drive?

GEORGE.

George.

No, no; fee me mount the box, handle the reins, my wrift turned down, fquare my elbows, ftamp with my foot---Gee up! off we go. Button, do you want to have us over! Do your work do---Awhi! awhi!---There we bowl away; fee how fharp they are---Gallows!---fofty up hill! (*whiftles*) there's a public-houfe. Give 'em a mouthful of water, do; and fetch me a dram---drink it off---Gee up! awhi! awhi!---There we go fcrambling altogether: reach Epfom in an hour and forty-three minutes, all Lombard-ftreet to an egg-fhell, we do. There's your work my girl!---Eh! damn me.

Old Philpot.

Mercy on me! What a profligate debauched young dog it is.

Enter Young Wilding.

Wilding.

Ha! my little Corinna---Sir, your fervant.

George.

Your fervant, Sir.

Wilding.

Sir, your fervant.

George.

Any commands for me, Sir?

Wilding.

For you, Sir?

George.

A COMEDY.

GEORGE.

Yes, for me, Sir?

WILDING.

No, Sir, I have no commands for you.

GEORGE.

What's your business?

WILDING.

Business!

GEORGE.

Ay, business.

WILDING.

Why, very good business I think---My little Corinna---My life---My angel!

GEORGE.

Is that your business?---Pray, Sir, not so free, if you please.

WILDING.

Not so free!

GEORGE.

No, Sir! that lady belongs to me.

WILDING.

To you?

GEORGE.

Yes, to me.

WILD-

WILDING.

Who are you?

GEORGE.

As good a man as you.

WILDING.

Upon my word! Who is this fellow, Corinna? Some journeyman-taylor, I suppose, who chuses to try on the gentleman's cloaths before he carries them home.

GEORGE.

Taylor!---What do you mean by that? You lie! I am no taylor.

WILDING.

You shall give me satisfaction for that!

GEORGE.

For what?

WILDING.

For giving me the lie.

GEORGE.

I did not.

WILDING.

You did, Sir.

GEORGE.

You lie; I'll bet you five pounds I did not. But
if

if you have a mind for a frolick, let me put by my sword: now, Sir, come on. *(in a boxing attitude)*

WILDING.

Why, you scoundrel, do you think I want to box? Draw, Sir, this moment.

GEORGE.

Not I---come on.

WILDING.

Draw, or I'll cut you to pieces.

GEORGE.

I'll give you satisfaction this way.
(clenches his fist)

WILDING.

Draw, Sir, draw; you won't draw! There, take that, Sirrah, and that, and that, you scoundrel.

OLD PHILPOT.

Ay, ay; well done; lay it on---*(peeps out)*

WILDING.

And there, you rascal; and there.

OLD PHILPOT.

Thank you; thank you. Could not he find in his heart to lay him on another for me?

CORINNA.

Pray, don't be in such a passion.

Wilding.

My dear Corinna, don't be frighten'd; I fhall not murder him.

Old Philpot.

I am fafe here---lie ftill Ifaac, lie ftill: I am fafe.

Wilding.

The fellow has put me out of breath. *(fits down)* (Old Philpot's *watch ftrikes under the table*) Whofe watch is that? *(looks round)* Hey! what is all this? *(looks under the table)* Your humble fervant, Sir! Turn out, pray, turn out. You won't? then I'll unfhell you. *(takes away the table)* Your very humble fervant, Sir.

George.

Confufion! my father there all this time! *(afide)*

Wilding.

I fuppofe you will give me the lie too?

Old Philpot. *(ftill on the ground)*

No, Sir; not I truly. But the gentleman there may divert himfelf again, if he has a mind.

George.

No, Sir, not I; I pafs.

Old Philpot.

George, you are there I fee.

George.

Yes, Sir, and you are there I fee.

WILDING.

Come rife----Who is this old fellow?

CORINNA.

Upon my word I don't know. As I live and breathe I don't: he came after my maid, I suppose; I'll go and ask her---let me run out of the way, and hide myself from this scene of confusion.

[*Exit* Corinna.

GEORGE.

What an imp of hell she is! (*aside*)

WILDING.

Come, get up, Sir; you are too old to be beat.

OLD PHILPOT. (*rising*)

In troth, so I am. But there you may exercise yourself again, if you please.

GEORGE.

No more for me, Sir, I thank you.

OLD PHILPOT.

I have made but a bad voyage of it. The ship is sunk, and stock and block loft. (*aside*)

WILDING.

Ha, ha! upon my soul, I can't help laughing. As for you, Sir, you have had what you deserv'd--- And you, reverend dad, must come here, tottering after a punk, ha, ha!

OLD PHILPOT.

Oh! George! George!

GEORGE.

Oh! father! father!

WILDING.

Ha, ha! what father and fon: And fo you have found one another out, have you?---Well, you may have bufinefs, and fo, gentlemen, I'll leave you to yourfelves. [*Exit.*

GEORGE.

This is too much to bear. What an infamous jade fhe is! All her contrivance! Don't be angry with me, Sir. I'll go my ways this moment, tie myfelf up in the matrimonial noofe, and never have any thing to do with thefe courfes again. *(going)*

OLD PHILPOT.

And hark you, George; tie me up in a real noofe, and turn me off as foon as you will. [*Exeunt.*

Enter BEAUFORT, *dreffed as a lawyer, and* SIR JASPER WILDING, *with a bottle and glafs in his hand.*

BEAUFORT.

No more, Sir Jafper, I can't drink any more.

SIR JASPER.

Why you be but a weezen-fac'd drinker, Mafter Quagmire: come, man, finifh this bottle.

BEAU-

Beaufort.

I beg to be excufed: you had better let me read over the deeds to you.

Sir Jasper.

Wounds! it's all about out-houfes, and meffuages, and barns, and ftables, and orchards, and meadows, and lands and tenements, and woods and underwoods, and commons, and backfides. I am o'the commiffion for Wilts, and I know the ley, and fo truce with your jargon, Mafter Quagmire.

Beaufort.

But, Sir, you don't confider, marriage is an affair of importance: it is contracted between perfons, firft confenting; fecondly, free from canonical impediments; thirdly, free from civil impediments, and can only be diffolved for canonical caufes or levitical caufes. See *Leviticus* xviii. and xxviii and 9th Harry VIII. chapter vii.

Sir Jasper.

You fhall drink t'other bumper, an you talk of ley.

Enter a Servant.

Servant.

Mr. Philpot, Sir, and his fon.

Sir Jasper.

I am glad of it: they will take me out of the hand of this lawyer here. [*Exit.*

Beau-

THE CITIZEN:

BEAUFORT, *solus.*

BEAUFORT.

Well done, Beaufort! thus far you have play'd your part, as if you had been of the pumple-hose family of Furnival's-Inn.

SIR JASPER. (*entering*)

Master Philpot, I be glad you are come; this man here has so plagued me with his ley, but now we'll have no more about it, but sign the papers at once.

Enter OLD PHILPOT *and* GEORGE.

OLD PHILPOT.

Sir Jasper, twenty thousand pounds you know is a great deal of money; a large fortune to give to your son with my daughter: but as George likes Maria, to forward the business, I'll advance the cash, provided you allow me discount for prompt payment, and so then we conclude a double match.

GEORGE.

Sir, I must beg to see the young lady once more before I embark; for to be plain, she appears to me a mere natural.

SIR JASPER.

I tell you what, youngster, I find my girl a notable wench: and here, here's zon Bob.

Enter YOUNG WILDING.

SIR JASPER.

Bob, gee us your hand. I ha' finished the business

nefs; and zo now, here, here, here's your vather-in-law.

OLD PHILPOT.
Of all the birds in the air, is that he? *(aside)*

SIR JASPER.
Go to un man: that's your vather:

WILDING.
This is the ftrangeft accident---Sir---Sir---*(ftifling a laugh)*---I---I---Sir---upon my foul, I can't ftand this. *(burfts out a laughing)*

OLD PHILPOT.
I deferve it: I deferve to be laughed at. *(aside)*

GEORGE.
He has behaved like a relation to me already. *(aside)*

SIR JASPER.
What's the matter, Bob? I tell you this is your vather-in-law. *(pulls* Old Philpot *to him)* Mafter Philpot, that's Bob---fpeak to un Bob; fpeak to un.

WILDING.
Sir---I---I am *(ftifles a laugh)* I fay, Sir---I am, Sir---extremely proud---of---

GEORGE.
Of having beat me, I fuppofe. *(aside)*

WILDING.
Of the honour, Sir---of---of---*(laughs)*

GEORGE.

GEORGE.

Ay! that's what he means. *(aside)*

WILDING.

And, Sir---I---I----this opportunity----I cannot look him in the face---*(burſts out into a laugh)* Ha, ha! I cannot ſtay in the room---*(going)*

SIR JASPER.

Why the volks are all mad, I believe. You ſhall ſtay, Bob; you ſhall ſtay. *(holds him)*

WILDING.

Sir I---I cannot poſſibly---*(whiſpers his father)*

OLD PHILPOT.

George, George! what a woeful figure do we make!

GEORGE.

Bad enough of all conſcience, Sir.

SIR JASPER.

An odd adventure, Bob. *(laughs heartily)*

OLD PHILPOT.

Ay! there now he's hearing the whole affair, and they are laughing at me.

SIR JASPER. *(to* Old Philpot*)*
Ha, ha! Po, never mind it: a did not hurt un.

OLD PHILPOT.

It's all diſcovered.

Sir Jasper.

Ha, ha!---I told ye zon Bob could find a hare fquat upon her form with any he in Chriftendom. Ha, ha! never mind it man, Bob meant no harm. Here, here, Bob, here's your vather, and there's your brother. I fhould like to ha'zeen un under the table.

Wilding.

Gentlemen, your moft obedient.
(ftifling a laugh)

Old Philpot.

Sir, your fervant. He has lick'd George well, and I forgive him.

Sir Jasper.

Well, young gentleman, which way is your mind now?

George.

Why, Sir, to be plain, I find your daughter an ideot.

Sir Jasper.

Zee her again then: zee her again. Here, you, firrah, fend our Moll hither.

Servant.

Yes, Sir.

Sir Jasper.

And then we'll go into t'other room, crack a bottle, and fettle matters there. Hoic! hoic---Our Moll---Tally over.

Enter MARIA.

MARIA.
Did you call me, papa?

SIR JASPER.
There, the gentleman wants to speak with you. Behave like a clever wench as you are. Come along good folks: Master Quagmire, come and finish the business.
[*Exit singing, with* Old Philpot *and* Beaufort, *manent* George *and* Maria.]

GEORGE.
I know she is a fool, and so I will speak to her without ceremony. Well, Miss, you told me you could read and write.

MARIA.
Read, Sir, Heavens!---*(looking at him)* Ha, ha, ha!

GEORGE.
What does she laugh at?

MARIA.
Ha, ha, ha, ha!

GEORGE.
What diverts you so, pray?

MARIA.
Ha, ha, ha, ha! What a fine tawdry figure you have made of yourself?

GEORGE.

George.
Figure, Madam!

Maria.
I shall die, I shall die! Ho! ho! ho!

George.
Do you make a laughing-stock of me?

Maria.
No, Sir, by no means---(*laughs*)

George.
Let me tell you, Miss, I don't understand being treated thus.

Maria.
Sir, I can't possibly help it---I---I---ha, ha!

George.
I shall quit the room, and tell your papa if you go on thus.

Maria.
Sir, I beg your pardon a thousand times. I am but a giddy girl. I cannot help it---I---I---ha, ha!

George.
Ma'am, this is downright insult.

Maria.
Sir, you look somehow or other---I don't know how, so---ha, ha, ha!

GEORGE.

Did you never ſee a gentleman dreſs'd before?

MARIA.

Never like you---I beg your pardon, Sir---ha, ha, ha!

GEORGE.

Now here is an ideot in ſpirits. I tell you this is your ignorance: I am dreſs'd in high taſte.

MARIA.

Yes, ſo you are---ha, ha, ha!

GEORGE.

Will you have done laughing?

MARIA.

Yes, Sir, I will---I will---there---there---there ---I have done.

GEORGE.

Do ſo then, and behave as you ought to do.

MARIA.

I will, Sir;---I won't look at him, and then I ſhan't laugh.

GEORGE.

Let me tell you, Miſs, that nobody underſtands dreſs better than I do.

MARIA.

Ho! ho! ho!

GEORGE.

George.
She's mad.

Maria.
No, Sir, I am not mad---I have done, Sir---I I have done---I assure you, Sir, that nobody is more averse from ill manners. I should be very sorry to affront a gentleman---Ha, ha, ha!

George.
Again! What do you mean? You'll put me in a passion, I can tell you, presently.

Maria.
I can't help it---indeed I can't---Beat me if you will, but let me laugh---I can't help it---ha, ha, ha!

George.
I am not used to such usage, Miss.

Maria.
I shall die---Do, Sir, let me laugh---it will do me good---Ha, ha, ha!
(sits down in a fit of laughing)

George.
If this is your way, I won't stay a moment longer in the room. I'll go this moment and tell your father.

Maria.
Sir, Sir, Mr. Philpot, don't be so hasty, Sir. I have done, Sir; it's over now. I have had my laugh out. I am a giddy girl, but I'll be grave. I'll compose myself and act a different scene with him
from

from what I did in the morning. I have all the materials of an impertinent wit, and I will now twirl him about the room, like a boy setting up his top with his finger and thumb. *(aside)*

George.

Miſs, I think you told me you can read and write.

Maria.

Read, Sir! Reading is the delight of my life. Do you love reading, Sir?

George.

Prodigiouſly. How pert ſhe is grown? I have read very little, and I'm reſolved for the future to read leſs. *(aside)* What have you read, Miſs?

Maria.

Every thing.

George.

You have?

Maria.

Yes, Sir, I have.

George.

Oh! brave---and do you remember what you read, Miſs?

Maria.

Not ſo well as I could wiſh. Wits have ſhort memories.

George.

George.
Oh! you are a wit too?

Maria.
I am: and do you know that I feel myself provoked to a simile now?

George.
A simile! Let us hear it.

Maria.
What do you think we are both like?

George.
Like! I played once at what's my thought like, and I could not make any thing of it.

Maria.
We are like Cymon and Iphigenia in Dryden's fable.

George.
Jenny in Dryden's fable!

Maria.
The fanning breeze upon her bosom blows;
To meet the fanning breeze her bosom rose.
That's me----now you.
He trudg'd along, unknowing what he sought,
And whistled as he went [mimicks] *for want of thought.*

George.
This is not the same girl. (*disconcerted*)

Maria.

Mark again, mark again:
The fool of nature stood with stupid eyes,
And gaping mouth, that testified surprize.

(*He looks foolish, she laughs at him*)

George.

I must take care how I speak to her; she is not the fool I took her for. (*aside*)

Maria.

You seem surprized, Sir: but this is my way. I I read, Sir, and then I apply. I have read every thing; Suckling, Waller, Milton, Dryden, Llandsdown, Gay, Prior, Swift, Addison, Pope, Young, Thompson.

George.

Hey! the devil---what a clack is here!
[*He walks away.*

Maria. (*following him eagerly*)

Shakespear, Fletcher, Otway, Southern, Rowe, Congreve, Wicherly, Farquhar, Cibber, Vanbrugh, Steel, in short every body; and I find them all wit, fire, vivacity, spirit, genius, taste, imagination, raillery, humour, character, and sentiment.---Well done, Miss Notable! you have played your part like a young actress in high favour with the town. (*aside*)

George.

Her tongue goes like a water-mill.

Maria.

What do you say to me now, Sir?

George.

Say!---I don't know what the devil to say.
(*Aside*)

Maria.

What's the matter, Sir? Why you look as if the stocks were fallen; or like London-bridge at low water; or like a waterman when the Thames is frozen; or like a politician without news; or like a prude without scandal; or like a great lawyer without a brief; or like some lawyers with one---or---

George.

Or like a poor devil of a husband hen-peck'd by a wit, and so say no more about it. What a capricious piece here is! (*aside*)

Maria.

Oh, fy! you have spoil'd all. I had not half done.

George.

There is enough of all conscience. You may content yourself.

Maria.

But I am not so easily contented. I like a simile half a mile long.

George.

I see you do.

Maria.

And I make verses too; verses like an angel; off hand, extempore. Can you give me an extempore?

George.

What does she mean!---No, Miss, I have never a one about me.

Maria.

You can't give an extempore? Oh! for shame, Mr. Philpot. I love an extempore of all things; and I love the poets dearly, their sense so fine, their invention rich as Pactolus.

George.

A poet rich as Pactolus! I have heard of Pactolus in the city.

Maria.

Very like.

George.

But you never heard of a poet as rich as he.

Maria.

As who?

George.

Pactolus---he was a great Jew merchant; lived in the ward of Farringdon without.

Maria.

Pactolus, a Jew merchant! Pactolus is a river.

George.

George.

A river!

Maria.

Yes---don't you underſtand geography?

George.

The girl's crazy!

Maria.

Oh! Sir---if you don't underſtand geography, you are nobody. I underſtand geography, and orthography; you know I told you I can write: and I can dance too---Will you dance a minuet?
(ſings and dances)

George.

You ſhan't lead me a dance, I promiſe you.

Maria.

Oh! very well, Sir: you refuſe me? Remember you'll hear immediately of my being married to another, and then you'll be ready to hang yourſelf.

George.

Not I, I promiſe you.

Maria.

Oh! mighty well: remember my words---I'll do it---you ſhall ſee---ha, ha!
(Runs off in a fit of laughing)

George.

Marry you! I would as ſoon carry my wife to live in Bow-ſtreet, and write over the door "Phil-"pot's punch-houſe."

Enter

Enter OLD PHILPOT *and* SIR JASPER.

SIR JASPER. (*singing*)
"So rarely so bravely we'll hunt him over the downs,
"and we'll hoop and we'll hollow." Gee us your hand, young gentleman; well, what zay ye to un now? Ben't she a clever girl?

GEORGE.
A very extraordinary girl indeed.

SIR JASPER.
Did not I tell un zo? Then you have nothing to do but to consummate as soon as you will.

GEORGE.
No, you may keep her, Sir: I thank you: I'll have nothing to do with her.

OLD PHILPOT.
What's the matter now, George?

GEORGE.
Po! she is a wit.

SIR JASPER.
Ay! I told un zo.

GEORGE.
And that's worse than t'other. I had rather marry a fool by half.

SIR JASPER.
Odds heart! I am afraid you are no great wit.

Enter

Enter MARIA.

MARIA.

Well, papa, the gentleman won't have me.

OLD PHILPOT.

The numfkull won't do as his father bids him; and fo, Sir Jafper, with your confent I'll make a propofal to the young lady myfelf.

MARIA.

How! what does he fay?

OLD PHILPOT.

I am in great vigour, and can be a brifk lover ftill. Fair lady, a glance of your eye is like the returning fun in the fpring: it melts away the froft of age, and gives a new warmth and vigour to all nature.

(falls a coughing)

MARIA.

Delightfull! I fhould like to have a fcene with him.

SIR JASPER.

Hey! what's in the wind now? This won't take. My girl fhall have fair play. No old fellow fhall totter to her bed. What fay you, my girl, will you rock his cradle?

MARIA.

Sir, I have one fmall doubt. Pray can I have two hufbands at a time?

GEORGE.

George.
There's a question now! She is grown foolish again.

Old Philpot.
Fair lady, the law of the land---

Sir Jasper.
Hold ye, hold ye; let me talk of law; I know the law better nor any on ye. Two husbands at once? No; no; men are scarce, and that's downright poaching.

Maria.
I am sorry for it, Sir: for then I can't marry him, I see.

Sir Jasper.
Why not?

Maria.
I am contracted to another.

Sir Jasper.
Contracted! To whom?

Maria.
To Mr. Beaufort, that gentleman, Sir.

Old Philpot.
That gentleman!

Beaufort.
Yes, Sir, (*throws open his gown*) my name is
Beau-

Beaufort. And I hope, Sir Jasper, when you consider my fortune, and my real affection for your daughter, you will generously forgive the stratagem I have made use of.

Sir Jasper.

Master Quagmire! what are you young Beaufort all this time?

Old Philpot.

All a trick; this will never do.

Beaufort.

But it will do, Sir. You have signed the deeds for your daughter's marriage to my friend Wilding; and Sir Jasper by this instrument has made me his son-in-law.

Old Philpot.

How is this? How is this? Then, Sir Jasper, you will agree to cancel the deeds, I suppose, for you know---

Sir Jasper.

Catch me at that, an ye can! I fulfilled my promise, and your son refused, and so the wench has looked out slily for herself elsewhere. Did I not tell you she was a clever girl? I ben't asham'd o' my girl. Our Moll, you have done no harm, and Mr. Beaufort is welcome to you with all my heart. I'll stand to what I have signed, though you have taken me by surprize.

Wilding.

Bravo! my scheme has succeeded rarely.

Old

Old Philpot.

And so here I am bubbled and choused out of my money. George! George! what a day's work have we made of it? Well, if it must be so, be it so. I desire, young gentleman, you'll come and take my daughter away to-morrow morning. And, I'll tell you what, here, here---Take my family watch into the bargain; and I wish it may play you just such another trick as it has me; that's all. I'll never go intriguing with a family watch again.

Maria.

Well, Sir! (*to* George) what do you think of me now? An't I a connoisseur, Sir! and a virtuoso? Ha! ha!

George.

Yes; and much good may it do your husband. I have been connoisseured among ye to some purpose. Bubbled at play; duped by my wench; cudgeled by a rake; laughed at by a girl; detected by my father; and there is the sum total of all I have got at this end of the town.

Old Philpot.

This end of the town! I desire never to see it again while I live. I'll pop into a hackney-coach this moment, drive to Mincing-lane, and never venture back to this side of Temple-bar. (*going*)

George.

And, Sir, Sir!---shall I drive you? I'll overturn him at the first corner. (*going*)

SIR JASPER.

No, no; you shan't go zo, neither. You shall stay and crack a bottle. [*stops them both.*

OLD PHILPOT *and* GEORGE *come forward and speak the*

EPILOGUE:

FATHER.

OH! George, George, George! *'tis such young rakes as you,*
That bring vile jokes, and foul dishonour too,
Upon our city youth.

GEORGE.

'Tis very true.

FATHER.

St. James's end o' th' town---

GEORGE.

No place for me.

FATHER.

No truly, no: their manners disagree
With ours intirely: yet you there must run,
To ape their follies.

George.
And am so undone.

Father.
There you all learn a vanity in vice,
You turn mere fops; you game.

George.
Oh damn the dice.

Father.
Bubbled at play---

George.
Yes, Sir.

Father.
By every common cheat.

George.
Ay! here's two witnesses---(pulls out his pockets)

Father.
You get well beat.

George.
A witness too of that, (shews his head) *and there's*
another. (to Young Wilding)

Father.
You dare to give affronts.

George.
Wounds such a pother!---

Father.
Affronts to gentlemen!

George.

EPILOGUE.

GEORGE.
'Twas a rash action.

FATHER.
Damn me, you lie! I'll give you satisfaction.
(mimicking)
Drawn in by strumpets, and detected too!

GEORGE.
That's a sad thing, Sir! I'll be judg'd by you.

FATHER.
The dog, he has me there.

GEORGE.
Think you it right,
Under a table------

FATHER.
Miserable plight!

GEORGE.
For grave threescore to sculk with trembling knees,
Aud envy each young lover that he sees!
Think you it fitting thus abroad to roam?

FATHER.
Wou'd I had stay'd to cast accounts at home.

GEORGE.
Ay! there's another vice! With anxious care---

FATHER.
Sirrah, have done: these taunts I cannot bear.

GEORGE.
You brood for ever o'er your much-lov'd store,
And scraping cent. per cent. *still pine for more.*

EPILOGUE.

At Jonathan's, where millions are undone,
Now cheat a nation, and now cheat your son.

FATHER.

Rascal, enough!

GEORGE.

I could but I am loth---

FATHER.

Enough! This jury (to the Audience*) will convict us both.*

GEORGE.

Then to the court we'd better make submission.
Ladies and gentlemen, with true contrition,
I here repent my faults. Ye courtly train,
Farewel!---farewel, ye giddy and ye vain!
I now take up; forsake the gay and witty,
To live henceforth a credit to the city.

FATHER.

You see me here quite cover'd o'er with shame,
I hate long speeches, but I'll do the same.
Come, George, *to mend is all the best can boast.*

GEORGE.

Then let us in---

FATHER.

And this shall be our toast:
May Britain's thunder on her foes be hurl'd,

GEORGE.

And London prove the market of the world!

No One's Enemy but His Own

No One's Enemy but his Own.

A
COMEDY,
IN TWO ACTS.

Performed at the

THEATRE ROYAL
IN
COVENT-GARDEN.

Scire tuum nihil est, nisi te scire hoc sciat alter.
PERSIUS.

Plenus rimarum sum : hac atque illac perfluo.
TER.

PROLOGUE.

Spoken by Mr. SMITH.

*B*OLD was the man, and fenc'd in ev'ry part
  With oak, and ten-fold brass about his heart,
To build a Play who tortur'd first his brain,
And then dar'd launch it on this stormy main.
What tho', at first, he spreads his little sails
To Heav'n's indulgent and propitious gales?
As the land gradual lessens to his eye,
He finds a troubled sea, and low'ring sky:
Envy, detraction, calumny, and spite,
Raise a worse storm than when the winds unite.
Around his bark, in many a dang'rous shoal,
Those monsters of the deep, the critics, prowl.
" She's a weak vessel, for these seas unfit,
" And has on board her not a spice of wit:
" She's French-built too; of foreign make," they cry;
Like geese, still cackling that the Gauls are nigh.
If thrown on rocks by the hoarse dashing wave,
Th' unhappy crew no hand is stretch'd to save;
But rouud the wreck, like Moors, with furious joy,
The witlings crowd, to murder and destroy.
  These are known dangers; and, still full as certain,
The bard meets other ills behind the curtain.
Little you think, ere yet you fix his fate,
What previous mischiefs there in ambush wait;
What plagues arise from all the mimic throng:
" My part's too short;---and, Sir, my part's too long."
This calls for incident; that repartee.
" Down the back stairs pen an escape for me.
" Give me a ladder, Mr. Bayes, of rope;
" I love to wear the breeches, and elope.
" Something for me the groundlings ears to split.
" Write a dark closet, or a fainting fit.
" Fix Woodward *in some whimsical disgrace*:
" Or be facetious with Ned Shuter's *face*."

This

PROLOGUE.

*This is our way, and yet our bard to-night
Removes each obstacle, and springs to light.
Some scenes, we hope, he brings to nature true,
Some gleams of humour, and a moral too;
No forms, grotesque and wild, are here at strife:
He boasts an etching from the real life;
Exerts his efforts in a polish'd age,
To drive the Smithfield muses from the stage;
By easy dialogue would win your praise
And on fair decency graft all his bays.*

Dramatis Personæ.

CARELESS,	Mr. WOODWARD.
SIR PHILIP FIGUREIN,	Mr. SHUTER.
WISELY,	Mr. ROSS.
BELLFIELD,	Mr. SMITH.
BLUNT,	Mr. CLARKE.
BRAZEN, servant to WISELY,	Mr. CUSHING.
CRIB, a Taylor,	Mr. COSTOLLO.
LA JEUNESSE, a French barber,	Mr. HOLTOM.
TOM, servant to CARELESS,	Mr. ****.

WOMEN.

LUCINDA,	Miss ELLIOT.
HORTENSIA,	Mrs. WARD.

Scene WINDSOR.

No One's Enemy but his Own.

ACT the FIRST.

Enter CARELESS *and* BLUNT.

CARELESS.

OH! ho! ho!---that laſt ſtroke I ſhall never ſurvive. My dear Blunt, you are no reader of character: the ſcience is beyond you: you don't know me.

BLUNT.

No man knows his own houſe better than I do you.

CARELESS.

Wrong, poſitively wrong.

BLUNT.

You may flatter yourſelf, Careleſs, but I wiſh you had a little of our friend Wiſely in your compoſition.

CARELESS.

Wrong again! Wiſely indeed has the name of a good ſort of a ſenſible kind of man; but the heart is never concerned in any one action of his life.

BLUNT.

Why, as to his heart---

Careless.

He has none; no heart at all: his affections are all contracted into a narrow regard for felf, and his underftanding points for ever to fchemes of intereft.

Blunt.

And your heart has made a window in your breaft, where every body may look and fee what paffes within. Shakefpeare has touched you to the life: " Your heart upon your fleeve, for daws to " peck at.

Careless.

There again! You obfervers of character are the ftrangeft characters yourfelves! I am grown very fecret of late: I don't believe there's even a ufurer about town can hold his tongue better.

Blunt.

S'death, man! you are the very fieve of your own intentions; the marplot of your own defigns; I would as foon truft a fecret with the printer of a daily paper. How did you lofe your election?

Careless.

Po! an old ftory: but that has taught me wifdom.

Blunt.

And your wifdom confifts in repenting of one folly, to commit a new one the next moment. Have you faid nothing of Lucinda lately.

Careless.

Not a fyllable.

Blunt.

Blunt.
You have not shewn her letter?

Careless.
Letter!---I!

Blunt.
You have shewn it, and there is Bellfield in a rage about a paragraph relating to himself.

Careless.
Well, now, that is very hard. I never shewed that letter to any body but Jack Tattle.

Blunt.
It was not he that betrayed you: when did you see Lady Betty Gabble?

Careless.
My Lady Betty? I---I repeated a passage to my Lady *Betty Gabble,* only by way of conversation.

Blunt.
And by way of conversation you are ever working your own ruin.

Careless.
Confusion! there is no trusting any body. My Lady Betty told me the whole affair between her and Sir George---

Blunt.
And you told it to Lucinda; she whispered half a dozen intimates, and so the story has gone on gathering like a snow ball.

Careless.

'Sdeath! the people that liften to idle ftories fhould be all hung up by the ear---

Blunt.

So the old poet has faid; but he adds, that all who fetch and carry ftories fhould be hung up by the tongue. Caution is neceffary: ridicule is the tafte of the age: every man you meet is a pleafant fellow: he has picked up a character, an incident, a ftory, a damned high ftory; he goes to the play with it; tells it in a fide box; buzz, it goes round the houfe; whifks away to the card table, and fo flies all over the town.

Careless.

All this is true, but I am a new man---

Blunt.

Po!---Bellfield has outwitted you: he will marry Lucinda.

Careless.

Ha! ha! now you fee I can keep a fecret. I have been engaged upon a better profpect this week paft; you have been here at Windfor in the fame houfe with me for three days, and yet not the wifer.

Blunt.

Three entire days!

Careless.

Yes; three entire days; and I have been clofe as oak. Ha! ha! you will be furprized. Ha! ha!

the

the greatest thing in the world! Ha! ha!---you will never guess it---ha! ha! a prodigious hit!

BLUNT.

Thou art an honest fellow, Careless, and no one's enemy but your own.

CARELESS.

Ha! ha!---I shall have the command of a borough.

BLUNT.

Very well! Keep your secret---

CARELESS.

The charming, blooming widow---

BLUNT.

Why speak of it?

CARELESS.

Only to you, man; only to you; my dear Blunt, if you will promise me---

BLUNT.

No; I promise nothing: I must step and write a letter: Wisely carries it to town for me: he will be here presently---

CARELESS.

Ha! ha!---Hortensia, my dear boy---

BLUNT.

There now!---how did you gain access to her?

CARE-

CARELESS.

I knew it would surprize you. Ha! ha!---I am ruined, if a syllable takes wind.

BLUNT.

Why she has broke off several matches already, because her fools were so imprudent as to make her the town talk.

CARELESS.

Very true: but she is come-at-able for all that: a warm amorous widow I can tell you, and---

Enter TOM.

TOM.

Your Honour's taylor from London, and your peruke-maker.

CARELESS.

Shew them in. [*Exit* Tom] Ha! ha!---Blunt--- preparations for my wedding! Bellfield may marry Lucinda; I shall lose no prize by it---ha! ha!--- have not I managed it well?

BLUNT.

You begin your triumph before the victory is gained.

Enter CRIB *and* LA JEUNESSE, *and Man with a Wig.*

CARELESS.

Walk in, Mr. Crib---Ha! La Jeunesse---Blunt, Blunt---a seal upon your lips.

BLUNT.

Blunt.
Keep your own secrets, if you can.   [*Exit.*

La Jeunesse.
Monsieur, I have l'honneur to make you such wig as will be de wonder of de town.

Crib.
And I have brought you such a suit of cloaths! I shall so admire them, when your Honour has them on: the greatest pleasure of my life is to admire my own cloaths.

La Jeunesse.
Me go to de Mall every Sunday to see my wig it walk by.

Crib.
And I go as often as I can to see my cloaths make a figure.

Careless.
Oh! you are both eminent in your vocations---

Crib.
Ah! Sir---you will be such a handsome bridegroom in this suit. Will your Honour try it on?

Careless.
I dare say it is elegance itself.---Monsieur La Jeunesse, you may fit on the wig.

La Jeunesse.
De tout mon cœur.---A ça---wid dis wig, you will look comme *un ange.*---Dis wig! It is not wig---it is head of hair---has it de honneur to sit easy upon your head?

Care-

CARELESS.
Perfectly easy.

LA JEUNESSE.
It is nature make dat, and not me.

CRIB.
When my cloaths are on, Madam Lucinda will so admire you---

CARELESS.
You think I am to be married to her, do you?

LA JEUNESSE.
It is all de talk of de great vorl.

CARELESS.
You are two very foolish fellows.

Enter BLUNT, *listening*.

LA JEUNESSE.
She will be so *en amour* wid my wig.

CARELESS.
You are a French coxcomb. An intrigue with Lucinda might amuse a body's time, and perhaps I am not without hopes of success.

LA JEUNESSE.
By gar, you may hope for intrigue wid who you will. My wig it is not easy resist. My wig it have more intrigue dan any gentleman in all de town. My Lady Brilliante,----my Lady Carmine,----my Lady Bell-

Bellair,---Madam Lurewell, it was my wig ruin dem all.

CRIB.

And my cloaths have had so many fine women---

CARELESS.

Well, when you hear of a rich blooming widow---

BLUNT.

'Sdeath! going to blab.---So: I have writ my letter---

CARELESS.

Have you?---Gentlemen, I have no further occasion---

CRIB.

Your Honour's most obedient--- [*Exit.*

LA JEUNESSE.

By gar I long to know my wig who it is to be marry to--- [*Exit.*

BLUNT.

Going to trust these fellows!---

CARELESS.

Po! two silly rascals! they will think no more about it.

BLUNT.

And thus you reconcile yourself to your follies. Hortensia will require different behaviour.

Careless.

Oh! yes, so she tells me in a dear charming letter
---(*searches his pockets*) Hey!---what have I done
with it? Confusion!---If it is lost---Here, Tom,
Richard, George---run to my dressing-room, and see
if I left a letter upon the table---

Blunt.

This is being qualified for a secret.

Careless.

Distraction!---I was upon the Terras last night---
If I dropt it there---no---no---no---I have it safe;
you see, Blunt, I am close; now you shall hear---

Enter Wisely.

Wisely.

Careless your servant: Blunt, is your letter ready?

Careless.

My dear Wisely, I am sorry we are to lose you:
but before you go, listen, thou dear rogue, to this
divine epistle----(*reads*) " Hortensia presents her
" compliments"

Wisely.

Hortensia to him!---Well, Sir.

Careless.

" Presents her compliments to Mr. Careless: she
" will meet him this evening at Sir Philip Figure-
" in's Mask; and in the mean time expects he will
" hide from the world this declaration of her heart,
" which

" which his merit has extorted from her."---There's a billet doux!

Blunt.
You obey the lady's commands most admirably.

Careless.
Po! this is only among ourselves.

Wisely.
Nothing more: he is very safe with us;--- (*aside*) not if I can help it---

Enter Tom.

Tom.
Sir Philip Figurein has sent to know if your Honour will meet him on the Terras before dinner---

Careless.
I'll wait on him. [*Exit* Tom] Blunt, will you take a turn with the Knight?

Blunt.
No, I am tired of his absurdities, and your's too.
[*Exit.*

Careless.
Well said philosopher!---Ha! ha!---he calls me the *Marplot* of my own designs; but I can confide in you.

Wisely.
I am obliged to you for the intelligence, and I shall make a very proper use of it.

Careless.

Come and take a turn with me on the Terras, before you set out: I will tell you more as we walk along: pleasure itself is insipid unless imparted to a friend. It is a rare conquest, is not it? This is enough to make Hortensia's discarded lovers challenge me, fight me, kill me---Oh! ho! ho!---

[*Exeunt.*

Scene the TERRAS.

Enter LUCINDA *and* BELLFIELD.

Bellfield.

You may depend upon it, Lucinda: in spite of all this raillery, you will make me the happy man at last.

Lucinda.

Can you go on, Sir?

Bellfield.

And so, like a good-natured General, I invite you to capitulate, when the town can hold out no longer.

Lucinda.

You mistake, Mr. Bellfield: the citadel (*laying her hand to her breast*) is still proof against all the artillery you have played off. I think you have not been able to throw in much fire, Mr. Bellfield.

Bellfield.

I have a secret friend there will betray the place to me.

Lucinda.

What if you have a secret enemy there? Nature, you will allow, knows where to plant her antipathies.

Bellfield.

Oh! certainly: she delights in blending contradictions to embellish the fair, and give her the graces of variety. A sort of Mosaic work, where folly is inlaid with talents; a love of pleasure with virtue, or with pride; a power of pleasing with a perverse delight in giving pain; and as the poet says,

> "Fix'd principles with fancy ever new;
> "Shakes all together, and produces---you."

Lucinda.

Upon my word, this is a little extraordinary: by convincing me that you can with curious discernment spy out every little foible, you think to recommend yourself to my notice. Take care, Sir: you know how Apollo served the critic, who collected all the faults in a celebrated poem.

Bellfield.

As how?

Lucinda.

Why, from a parcel of wheat he ordered him to separate the chaff, and take it for his pains.

Bellfield.

Oh! that was because the man had no relish for the beauties, whereas my admiration---

Lucinda.

Is all engroffed by yourfelf; and for that reafon, you have been in my black lift---let me fee how long (*takes out a pocket book*)---" A lift of the men I never " will marry"---Let me fee---(*turns over the leaves*) let me fee----(*reads*) Mr. Worthlefs condemned May the 19th.---

Bellfield.

Worthlefs!---he married a rich heirefs, I think---

Lucinda.

And took on prodigioufly at her death---he made love to me in his weepers, and I hated him for an impoftor, worfe than Maria does Doctor Wolf in the Nonjuror.---(*reads*) Lord Hazard! he had a pale quality-face, and a genteel emaciated figure. I faw that the queen of trumps was the greateft beauty in his eyes, and fo I difmiffed him from my fervice, and he told the world that he refigned.

Bellfield.

Ha! ha!---I fee fhe will drop into my arms.

Lucinda.

Where the deuce is your name?---Morelove---Dorimant--Blackacre.---Oh! this Mr. Blackacre was a curiofity!---Not one civil word to my perfon, but all about my eftate, and when the prefent leafes expire, he would let it at an improved rent.

Bellfield.

A fellow fit only to be the fteward of your manor.

Lucinda.

The man was counted handsome, but I never thought so---a florid bloom, and a certain insipidity that I hated---He brought me all the news---

Bellfield.

Ay!

Lucinda.

Oh! all; but none that I valued; no news about the little victories this figure obtained in the world; no advices of what was said about my last new cap; he never came with " We hear from Ranelagh that Lucinda's eyes scattered death and torment among the beaux last Friday night"-----his was all political intelligence---At ten in the morning a battle was fought, and the French lost three Princes of the Blood, and five Mareshalls of France.---At twelve, the news was doubtfull---At two, an express arrived at the Secretary of State's office.---In the evening the victory was not quite so compleat, and a noble Lord was heard to say, if a certain General had done his duty, the ballance of Europe had been settled.---At night, the whole report was false, and there was no battle at all.

Bellfield.

You would have had a mere newspaper for your husband.

Lucinda.

Oh! horrid! So I told him, and that whenever he was out of hand, or not bespoke, that I should order my servants to take him in by way of the Morning Chronicle, or the Gazetteer.

Bellfield.

A pretty group of humourists you have collected.

Lucinda.

Enough to furnish out a comedy. The vain, the proud, the dull, the brisk, every species of absurdity has been my most humble servant. But where is your name?---Oh! here---Mr. Bellfield!---

Bellfield.

Now bring him on the stage---

Lucinda.

Condemned for looking at himself in the glass for a full half hour, while he was directing his discourse to me---

Bellfield.

How can you run on thus? You know I have worshipped you even to idolatry, and have offered up vows on my very knees.

Lucinda.

But I require true devotion in your prayers. Would it not provoke the patience of a saint, to have a powdered fop kneel at his shrine, with "There's a "handsome fellow for you; mind my dress, Bruf- "sels' lace, diamond ring, saucy snuff-box, and im- "pudent face." And this too under the notion of asking a blessing.

Bellfield.

I never knew you so much out: would not you have me approach you with a good conscience? And what are the pleasures of a good conscience? Self-approbation. Besides, darts and flames, and Cupid are all out of fashion now, and therefore in plain English, I love you: I shall study your happiness; and so let me call the parson.

LUCINDA.

I am frightened at you: you are a very free-thinker in love: preach this doctrine to the ladies, and you will be thought an infidel. Love's religion is a sort of popery, and requires penance, and fasting, and prayers in a language almost unintelligible. But you say your prayers in the vulgar tongue; " and so let me call the parson."---

BELLFIELD.

And as sighs, verses, and fine things, must end in that at last, you may as well wave ceremony, for as to Careless,---

LUCINDA.

Careless! I desire you will never mention him.--- Even from such a wretch as *La Jeuensse*, I could hear the scandal he talks of me.

BELLFIELD.

Scandal of you!

LUCINDA.

An intrigue will serve his turn, and my character ensures him success.

BELLFIELD.

He shall answer it to me: pronounce me unworthy of your love, if the injury is not redressed within this hour. [*Exit.*

Lucinda.

A fcurrilous wretch !----Hey !----Mr. Bellfield gone !---Did not he talk of calling the bafe man to an account ?---I hope he will not be fo mad.---So---fo---Mr. Carelefs this way ---I believe I fhall refign my perfon to Bellfield in order to pique the wretch.
[*Exit.*

Enter Careless *and* Wisely.

Careless.

Ha! ha!---poor Sir Philip---I am glad we have got rid of him. A paffion for dancing when the ufe of his limbs has almoft left him! He is feventy, is not he?

Wisely.

Not very fhort of it, and in high fpirits ftill.

Careless.

Spirits! he dances about the world as if he was bit by a tarantula. He has not a fingle idea but what is derived from dancing. Afk what fort of a place fuch a town is---" They have a very good " Monday night Affembly."---How many miles from London?---" They often dance forty couple."

Wisely.

You have him exactly.

Careless.

Well, but now we have a moment to ourfelves, have not I fucceeded rarely with Hortenfia?

WISELY.

To my astonishment.

CARELESS.

I thought so. Now, as you are going to town, here is a snuff-box with her picture in it: she gave it to me as a pledge of her love: I let it fall last night upon the Terras, and have damaged it a little: leave it at *Deards'* as you pass by, and order it to be mended.

WISELY.

With all my heart: let me see.

CARELESS.

There---is not it a beautiful picture?

WISELY.

Admirable!---This picture (*aside*) shall be his ruin.

CARELESS.

But not a word, my dear fellow.---(Sir Philip *sings*) 'Sdeath!---Sir Philip again to interrupt us. He gives a masked ball to-night: I shall have some business upon my hands there: he little suspects his lady: I could tell you a secret about her---

WISELY.

She is young, he is old, and you are well with her ladyship--

CARELESS.

Yes, I am much in her good graces: if you see hereafter the likeness of your humble servant in a boy a boy of her's, tip me a smile, but keep your mind to yourself---Hush! here comes Sir Philip, with St. Vitus strong upon him---

Enter SIR PHILIP FIGUREIN.

SIR PHILIP. *(in a minuet step)*

I forgot to tell you, Careless; Mr. Wisely, I forgot to tell you; the mask begins at six in the evening.

CARELESS.

So your lady has informed me.

SIR PHILIP.

Has she?---*(turning out his toes)* I recollect; so she told me---a little *Fete Champetre* that I have devised---You intend to---La! loll *(singing and dancing)* you intend to come early---la! loll---

CARELESS.

By all means---

SIR PHILIP. *(advancing in a minuet step)*

We shall be all gaiety, briskness, and activity of spirit.---Mr. Wisely, you intend to honour us?

WISELY.

I am afraid not, Sir: I have not your spirits---

SIR PHILIP.

(throwing back his shoulders, turning out his toes, and sinking and rising)

All owing to the exercise I take. I dance three thousand miles a year.

WISELY.

So much!

CARELESS.

More; he dances more; he danced to Italy and back again in a shorter time than ever was performed.

SIR PHILIP.

Yes, I was expeditious: did you never hear of it? I was resolved to have a *cotillon* upon the continent: I was brisk in my career. I left England on the 15th of August, went over the Alps, reached Naples, saw the Vesuvius, and eat my Michaelmas goose in London.

CARELESS.

Besides this, he goes to all the Assemblies within sixty miles of London.

SIR PHILIP.

Yes, I go to all: I call it sacrificing to the Graces. SOCRATES the philosopher called it so before me.

CARELESS.

I should like to see the old philosopher turning out his toes.

SIR PHILIP.

The old philospher loved the elegant arts. And there was Scaliger---a great critic! he danced a Pyrrhic dance,---a dance well known to the ancients, ---to the astonishment of all Germany. We have his own word for it.

WISELY.

And well they might be aftonifhed.

SIR PHILIP.

Why fo, Sir, why fo?

CARELESS.

Very true, Knight. It is a noble exercife---

SIR PHILIP.

Give me your hand: do you know Mifs Charlotte Cherry?

CARELESS.

She is the youngeft daughter, is not fhe?---

SIR PHILIP.

The fame, Sir: juft turned of fourteen: I danced with her at the laft Affembly at Sunning Hill. Was it not bold to undertake her fo young? I can match Hercules for labour in a country dance. I began the minuets with my Lady Portfoken: a comely, refponfible woman my Lady Portfoken! fhe moves a minuet like a cathedral: indeed a flight accident happened.

CARELESS.

What was that?

SIR PHILIP.

Why, Sir, as I was gliding along in the harmonious movement---you know my way---gliding along!---an unlucky hook in the great branch under the middle of the room took a fancy to my wig. I
loft

lost the honours of my head, but did not know it. I moved on; the room tittered and laughed; I did not mind; lost none of my dignity, and finished my dance before I made the discovery.

CARELESS.
My dear Knight, an unlucky disaster.

SIR PHILIP.
Oh! no; nothing; a few lampoons, epigrams, and slight lutestring verses for the summer season flew about: I danced on, and answered them out of Horace, *Nunc pede libera*---Hey! lads!

CARELESS.
Very well, Knight; an excellent repartee.

WISELY.
I think I heard something of this from your daughter Harriet.

SIR PHILIP.
Ay! poor girl---Heigho! (*sinks and rises*) she did not live long (*turning out his toes*) never took to her dancing; it was the death of her.

WISELY.
I beg pardon for mentioning her, since it seems to grieve you so much.

SIR PHILIP. (*in a minuet step*)
It was a great shock.

CARELESS.
But my favourite, your son, I hope is well.

Sir Philip.

He is at school at *Stockbridge*, but he learns nothing; when he comes home, I shall take care of his dancing myself.

Careless.

Vive la dance, Sir Philip.

Sir Philip.

Ay, Sir, vive la dance. Well, you will be at the Mask: Wisely, I shall expect you: you may go to town to-morrow. Be in at the diversions of the place, man; Careless, you won't fail; *Nunc pede libero*---Toll-der-a. [*Exit.*

Careless.

Ha! ha! was there ever such a ridiculous character? But not a word of Hortensia. You see it all depends upon secresy. Take care of my picture; yours---I must follow the Knight. [*Exit.*

Wisely. *(alone)*

Yes, I shall take care of the picture. Successful coxcomb! how could he bring her to this?

Enter Brazen.

Brazen.

The horses are put to, and the chaise is waiting.

Wisely.

Very well, Brazen: they may be put up again: I shan't leave Windsor to-day.

Brazen.

No, your Honour?

Wisely.

No: I have business for you. I have found out my rival.

Brazen.

Joy, Sir, victory! To know him, is to defeat him. What's his name?

Wisely.

Careless.

Brazen.

The gentleman I have heard you laugh at so often? I saw him go down street yesterday evening: ---comely, well built, good figure!

Wisely.

Slave, villain!---(*collars him*)

Brazen.

For Heaven's sake, Sir, don't strangle me---

Wisely.

Rascal! he handsome!---

Brazen.

That is, Sir---a little more tenderly on my wind-pipe---that is to say, Sir---not quite so hard---he seems at a distance---a little too tight still---but when you are near him---that will do, Sir---he looks quite another thing, and very unpromising---

WISELY.

What am I doing?---The rage of jealousy.---

BRAZEN.

Lord, Sir, he will be nothing in our hands.

WISELY.

Well, rascal, how to counterplot him?

BRAZEN.

Only think what you expect of me, Sir: to stop the course of a river, a bird in the air, or a lawyer at Westminster, or thunder and lightning, or a poet repeating his own verses, or a critic abusing them, or---in short, Sir, any one of these things is easier than to silence a coxcomb of wit and parts.

WISELY.

Wit and parts, villain!

BRAZEN.

Wit and parts to expose himself: no real parts.

WISELY.

To the purpose:---what must be done?

BRAZEN.

With submission, Sir, I am but a poor, ingenious good clever kind of a fellow, who pretend to no more than a tolerable share of mother-sense, to obey the happier talents of my master.

WISELY.

Oh! Hortensia, to favour this coxcomb, and send me a letter of dismission, in such abrupt terms! (*reads*) "To listen any longer to your addresses, "when I cannot comply with them, would be un- "generous. I must, therefore, by this letter, which "will be my last, wish you all happiness, and freely "declare I never can be yours,---Hortensia." I cannot lose her thus:---a lucky thought! I'll send this letter under a cover directed to Careless.---Right! right!---and this snuff-box shall be conveyed back to Hortensia. Well, hit off! Brazen, I have work for you.

BRAZEN.

The more the better, Sir: I love an active campaign.

WISELY.

Follow me this moment: can you procure a livery from one of Careless's servants?

BRAZEN.

I can give one of them his dose of liquor, and then---

WISELY.

That will do: come this way: I'll give you your instructions: an admirable project this, to supplant my rival,---to alarm Hortensia,--to throw them all into confusion, to---This way Brazen: Hortensia still is mine.

End of the FIRST ACT.

ACT the SECOND.

Enter LUCINDA *and* HORTENSIA.

LUCINDA.

MY dear Hortensia, I am astonished at you: how can you be so captious?---This is carrying it too far: there is no harm in a little raillery.

HORTENSIA.

Won't you allow me to be deeper in my own secrets, than any body else can pretend to be?

LUCINDA.

By no means: we are all very ingenious in deceiving ourselves: our passions wear so many cunning disguises, we hardly know them. Spleen shall pass for wit; avarice for œconomy; and the love of a man shall often be thought nothing more than pure friendship, or perhaps a mere delight in hearing our own praise.

HORTENSIA.

So that if I suffer a civil thing to be said to me, the pleasure I feel from the compliment, converts itself into a liking of the man's person.

LUCINDA.

Instantly, and almost imperceptibly to ourselves; and when we think we are putting him off with cold delay, it is, at the bottom, but mere coquetry to draw him on the more: like playing with edge tools, till we cut ourselves.

HOR-

Hortensia.
Still I am not wounded.

Lucinda.
I'll lay you a pot of coffee you have your second husband, before I yield to the first.

Hortensia.
You will lose: there it no room to infer any thing of this sort from my conduct.

Lucinda.
I beg your pardon: there is in your serious people a demure love of pleasure, which we giddy creatures never come up to. We receive slight impressions, and slight impressions wear away, and evaporate in the whirl of fancy. Now you are a young widow; you grieve for the loss of your husband, and grief is very amorous, my dear.

Hortensia.
Mighty well: this rattle seems to please you: but let me tell you, the man who prevails with me, must have extraordinary merit.

Lucinda.
There again now! another of the masquerade habits our passions wear: —when you are in love with a man's person, you fancy it is a refined esteem for his merit.

Hortensia.
O fy, Lucinda!—

LUCINDA.

O fy, hypocrite!---I proteſt, I did not think a briſk widow ſo unlettered in matters of love.

HORTENSIA.

Oh! a few lectures on the ſubject from Mr. Careleſs will much improve a young lady's ideas.

LUCINDA.

That's right: do you know---Well,---I adore my own eaſe upon the occaſion---I forgot to tell you---Every thing is quite at an end between me and Careleſs.

HORTENSIA.

You amaze me: was not the wedding-day fixed?

LUCINDA.

Yes, I was under ſentence of matrimony, but he has ſent me a reprieve. He is going to be married to another.

HORTENSIA.

To another! no woman of delicacy would liſten to him, conſidering how far matters have been carried with you.

LUCINDA.

Oh! if there is any body ſo inclined, the diſpute between her love and her delicacy will not laſt long. ---Delicacy may talk of nice points of honour, but that will only reach the head, while every ſyllable from that ſly urchin Love, will make it's way directly to the heart; and while Delicacy is reading lectures, Love will perſuade, and ſo the buſineſs is over. But

pray,

pray, my dear, have not you heard that Carelefs and I have declared off?

HORTENSIA.

I, my dear!---I hope (*afide*) fhe does not fufpect me---no; I have heard nothing:---how can you afk me fuch a queftion? I am not in a courfe of town news.

LUCINDA.

Well! let us change the fubject. The man is not worth a moment's thought. His indifcretion is the fmalleft of his faults.

HORTENSIA.

Give me your hand, Lucinda. If the falfe man deferts you, fhew yourfelf a girl of fpirit upon the occafion. To truft him, is taking up water with a fieve: fo refolve at once to look down with fcorn both on him, and the proud beauty, who values herfelf for the conqueft. Wifh her joy of her bargain, and think no more about him.

Enter BRAZEN, *in a livery.*

BRAZEN.

Madam Hortenfia, my mafter prefents his compliments.

HORTENSIA.

To me!---who is your mafter?

BRAZEN.

Mr. Carelefs, Madam: upon confulting his heart, he finds his inclinations fixed elfewhere, upon Madam Lucinda. (*bows to her*) I endeavoured to foften his proud heart---" Wont you confider, Sir,
" that

"that Madam Hortensia has privately given you
"every kind of encouragement?"

LUCINDA.
How! how! how!---This is worth hearing.

BRAZEN.
Rascal, says my Master, do as I bid you, and so off he brushed to the tune of an old song.

LUCINDA.
Oh! ho! ho! this is worth all the discoveries of all the philosophers for a thousand years.

HORTENSIA.
Who bribed you, Sir, to be guilty of this rudeness? Lucinda, I assure you---

LUCINDA.
And so, you are the happy lady?

HORTENSIA.
Nay, if you won't give me leave to speak---Begone, Sir, this moment: I know nothing of your master.

BRAZEN.
Before I go, Madam, permit me to return the present you made my master; this snuff-box here, with your picture in it---

LUCINDA.
Her picture too!---let me see, let me see.

HORTENSIA. *(snatches it.)*
No, Madam, it is not my picture.

BRAZEN.
Carry back her snuff-box, says he, and as I have done it a mischief, if she will get it mended, and send in her bill, I will pay the damage.

LUCINDA.
Oh! ho! ho! I shall die; I shall die.

HORTENSIA.
Vexation!---this absurd man. *(aside)*

BRAZEN.
Any commands for my master, Madam?

HORTENSIA.
No more of your impertinence.

BRAZEN.
So I shall tell my master, Madam---Well done Brazen; you are a great officer in this business---
[*Exit.*

LUCINDA.
The man who prevails with you, must have extraordinary merit---Oh! ho! ho!

HORTENSIA.
Let me tell you, there is no argument in a laugh.

LUCINDA.
Very true; I will command myself---Do you know

know (*ſtifling a laugh*) that I was weak enough to imagine, that no woman of delicacy (*ſtill ſtifling a laugh*)---conſidering---conſidering how far (*burſts into a laugh*) matters have been carried with me---Oh! ho ho!---

HORTENSIA.
Shame! diſtraction!---Will you liſten?

LUCINDA.
To truſt him, is taking up water with a ſieve.

HORTENSIA.
Inſupportable!---I will not ſtay to be inſulted thus---(*going*) If you will but hear me for a moment---

LUCINDA.
I can look down with ſcorn on the proud beauty---

HORTENSIA.
O very well---your ſervant--- [*Exit.*

LUCINDA. (*alone*)
And has your Æneas left you? Poor diſconſolate Dido!---Oh! I feel my heart much lighter. Certainly, revenge is the ruling paſſion of every female breaſt: it is the ſecond paſſion at leaſt. But---ſtay---ſtay---ſtay. What is to be done?---what's to be done?---Shall I,---to complete my triumph,---give my hand to Careleſs?---Why,---Revenge ſays, Yes: but Love ſlily whiſpers,---Have not you a *ſecret tendre* for Mr. Bellfield?---I don't know what to ſay to that?---Let me examine myſelf---How ſay you my heart? (*lays her hand to her breaſt*)---You ſhall true anſwer make to all ſuch queſtions as ſhall

be

be afked of you.---Ah!---thofe flutterings are fufpicious.---Eyes, how fay you?---We have feen the gentleman---But is that all? Have not you indulged in many a ftolen glance, and have not you gazed with pleafure on him?---It is too true:---Lips, what do you fay?---Why the gentleman has rudely forced a kifs, and though we forbade him---Forbid him!---don't equivocate.---Have not you been pleafed with his rudenefs?---Guilty---Guilty.---What fay my hands?---When he has drawn a glove on you *(looking at one hand)*---or, when he has clafped you *(looking at her other hand)* to lead me to my coach---Ah! thofe tremblings were a foft fymptom I fear.---Ears---Oh! they were delighted with his flattery---I muft call no more witneffes: fairly in for it.---Well, but what muft be done?---Hortenfia will be fo picqued if I marry Carelefs: yes, and fo will Carelefs, if I marry Bellfield. One match has been talked of; fo has the other. I have coquetted on this fide: fo I have on that. I am in a fine condition; Revenge and Love have got poor weak woman's will between them, and they beat it about like a fhuttle-cock, to and fro, backwards and forwards; tick, tack; and on which fide it will fall, Heaven only knows.

Enter CARELESS.

CARELESS. *(repeating)*
Bleft as th' immortal Gods is he,
The youth who fondly---

Hey! Lucinda here!---poor girl!---fhe may now fet her cap at me in vain.

LUCINDA.

You wretch what brings you?---Could not you ftay till the game was out?---You have interrupted fuch a battle about yourfelf.

Careless.
About me!

Lucinda.
Yes, my head and my heart were at open war about you, but you would not let them fight it out. Well, I'll retire to solitude, and let them go to cuffs again. In my absence, I suppose, my character will be finely handled by you.

Careless.
Madam, your character---

Lucinda.
Is a strange one; I know that is what you will say; have you no scraps and ends of verse?
"*Most women have no character at all.*"

Careless.
You will prove an exception to the general rule--

Lucinda. (*repeating affectedly*)
"*Matter too soft a lasting mark to bear*"---

Careless.
Wound up, I see, to your usual extravagance of spirit.

Lucinda.
That's a fault that will mend you know. My spirits in time will be under due restraint, as flowers contract with the setting sun.

CARELESS.

And folly will still encreafe, as shadows lengthen with the setting sun.

LUCINDA.

Satyrical Carelefs! But you should not have said that to my face. Would not that do better for your friends at the tavern? And La Jeuneffe, the *friſeur*, would not he be a proper person to hear your secrets?

CARELESS.

La Jeuneffe!---He has not (*aside*) repeated any thing, I hope---Another of your wild flights! Why you mount like a pheafant---Whur!

LUCINDA.

And do you vainly hope to bring me down?

CARELESS.

The gun of wit may reach you: take care.

LUCINDA.

But you have not eftate enough in Parnaffus to entitle you to kill game.

CARELESS.

You shine, Ma'am, and it is a pity you have not a train of beaux to edify by all this.

LUCINDA.

You frighten them away: let the fruit be ever fo fine, the birds will not nibble, when there is a scarecrow at hand.

CARE-

Careless.

Oh! you want no assistance to disperse them. A lover with you has as bad a time as a poor animal in a philosopher's air-pump: when your false refinements are too thin for him to subsist upon, you let in a little substantial air of common sense, merely to have the pleasure of rarifying all away again, and so leave a poor deluded fellow panting for his existence.

Lucinda.

By way of experiment, you know, one does a number of things---Oh!---your experiment to-day was the very best that ever was heard of. I must laugh with you, though you don't deserve it.

Careless.

What are you driving at?

Lucinda.

And your servant played his part with such address, and she did so bite her lips with vexation.

Careless.

I am in a wood here: unriddle pray.

Lucinda.

Oh!---you have seen her since, perhaps, and made up the quarrel.

Careless.

May I never have the fan of enraged beauty lifted to my throat, if I understand one word of all this.

Lucinda.

You don't understand? Then I'll leave you to
medi_

meditate upon it, and so I'll go and prepare for the Masquerade. [*Exit.*

CARELESS.

A l'honneur---How that pretty face will fret itself into a thousand wrinkles, when she hears of Hortensia!

Enter BELLFIELD *and* BLUNT.

BELLFIELD.

I have been in quest of you, Sir.

CARELESS.

What, with that that frozen face of care?

BELLFIELD.

My business is serious: that gentleman is in your secrets, and will, I suppose, be your friend upon the occasion: chuse your weapon, Sir.

CARELESS.

Laconic!---for what? Explain the cause.

BELLFIELD.

The cause of injured beauty, injured innocence, and violated honor.

CARELESS.

Still I am in the dark.

BELLFIELD.

Lucinda! does light break in upon you now? You chose your companions well, when you could traduce her to such a powder-puff as La Jeunesse.

BLUNT.

BLUNT.

I foresaw this. (*aside*)

CARELESS.

I am glad you are so well with the lady, as to become her champion.

BELLFIELD.

I have the applause of my own heart for it. Every honest man is concerned, when calumny draws a tear from the soft eye of injured beauty.

CARELESS.

If I have injured the lady, I beg her pardon, but strike me stupid if I can marry her.

BELLFIELD.

The lady, Sir, is worthy of---not marry her! Why not? Explain yourself.

CARELESS.

Would you compel me into a marriage?

BELLFIELD.

Compel! no---'sdeath! what am I about? (*aside*)

CARELESS.

It is impossible: I am engaged to Hortensia.

BLUNT. (*aside*)

Fool! blockhead! madman!

BELLFIELD.

Engaged to Hortensia?

CARE

A COMEDY.

CARELESS.

Pofitively, fixed, determined: the licence is fent for.

BELLFIELD.

Carelefs, give me your hand. Thou art an honeft fellow.—I challenge you!---you have done Lucinda no injury, and fo I fhall tell her. Hey! here fhe comes, and Sir Philip, and---

Enter SIR PHILIP, LUCINDA, HORTENSIA.

SIR PHILIP. *(finging)*

Lads for fhame! not ready for the Mafk? Carelefs, I have made a new dance, fince I faw you.

CARELESS.

You employ your time to advantage. Blunt, mind Hortenfia: how fhe frowns upon me!---fhe carries it with difcretion, does not fhe?

LUCINDA.

They take no notice of each other, but I will embroil them. (*afide*)---Sir Philip, Mr. Carelefs has fo peftered me with fine things, and has talked of tender pain, and pleafing anguifh, and---

BELLFIELD.

How, Carelefs! (*afide*)

CARELESS. *(to* BELLFIELD)

Never mind her: fhe is pleafed to be merry.

Lucinda.

That air of indifference! Hortensia, the wretch was down on his knees, sighing, vowing, and protesting that he loved me, and only me.

Hortensia.

False, perfidious man! (*aside*)

Lucinda.

Are you ashamed of your passion for a fine woman?

Sir Philip.

Refuse to be his partner at Sunning Hill.

Hortensia.

Refuse to be his partner every where.

Careless.

Blessings on her discretion!---Blunt, she does not pretend the least regard for me. (*aside*)

Hortensia.

Come, Lucinda, we shall be too late---the ball begins presently. [*Exit.*

Lucinda.

Mr. Bellfield, won't you squire us?
[*Exit with* Bellfield.

Sir Philip.

That's right; make you ready. Careless, dispatch; we shall want you in my new dance. I heard
bad

bad news, and so I composed it to dance away thought.

BLUNT.

Hang him; a troublesome coxcomb. *(aside)*

SIR PHILIP.

All life; all vivacity: foot it at top, cast off two couple, foot it at bottom, dance corners, cross over, turn your partner, right hand and left.
(sings and dances away)

CARELESS.

My affairs are in a fine train you see. We have both shewn our prudence.

BLUNT.

You'll be undone.

CARELESS.

Suspicious to the last. Whom have we here?

Enter BRAZEN, *in a different livery.*

CARELESS.

Hortensia's livery!---this is a message from her.

BRAZEN.

Madam Hortensia ordered me to deliver this letter into your own hands, Sir.

CARELESS.

A letter! let me press it close. *(kissing it)*--- Here,

Here, friend, a reward for your diligence. (*gives him money*) You may wait an anfwer.

Brazen.

I dare not ftay, Sir; fecrecy is the word: I muft be gone. [*Exit.*

Careless.

You fee I am in high favour. And here, here is a proof of my approaching joys. (*opens the letter*) Now—now—(*reads*) cannot comply—Ungenerous —be my laft—never—yours—(*ftands in confufion*)

Blunt.

What's the matter now?

Careless.

I never was fo let down in all my days.

Blunt. (*taking the letter*)

A proof of your approaching joys! (*reads*) "To liften any longer to your addreffes, when I cannot "comply with them, would be ungenerous. I muft, "therefore, by this letter, which will be my laft, wifh "you all happinefs, and freely declare I never can be "yours. *Hortenfia*."——Your affairs are in a fine train!

Careless.

This muft be fome bufy intermeddler.

Blunt.

Your own tongue has intermeddled.

A COMEDY. 349

CARELESS.

Hell and confusion!—what does all this mean? I never shall be able to shew my face: my friends will blame me, my enemies will rejoice, and every female tongue will clack, clack.—I'll meet her at the mask: this shall be explained. That's what she means: it will be a renewal of love: Blunt, I shall succeed still. Come, our dresses are at hand: and from this moment not one unguarded word shall escape me. [*Exeunt.*

Scene, *an* APARTMENT *at* SIR PHILIP*'s*.

Enter SIR PHILIP, WISELY, BELLFIELD.

SIR PHILIP. (*in a minuet step*)
You amaze me, Mr. Wisely. Careless form a design upon my wife!

WISELY.
The plot lies as I tell you.

SIR PHILIP. (*turning out his toes*)
This is enough to put a man out of tune.

WISELY.
Be directed by me, and you shall have full proof, and at the same time prevent the mischief.

SIR PHILIP. (*dancing*)
I never was so disconcerted in all my days.

BELL-

BELLFIELD.
Your own eyes, your own ears shall convince you. Wisely (*aside to him*) I'll step and see if Lucinda is ready.

WISELY. (*aside to* BELLFIELD)
Does she enter with spirit into the scheme?

BELLFFIELD.
Most chearfully: the frolick pleases her of all things: she is dressed by this time.

WISELY.
Step and speak to her once more. [*Exit* Bellfield] The folly of this man, Sir Philip, has put it in my power to do you this service. Hark! he comes this way: I know his dress.

SIR PHILIP.
And here comes my wife to meet him: I know her dress. *(rising and sinking)*

WISELY.
Place yourself in this bow window: I'll let down the curtain: you may hear all unseen and unsuspected: quick, dispatch; this will save you from dishonour.

SIR PHILIP.
I shall be ever thankful to you.
(walks in a minuet step)

WISE-

WISELY. *(letting down the curtain)*
Now, this is the very crisis of your fortune. So;
I have stationed him, and now to find Hortensia.
[*Exit.*

Enter CARELESS *and* LUCINDA, *at opposite doors, and both masked.*

CARELESS. *(unmasking)*
Her Ladyship is true to her appointment.—My Lady Figure-In, this is generous indeed.

LUCINDA.
The ball-room is quite full. *(in a feigned voice)*

CARELESS.
We are safe here: nobody will come this way. You may throw off all restraint: let me hear the accents of your own sweet voice.

LUCINDA.
No; I love to practise.

SIR PHILIP. *(peeping)*
I never knew such treachery.

CARELESS.
The opportunity is now favourable to our mutual loves: you have encouraged me to hope for one kind moment, and in return I here vow eternal constancy and love.

SIR PHILIP. *(peeping)*
You shall dance to another tune presently.

LUCINDA.
How can I believe you, when you are upon the very brink of marriage with Lucinda?

CARELESS.
Lucinda! that will never be.—Marry her! a giddy insolent, who over-rates both her beauty and her fortune—But she never was to my taste, I assure you.

LUCINDA.
You have had a lucky escape: her character, I fear, is not without a blemish.

CARELESS.
Mere broken china: but she patches it up, and turns the best side to view, in order to conceal the flaw.

LUCINDA.
I am glad you know her: but then, Hortensia will seduce you from me.

CARELESS.
She will be of no inconvenience to our happiness. I begin to know her too: an artful, sly, designing, amorous widow: she occasioned the death of her first husband, and that is no encouraging circumstance to a second.

Sir Philip. (*peeping*)

Such a villain never entered a gentleman's house.

Lucinda.

I am very faint all of a sudden: the heat has overpowered me: draw up that curtain, and give me a little air.

Careless.
(*drawing up the curtain and looking at her*)

Your Ladyship will be well in a moment. Sir Philip will be busy among the masks; he will never suspect us, and if he should, he will dance away his horns. He will sacrifice to the graces. (*making fast the string, he sees Sir Philip*) Confusion! [*Walks away.*

Sir Philip. (*following him*)

Mr. Careless, this is the vilest proceeding; the basest usage, Sir;—the most ungenerous design—it sets me all on fire. (*dancing*)

Careless.

I am blown: what shall I do now?

Sir Philip.

I did not think you capable of this perfidy: nor did I think your Ladyship such a Jezabel: come, shew your face, Madam, and let me see how guilt becomes it.

Lucinda. (*unmasking*)

How innocence becomes it.

Sir Philip.
Lucinda all this time!

Careless.
Ay! more misfortunes. *(aside)*

Sir Philip.
And my wife innocent!

Lucinda.
Yes, she is innocent: she was willing to let you see the honour of your friend there: I am sorry you have found a flaw in my character, Mr. Careless.

Careless.
I deserve it all. *(aside)*

Lucinda.
And was you so kind as to flatter me with hopes? Oh! ho! ho!

Enter Wisely *and* Bellfield.

Both.
Your humble servant, Mr. Careless.

Careless.
A swarm of enemies upon me at once!

Sir Philip. *(dancing up to him)*
You see what a false step you have made.

Careless.

I shall take an opportunity to explain all, and for the present—I—(*going*)

Enter Hortensia *and* Blunt.

Careless.

She too here! all my ill stars combined!

Lucinda.

Hortensia, here has been such a discovery!

Hortensia.

I have heard it all, my dear.

Careless.

I cannot stand it:—this is not a proper time—I shall now take my leave—(*going*)

Hortensia. (*stopping him*)

Your presence is necessary: you shall be witness to an act of justice: Mr. Wisely, I acknowledge the errors of my conduct, and if my picture in this box can be acceptable—

Wisely.

Say, you give your heart with it.

Careless.

As to that snuff box, if you will but permit me to speak—

HORTENSIA.

No explanations: you have betrayed me, and that determines every thing.

LUCINDA.

And Mr. Wifely reaps the juft reward of his fecrecy: Mr. Carelefs, I have been a very tyrant to your friend Bellfield: my airs are too thin for a lover to fubfift upon, and fo now, I'll let in a little common fenfe to keep him alive. (*gives her hand*)

BELLFIELD.

Thus I am bleffed indeed.

SIR PHILIP.

Poor Carelefs! he has had his devil's dance, and now he pays the piper.

ALL.

Ha! ha! ha!

CARELESS.

You may all laugh: I fhall leave you in poffeffion of your mirth: I fhall drop no hint of my future fchemes: I fhall fet out for the country, and in a few days you may, perhaps, read in the Bath Journal—

LUCINDA.

Oh! brave! a fieve to the very laft.

SIR PHILIP.

The Bath Journal, did he fay?—I have known them dance fixty couple at Bath.

CARELESS.

Wifely, you have been at the bottom of all this: I deferve it for putting myfelf in your power. Spare your reproaches, Blunt; I have been a very filly fellow: but fince matters are come to this iffue, I have the confolation to feel,—whatever may have been my indifcretions, that I am above a felfifh and ungenerous character:—I fcorn a bafe action as much as any man in England.

The Carelefs Indifcreet (this day has fhewn)
Is No Ones Enemy, Except his Own.

FINIS.

Three Weeks after Marriage

Three Weeks after Marriage;

A

COMEDY.

Three Weeks after Marriage;

A

COMEDY,

IN TWO ACTS.

Performed at the

THEATRE ROYAL

IN

COVENT-GARDEN.

―――

――――― Otium & oppidi
Laudat rura sui ―――――

                                        Hor.

――――― Nugæ feria ducent
In mala ―――

                                        Hor.

ADVERTISEMENT.

THE following scenes were offered to the Public in January 1764; but a party of that species of CRITICS, whom the love of mischief sometimes assembles at the theatre, being unwilling to hear, the piece was *damned*. Mr. LEWIS, of Covent Garden Theatre, had the courage to revive it for his benefit in March 1776, with an alteration of the title, and it has been since frequently repeated with success. A similar incident happened to VOLTAIRE at PARIS. That writer, in the year 1734, produced a tragedy, intitled ADELAIDE DU GUESCLIN, which was hissed through every act. In 1765, LE KAIN, an actor of eminence, revived the play, which had lain for years under condemnation. Every scene was applauded. What can I think, says VOLTAIRE, of these opposite judgments? He relates the following anecdote. A banker at Paris had orders to get a new march composed for one of the regiments of Charles XII. He employed a man of talents for the purpose. The march was prepared, and a practice of it had at the banker's house before a numerous assembly. The music was found detestable. MOURET (that was the composer's name) retired with his performance, and soon after inserted it in one of his operas. The banker and his friends went to the opera: the march was universally admired. Ah, says the banker, *that's what we wanted: why did not you give us something in this taste?* Sir, replied MOURET, the march, which you now applaud, is the very same that you condemned before.

Dramatis Personæ.

MEN.

Sir Charles Rackett,	Mr. Lewis.
Drugget,	Mr. Quick.
Lovelace,	Mr. Booth.
Woodley,	Mr. Young.

WOMEN.

Lady Rackett,	Mrs. Mattocks.
Mrs. Drugget,	Mrs. Pitt.
Nancy,	Miss Dayes.
Dimity,	Mrs. Green.

Three Weeks after Marriage.

ACT the FIRST.

Enter WOODLEY *and* DIMITY.

DIMITY.

PO! po!—no such thing: I tell you, Mr. Woodley, you are a mere novice in these affairs.

WOODLEY.

Nay, but listen to reason, Mrs. Dimity: has not your master, Mr. Drugget, invited me down to his country-seat? has not he promised to give me his daughter Nancy in marriage? and with what pretence can he now break off?

DIMITY.

What pretence!—you put a body out of all patience. Go on your own way, Sir; my advice is lost upon you.

WOODLEY.

You do me injustice, Mrs. Dimity. Your advice has governed my whole conduct. Have not I fixed an interest in the young lady's heart?

DIMITY.

An interest in a fiddlestick!—You ought to have made sure of the father and mother. What, do you think the way to get a wife, at this time of day, is by speaking fine things to the lady you have a fancy for?

for? That was the practice, indeed; but things are altered now. You muſt addreſs the old people, Sir; and never trouble your head about your miſtreſs. None of your letters, and verſes, and ſoft looks, and fine ſpeeches,—" Have compaſſion, thou angelic creature, on a poor dying"—Pſhaw! ſtuff! nonſenſe! all out of faſhion. Go your ways to the old curmudgeon, humour his whims—" I ſhall eſteem it an honour, Sir, to be allied to a gentleman of your rank and taſte." "Upon my word, he's a pretty young gentleman."——Then wheel about to the mother: "Your daughter, ma'am, is the very model of you, and I ſhall adore her for your ſake." " Here, come hither, Nancy, take this gentleman for better for worſe." " La, mama, I can never conſent."—" I ſhould not have thought of your conſent: the conſent of your relations is enough: why, how now, huſſey!" So away you go to church; the knot is tied; an agreeable honey-moon follows; the charm is then diſſolved; you go to all the clubs in St. James's ſtreet; your lady goes to the Coterie; and, in a little time you both go to Doctor's Commons; the *Morning Poſt* diſplays you in black and white; *Poets Corner* treats you with a ballad or an epigram; your friends pity you; the town laughs at you; the lawyers abuſe you; and if faults on both ſides prevent a divorce, you quarrel like contrary elements all the reſt of your lives: that's the way of the world now.

Woodley.

But you know, my dear Dimity, the old couple have received every mark of attention from me.

Dimity.

Attention! to be ſure you did not fall aſleep in their company; but what then? You ſhould have
en-

entered into their characters, play'd with their humours, and sacrificed to their abfurdities.

WOODLEY.

But if my temper is too frank——

DIMITY.

Frank, indeed! yes, you have been frank enough to ruin yourself. Have not you to do with a rich old shopkeeper, retired from business with an hundred thousand pounds in his pocket, to enjoy the dust of the London road, which he calls living in the country? and yet you must find fault with his situation! What if he has made a ridiculous gimcrack of his house and gardens? you know his heart is set upon it; and could not you have commended his taste? But you must be too frank! " Those walks and alleys are too regular: those evergreens should not be cut into such fantastic shapes."—And thus you advise a poor old mechanic, who delights in every thing that's monstrous, to follow nature. Oh, you are likely to be a successful lover!

WOODLEY.

But why should I not save a father-in-law from being a laughing-stock?

DIMITY.

Make him your father-in-law first.

WOODLEY.

Why, he can't open his windows for the dust: he stands all day, looking through a pane of glass, at the carts and stage-coaches, as they pass by, and he calls that living in the fresh air, and enjoying his own thoughts.

DIMITY.

Dimity.

And could not you let him go on his own way? You have ruined yourself by talking sense to him; and all your nonsense to the daughter won't make amends for it. And then the mother; how have you played your cards in that quarter? She wants a tinsel man of fashion for her second daughter. "Don't you see (says she) how happy my eldest girl is made by her match with Sir Charles Rackett? She has been married three entire weeks, and not so much as one angry word has passed between them! Nancy shall have a man of quality too."

Woodley.

And yet I know Sir Charles Rackett perfectly well.

Dimity.

Yes, so do I; and I know he'll make his lady wretched at last. But what then? You should have humoured the old folks: you should have been a talking empty fop to the good old lady; and to the old gentleman, an admirer of his taste in gardening. But you have lost him: he is grown fond of this beau Lovelace, who is here in the house with him: the coxcomb ingratiates himself by flattery, and you're undone by frankness.

Woodley.

And yet, Dimity, I won't despair.

Dimity.

And yet you have reason to despair, a million of reasons: to-morrow is fixed for the wedding-day; Sir Charles and his lady are to be here this very night;

night; they are engaged, indeed, at a great rout in town, but they take a bed here, notwithſtanding. The family is ſitting up for them; Mr. Drugget will keep you all in the next room there, till they arrive; to-morrow the buſineſs is over; and yet you don't deſpair!—Huſh! hold your tongue; here comes Lovelace, and Mr. Drugget with him; ſtep in, and I'll deviſe ſomething, I warrant you. [*Exit* Woodley.] The old folks ſhall not have their own way. It is enough to vex a body, to ſee an old father and mother marrying their daughter as they pleaſe, in ſpite of my judgment, and all I can do.

[*Exit.*

Enter DRUGGET *and* LOVELACE.

DRUGGET.

And ſo you like my houſe and gardens, Mr. Lovelace.

LOVELACE.

Oh! perfectly, Sir; they gratify my taſte of all things. Ones ſees villas where Nature reigns in a wild kind of ſimplicity: but then they have no appearance of art, no art at all.

DRUGGET.

Very true, rightly diſtinguiſhed: now mine is all art; no wild nature here; I did it all myſelf.

LOVELACE.

Indeed! I thought you had ſome of the great proficients in gardening to aſſiſt you.

DRUGGET.

Lackaday! no. Ha! ha! I underſtand theſe things.

things. I love my garden. The front of my houfe, Mr. Lovelace, is not that very pretty?

Lovelace.

Elegant to a degree!

Drugget.

Don't you like the fun-dial, placed juft by my dining-room windows!

Lovelace.

A perfect beauty!

Drugget.

I knew you'd like it: and the motto is fo well adapted—*Tempus edax & index rerum.* And I know the meaning of it. Time eateth and difcovereth all things. Ha! ha! pretty, Mr. Lovelace! I have feen people fo ftare at it as they pafs by! Ha! ha!

Lovelace.

Why now, I don't believe there's a nobleman in the kingdom has fuch a thing.

Drugget.

Oh no; they have got into a falfe tafte. I bought that bit of ground on the other fide of the road, and now it is a perfect beauty. I made a duck-pond there, for the fake of the profpect.

Lovelace.

Charmingly imagined!

Drugget.

My leaden images are well!

Lovelace.

They exceed antient statuary.

Drugget.

I love to be surprized at the turning of a walk with an inanimate figure, that looks you full in the face, and can say nothing at all, while one is enjoying one's own thoughts. Ha! ha!—Mr. Lovelace, I'll point out a beauty to you. Just by the haw-haw, at the end of my ground, there is a fine Dutch figure, with a scythe in his hand, and a pipe in his mouth. That's a jewel, Mr. Lovelace!

Lovelace.

That escaped me: a thousand thanks for pointing it out. I observe you have two very fine yew trees before the house.

Drugget.

Lackaday, Sir! they look uncouth. I have a design about them. I intend—ha! ha! it will be very pretty, Mr. Lovelace—I intend to have them cut into the shape of the two giants at Guildhall!

Lovelace.

Exquisite!—Why then they won't look like trees.

Drugget.

No, no; not in the least; I won't have any thing in my garden that looks like what it is.

Lovelace.

Nobody understands these things like you, Mr. Drugget.

Drugget

Lackaday! it's all my delight now. This is what I have been working for. I have a great improvement to make ftill: I propofe to have my evergreens cut into fortifications; and then I fhall have the Moro caftle, and the Havanna; and then near it fhall be fhips of myrtle, failing upon feas of box to attack the town: won't that make my place look very rural, Mr. Lovelace?

Lovelace.

Why you have the moft fertile invention, Mr. Drugget.

Drugget.

Ha! ha! this is what I have been working for. I love my garden. But I muft beg your pardon for a few moments: I muft ftep and fpeak with a famous nurfery-man, who is come to offer me fome choice rarities. Go and join the company, Mr. Lovelace: my daughter Rackett and Sir Charles will be here prefently. I fhan't go to bed till I fee them. Ha! ha!—my place is prettily variegated. This is all I delight in now. I fined for Sheriff to enjoy thefe things—ha! ha! [*Exit.*

Lovelace.

Poor Mr. Drugget! Mynkeer Van Thundertentrunck, in his little box at the fide of a dyke, has as much tafte and elegance. However, if I can but carry off his daughter, if I can but rob his garden of that flower; why then I fhall fay, " This is what I have been working for."

Dimity.

Enter DIMITY.

DIMITY.

Do lend us your affiftance, Mr. Lovelace. You are a fweet gentleman, and love a good-natured action.

LOVELACE.

Why how now! what's the matter?

DIMITY.

My mafter is going to cut the two yew-trees into the fhape of two devils, I believe; and my poor miftrefs is breaking her heart for it. Do, run and advife him againft it. She is your friend, you know fhe is, Sir.

LOVELACE.

Oh, if that's all, I'll make that matter eafy directly.

DIMITY.

My miftrefs will be for ever obliged to you; and you will marry her daughter in the morning.

LOVELACE.

Oh, my rhetoric fhall diffuade him.

DIMITY.

And, Sir, put him againft dealing with that nurfery-man; Mrs. Drugget hates him.

LOVELACE.

Does fhe?

DIMITY.

Dimity.
Mortally.

Lovelace.
Say no more, the bufinefs is done. [*Exit.*

Dimity.
If he fays one word againft the Giants at Guildhall, he is undone. Old Drugget will never forgive him. My brain was at its laft fhift; but if this plot takes—So, here comes our Nancy.

Enter Nancy.

Nancy.
Well, Dimity, what's to become of me?

Dimity.
My ftars! what makes you up, Mifs? I thought you were gone to bed.

Nancy.
What fhould I go to bed for? only to tumble and tofs, and fret, and be uneafy. They are going to marry me, and I am frighted out of my wits.

Dimity.
Why then you are the only young lady within fifty miles round, that would be frightened at fuch a thing.

Nancy.
Ah! if they would let me chufe for myfelf.

Dimity.

DIMITY.

Don't you like Mr. Lovelace?

NANCY.

My mama does, but I don't; I don't mind his being a man of fashion, not I.

DIMITY.

And, pray, can you do better than to follow the fashion?

NANCY.

Ah! I know there's a fashion for new bonnets, and a fashion for dressing the hair: but I never heard of a fashion for the heart.

DIMITY.

Why then, my dear, the heart mostly follows the fashion now.

NANCY.

Does it! Pray who sets the fashion of the heart?

DIMITY.

All the fine ladies in London, o'my conscience.

NANCY.

And what's the last new fashion, pray?

DIMITY.

Why to marry any fop that has a few deceitful agreeable appearances about him; something of a pert phrase, a good operator for the teeth, and tolerable taylor.

NANCY.

Nancy.

And do they marry without loving?

Dimity.

Oh! marrying for love has been a great while out of fashion.

Nancy.

Why then I'll wait till that fashion comes up again.

Dimity.

And then, Mr. Lovelace, I reckon——

Nancy.

Pshaw! I don't like him: he talks to me as if he was the most miserable man in the world, and the confident things looks so pleased with himself all the while. I want to marry for love, and not for card-playing. I should not be able to bear the life my sister leads with Sir Charles Rackett. Shall I tell you a secret? I will forfeit my new cap if they don't quarrel soon.

Dimity.

Oh fie! no! they won't quarrel yet a-while. A quarrel in three weeks after marriage, would be somewhat of the quickest. By and by we shall hear of their whims and their humours. Well, but if you don't like Mr. Lovelace, what say you to Mr. Woodley?

Nancy.

NANCY.

Ah!—I don't know what to fay—but I can fing fomething that will explain my mind.

SONG.

I.

WHEN firſt the dear youth paſſing by,
  Diſclos'd his fair form to my ſight,
I gaz'd, but I could not tell why;
  My heart it went throb with delight.

II.

As nearer he drew, thoſe ſweet eyes
  Were with their dear meaning ſo bright,
I trembled, and, loſt in ſurprize,
  My heart it went throb with delight.

III.

When his lips their dear accents did try
  The return of my love to excite,
I feign'd, yet began to gueſs why
  My heart it went throb with delight.

IV.

We chang'd the ſtol'n glance, the fond ſmile,
  Which lovers alone read aright;
We look'd, and we ſigh'd, yet the while
  Our hearts they went throb with delight.

V.

Conſent I ſoon bluſh'd, with a ſigh
  My promiſe I ventur'd to plight;
Come, Hymen, we then ſhall know why
  Our hearts they go throb with delight.

Enter WOODLEY.

WOODLEY.

My sweetest angel! I have heard it all, and my heart overflows with love and gratitude.

NANCY.

Ah! but I did not know you was listening. You should not have betrayed me so, Dimity: I shall be angry with you.

DIMITY.

Well, I'll take my chance for that. Run both into my room, and say all your pretty things to one another there, for here comes the old gentleman—make haste away. [*Exeunt* Woodley *and* Nancy.

Enter DRUGGET.

DRUGGET.

A forward presuming coxcomb! Dimity, do you step to Mrs. Drugget, and send her hither.

DIMITY.

Yes, Sir;—it works upon him I see. [*Exit.*

DRUGGET.

The yew trees ought not to be cut, because they'll help to keep off the dust, and I am too near the road already. A sorry ignorant fop! When I am in so fine a situation, and can see every cart, waggon, and stage-coach that goes by. And then to abuse the nursery-man's rarities! A finer sucking pig in lavender, with sage growing in his belly, was never seen! And yet he wants me not to have it. But

have

have it I will.—There's a fine tree of knowledge, with Adam and Eve in juniper; Eve's nofe not quite grown, but it's thought in the fpring will be very forward: I'll have that too, with the ferpent in ground ivy. Two Poets in wormwood! I'll have them both. Ay; and there's a Lord Mayor's feaſt in honey-fuckle; and the whole court of Aldermen in hornbeam: and three modern beaux in jeffamine, fomewhat ſtunted: they all ſhall be in my garden, with the Dragon of Wantley in box, all, all; I'll have them all, let my wife and Mr. Lovelace fay what they will.

Enter Mrs. DRUGGET.

MRS. DRUGGET.
Did you fend for me, lovey?

DRUGGET.
The yew-trees ſhall be cut into the giants at Guildhall, whether you will or not.

Mrs. DRUGGET.
Sure my own dear will do as he pleaſes.

DRUGGET.
And the pond, though you praife the green banks, ſhall be walled round, and I'll have a little fat boy in marble, fpouting up water in the middle.

Mrs. DRUGGET.
My fweet, who hinders you?

DRUGGET.
Yes, and I'll buy the nurfery-man's whole catalogue. Do you think, after retiring to live all the

way here, almoſt four miles from London, that I won't do as I pleaſe in my own garden?

Mrs. Drugget.

My dear, but why are you in ſuch a paſſion?

Drugget.

I'll have the Lavender Pig, and the Adam and Eve, and the Dragon of Wantley, and all of 'em: and there ſhan't be a more romantic ſpot on the London road than mine.

Mrs. Drugget.

I'm ſure it is as pretty as hands can make it.

Drugget.

I did it all myſelf, and I'll do more. And Mr. Lovelace ſhan't have my daughter.

Mrs. Drugget.

No! what's the matter now, Mr. Drugget?

Drugget.

He ſhall learn better manners than to abuſe my houſe and gardens. You put him in the head of it, but I'll diſappoint ye both. And ſo you may go and tell Mr. Lovelace that the match is quite off.

Mrs. Drugget.

I can't comprehend all this, not I. But I'll tell him ſo, if you pleaſe, my dear. I am willing to give myſelf pain, if it will give you pleaſure: muſt I give myſelf pain? Don't aſk me, pray don't; I can't ſupport all this uneaſineſs.

Drug-

Drugget.
I am refolved, and it fhall be fo.

Mrs. Drugget.
Let it be fo then. (*cries*) Oh! oh! cruel man! I fhall break my heart if the match is broke off. If it is not concluded to-morrow, fend for an undertaker, and bury me the next day.

Drugget.
How! I don't want that neither.

Mrs. Drugget.
Oh! oh!

Drugget.
I am your lord and mafter, my dear, but not your executioner. Before George, it muft never be faid that my wife died of too much compliance. Chear up, my love; and this affair fhall be fettled as foon as Sir Charles and Lady Rackitt arrive.

Mrs. Drugget.
You bring me to life again. You know, my fweet, what an happy couple Sir Charles and his Lady are. Why fhould not we make our Nancy as happy?

Enter Dimity.

Dimity.
Sir Charles and his Lady, Ma'am.

Mrs.

Mrs. Dimity.

Oh! charming! I'm transported with joy! where are they? I long to see 'em. [*Exit.*

Dimity.

Well, Sir; the happy couple are arrived.

Drugget.

Yes, they do live happy indeed.

Dimity.

But how long will it last?

Drugget.

How long! Don't forbode any ill, you jade; don't, I say. It will last during their lives, I hope.

Dimity.

Well, mark the end of it. Sir Charles, I know, is gay and good-humoured; but he can't bear the least contradiction, no, not in the merest trifle.

Drugget.

Hold your tongue; hold your tongue.

Dimity.

Yes, Sir, I have done; and yet there is in the composition of Sir Charles a certain humour, which, like the flying gout, gives no disturbance to the family till it settles in the head: when once it fixes there, mercy on every body about him! But here he comes. [*Exit.*

Enter

Enter Sir Charles.

Sir Charles.

My dear Sir, I kifs your hand. But why ftand on ceremony? To find you up at this late hour mortifies me beyond expreffion.

Drugget.

'Tis but once in a way, Sir Charles.

Sir Charles.

My obligations to you are inexpreffible; you have given me the moft amiable of girls; our tempers accord like unifons in mufic.

Drugget.

Ah! that's what makes me happy in my old days; my children and my garden are all my care.

Sir Charles.

And my friend Lovelace—he is to have our fifter Nancy, I find.

Drugget.

Why my wife is fo minded.

Sir Charles.

Oh, by all means, let her be made happy. A very pretty fellow Lovelace; as to that Mr.— Woodley, I think you call him—he is but a plain, underbred, ill-fafhioned fort of a—Nobody knows him; he is not one of us. Oh, by all means marry her to one of us.

Drugget.

I believe it muft be fo. Would you take any refrefhment?

Sir Charles.

Nothing in nature—it is time to retire to reft.

Drugget.

Well, well! good night Sir Charles. Ha! here comes my daughter. Good night, Sir Charles.

Sir Charles.

Bon repos.

Enter Lady Racket.

Lady Racket.

Dear Sir! I did not expect to fee you up fo late.

Drugget.

My Lady Racket, I am glad to hear how happy you are: I won't detain you now. There's your good man waiting for you: good night, my girl.
[*Exit.*

Sir Charles.

I muft humour this old putt, in order to be remembered in his will.

Enter Lady Racket.

Lady Rackett.

O la! I am quite fatigued. I can hardly move. Why don't you help me, you barbarous man?

Sir

A COMEDY. 385

Sir Charles.

There; take my arm—"Was ever thing so pretty made to walk?"

Lady Racket.

But I won't be laughed at. (*looking tenderly at him*) I don't love you.

Sir Charles.

Don't you?

Lady Rackett.

No. Dear me! this glove! why don't you help me off with my glove? Pshaw! you aukward thing, let it alone; you an't fit to be about my person. I might as well not be married, for any use you are of. Reach me a chair. You have no compassion for me. I am so glad to sit down. Why do you drag me to routs? You know I hate them.

Sir Charles.

Oh! there's no existing, no breathing, unless one does as other people of fashion do.

Lady Rackett.

But I am out of humour: I lost all my money.

Sir Charles.

How much?

Lady Rackett.

Three hundred.

SIR CHARLES.

Never fret for that. I don't value three hundred pounds to contribute to your happinefs.

LADY RACKETT.

Don't you?—not value three hundred pounds to pleafe me?

SIR CHARLES.

You know I don't.

LADY RACKETT.

Ah! you fond fool!—But I hate gaming: it almoft metamorphofes a woman into a fury. Do you know that I was frighted at myfelf feveral times tonight? I had an huge oath at the very tip of my tongue.

SIR CHARLES.

Had ye?

LADY RACKETT.

I caught myfelf at it; but I bit my lips, and fo I did not difgrace myfelf. And then I was crammed up in a corner of the room with fuch a ftrange party at a whift-table, looking at black and red fpots: did you mind them?

SIR CHARLES.

You know I was bufy elfewhere.

LADY RACKETT.

There was that ftrange, unaccountable woman, Mrs. Nightfhade: fhe behaved fo fretfully to her hufhusband, a poor, inoffensive, good-natured, good sort of a good for nothing kind of man: but she so teized him—" How could you play that card? Ah, you've a head, and so has a pin—You're a numscull, you know you are—Ma'am, he has the poorest head in the world, he does not know what he is about; you know you don't—Oh fye!—I'm ashamed of you!"

SIR CHARLES.
She has served to divert you, I see.

LADY RACKETT.
And to crown all, there was my Lady Clackit, who runs on with an eternal larum about nothing, out of all season, time, and place—In the very midst of the game she begins, " Lard, Ma'am, I was apprehensive I should not be able to wait on your La'ship; my poor little dog, Pompey—the sweetest thing in the world,—a spade led!—there's the Knave—I was fetching a walk, Me'm, the other morning in the Park; a fine frosty morning it was; I love frosty weather of all things. Let me look at the last trick—and so, Me'm, little Pompey—Oh! if your La'ship was to see the dear creature pinched with the frost, and mincing his steps along the Mall, with his pretty innocent face—I vow I don't know what to play—And so, Me'm, while I was talking to Captain Flimsey — Your La'ship knows Captain Flimsey—Nothing but rubbish in my hand—I can't help it—And so, Me'm, five odious frights of dogs beset my poor little Pompey—the dear creature has the heart of a lion, but who can resist five at once? And so Pompey barked for assistance. The hurt he received was upon his chest: the doctor would not advise him to venture out till the wound is healed, for fear of an inflammation—Pray what's trumps?

SIR CHARLES.
My dear, you'd make a moſt excellent actreſs.

LADY RACKETT.
Why don't you hand me up ſtairs? Oh!—I am ſo tired: let us go to reſt.

SIR CHARLES. *(aſſiſting her)*
You complain, and yet raking is the delight of your little heart.

LADY RACKETT.
(leaning on him as ſhe walks away)
It is you that make a rake of me. Oh! Sir Charles, how ſhockingly you played that laſt rubber, when I ſtood looking over you!

SIR CHARLES.
My love, I played the truth of the game.

LADY RACKETT.
No, indeed, my dear, you played it wrong. Ah! Sir Charles, you have a head.

SIR CHARLES.
Po! nonſenſe! you don't underſtand it.

LADY RACKETT.
I beg your pardon: I am allowed to play better than you.

SIR CHARLES.
All conceit, my dear: I was perfectly right.

Lady Rackett.

No fuch thing, Sir Charles. How can you difpute it? The diamond was the play.

Sir Charles.

Po! ridiculous! the club was the card againſt the world.

Lady Rackett.

Oh, no, no, no, I ſay it was the diamond.

Sir Charles.

Zounds! Madam, I ſay it was the club.

Lady Rackett.

What do you fly into ſuch a paſſion for?

Sir Charles.

Death and fury, do you think I don't know what I am about? I tell you once more, the club was the judgment of it.

Lady Rackett.

May be ſo. Have it your own way, Sir.

(walks about and ſings)

Sir Charles.

Vexation! You're the ſtrangeſt woman that ever lived; there's no converſing with you. Look'ye here, my Lady Rackett: it is the cleareſt caſe in the world: I'll make it plain to you in a moment.

Lady Rackett.

Very well, Sir. To be sure you must be right.
(with a sneering laugh)

Sir Charles.

Listen to me, Lady Racket : I had four cards left. Trumps were out. The lead was mine. They were six—no, no, no, they were seven, and we nine ; then you know, the beauty of the play was to—

Lady Rackett.

Well, now it's amazing to me, that you can't perceive : give me leave, Sir Charles. Your left hand adversary had led his last trump, and he had before finessed the club, and roughed the diamond : now if you had led your diamond—

Sir Charles.

Zoons! Madam, but we played for the odd trick.

Lady Rackett.

And sure the play for the odd trick—

Sir Charles.

Death and fury! can't your hear me?

Lady Rackett.

And must not I be heard, Sir?

Sir Charles.

Zoons, hear me, I say. Will you hear me?

LADY RACKETT.
I never heard the like in my life.
(*hums a tune, and walks about fretfully*)

SIR CHARLES.
Why then you are enough to provoke the patience of a Stoick.—(*looks at her; she walks about, and laughs*) Very well, Madam; you know no more of the game than your father's leaden Hercules on the top of the house. You know no more of whist than he does of gardening.

LADY RACKETT.
Go on your own way, Sir.
(*takes out a glass and settles her hair*)

SIR CHARLES.
Why then, by all that's odious, you are the most perverse, obstinate, ignorant—

LADY RACKETT.
Polite language, Sir!

SIR CHARLES.
You are, Madam, the most perverse, the most obstinate—you are a vile woman!

LADY RACKETT.
I am obliged to you, Sir.

SIR CHARLES.
You are a vile woman, I tell you so, and I will never sleep another night under one roof with you.

LADY RACKETT.

As you pleafe.

SIR CHARLES.

Madam, it fhall be as I pleafe. I'll order my chariot this moment. *(going)* I know how the cards fhould be played as well as any man in England, that let me tell you. *(going)*—And when your family were ftanding behind counters, meafuring out tape, and bartering for Whitechapel needles, my anceftors, my anceftors, Madam, were fquandering away whole eftates at cards; whole eftates, my Lady Rackett. *(fhe hums a tune, and he looks at her)* Why then, by all that's dear to me, I'll never exchange another word with you, good, bad, or indifferent. *(goes and turns back)* Will you command your temper, and liften to me?

LADY RACKETT.

Go on, Sir.

SIR CHARLES.

Can't you be cool as I am?—Lookye, my Lady Racket: thus it ftood. The trumps being all out, it was then my bufinefs—

LADY RACKETT.

To play the diamond to be fure.

SIR CHARLES.

Damnation! I have done with you for ever; for ever, Madam, and fo you may tell your father.

(going)

LADY RACKETT.

What a paffion the gentleman is in!

SIR

SIR CHARLES.
Will you let me speak?

LADY RACKETT.
Who hinders you, Sir?

SIR CHARLES.
Once more then out of pure good nature—

LADY RACKETT.
Oh, Sir, I am convinced of your good nature.

SIR CHARLES.
That, and that only prevails with me to tell you, the club was the play.

LADY RACKETT.
I am prodigiously obliged to you for the information. I am perfectly satisfied, Sir.

SIR CHARLES.
It is the clearest point in the world. Only mind now. We were nine, and—

LADY RACKETT.
And for that reason, the diamond was the play. Your adversary's club was the best in the house.

SIR CHARLES.
Why then, such another fiend never existed. There is no reasoning with you. It is in vain to say a word. Good sense is thrown away upon you. I now see the malice of your heart. You are a base woman, and I part from you for ever. You may live

live here with your father, and admire his fantaſtical evergreens, till you become as fantaſtical yourſelf. I'll ſet out for London this moment. Your ſervant, Madam. (*turns and looks at her*) The club was not the beſt in the houſe.

LADY RACKETT.

How calm you are!—Well, I'll go to bed. Will you come? You had better. Not come when I aſk you?—Oh! Sir Charles. (*going*)

SIR CHARLES.

That eaſe is ſo provoking. I deſire you will ſtay and hear me. Don't think to carry it in this manner. Madam, I muſt and will be heard.

LADY RACKETT.

Oh! Lud! with that terrible countenance! you frighten me away. (*runs in and ſhuts the door*)

SIR CHARLES. (*following her*)

You ſhall not fly me thus. Confuſion!—open the door—will you open it? This contempt is beyond enduring. (*walks away*) I intended to have made it clear to her, but now let her continue in her abſurdity. She is not worth my notice. My reſolution is taken. She has touched my pride, and I now renounce her for ever; yes for ever; not to return, though ſhe were to requeſt, beſeech and implore on her very knees. [*Exit.*

LADY RACKETT. (*peeping in*)

Is he gone? (*comes forward*) Bleſs me! what have I done?—I have carried this too far, I believe. I had better call him back. For the ſake of peace I'll give up the point. What does it ſignify which

was

was the beſt of the play?—It is not worth quarrelling about.—How!—here he comes again.—I'll give up nothing to him. He ſhall never get the better of me: I am ruined for life, if he does. I will conquer him, and I am reſolved he ſhall ſee it.
(runs in and ſhuts the door)

SIR CHARLES. *(looking in)*

No; ſhe won't open it. Headſtrong and poſitive! —If ſhe could but command her temper, the thing would be as clear as day-light. She has ſenſe enough, if ſhe would but make uſe of it. It were pity ſhe ſhould be loſt. *(advances towards the door)* All owing to that perverſe ſpirit of contradiction. —I may reclaim her ſtill—*(peeps through the keyhole)* Not ſo much as a glimpſe of her. *(taps at the door)* Lady Rackett—Lady Rackett—

LADY RACKETT. *(within)*
What do you want?

SIR CHARLES. *(laughing affectedly)*

Come, you have been very pleaſant. Open the door: I cannot help laughing at all this.——Come, no more foolery: have done now, and open the door.

LADY RACKETT. *(within)*
Dont be ſuch a torment.

SIR CHARLES.
Will you open it?

LADY RACKETT. *(laughing)*
No—no——ho! ho!

Sir Charles.

Hell and confufion! what a puppy I make of myfelf! I'll bear this ufage no longer. To be trifled with in this fort by a falfe, treacherous——— (*runs to the door and speaks through the key-hole*) The diamond was NOT the play. (*walks away as faſt as he can*) I know what I am about, (*looks back in a violent rage*) and the club was NOT the beſt in the houſe.

[*Exit.*

End of the FIRST ACT.

ACT the SECOND.

Enter DIMITY.

DIMITY. (*laughing violently*)

OH! I shall die; I shall expire in a fit of laughing. This is the modish couple that were so happy! Such a quarrel as they have had; the whole house is in an uproar. Ho! ho! ho! a rare proof of the happiness they enjoy in high life. I shall never hear people of fashion mentioned again, but I shall be ready to crack my sides. They were both—Ho! ho! ho! This is three weeks after marriage, I think.

Enter DRUGGET.

DRUGGET.

Hey! how! what's the matter, Dimity? What am I called down stairs for?

DIMITY.

Why there's two people of fashion—
(*stifles a laugh*)

DRUGGET.

Why, you malapert hussey! explain this moment.

DIMITY.

The fond couple have been together by the ears this half hour. Are you satisfied now?

Drugget.

Ay!—what, have they quarrelled? What was it about?

Dimity.

Something too nice and fine for my comprehenfion, and your's too, I believe. People in high life underftand their own forms beft. And here comes one that can unriddle the whole affair. *Exit.*

Enter Sir Charles.

Sir Charles. (*to the people within*)
I fay, let the horfes be put-to this moment. So, Mr. Drugget!

Drugget.

Sir Charles, here's a terrible buftle. I did not expect this. What can be the matter?

Sir Charles.

I have been ufed by your daughter in fo bafe, fo contemptuous, fo vile a manner, that I am determined not to ftay in this houfe to-night.

Drugget.

This is a thunderbolt to me! After feeing how elegantly and fafhionably you lived together, to find now all funfhine vanifhed! Do, Sir Charles, let me heal this breach if poffible.

Sir Charles.

Sir, it is impoffible. I'll not live with her an hour longer.

Drugget.

Nay, nay, don't be too hasty. Let me intreat you, go to bed and sleep upon it. In the morning, when you are cool——

Sir Charles.

Oh, Sir, I am very cool, I assure you. Ha! ha! ---it is not in her power, Sir, to---a---a---to disturb the serenity of my temper. Don't imagine that I'm in a passion. I am not so easily ruffled as you imagine. But quietly and deliberately, I can repay the injury done me by a false, ungrateful, deceitful woman.

Drugget.

The injuries done you by a false, ungrateful! My daughter I hope, Sir—

Sir Charles.

Her character is now fully known to me. I understand her perfectly. She is a vile woman! that's all I have to say, Sir!

Drugget.

Hey! how!---a vile woman! what has she done? I hope she is not capable---

Sir Charles.

I shall enter into no detail, Mr. Drugget; the time and circumstances will not allow it at present. But depend upon it, I have done with her. A low, unpolished, uneducated, false, imposing——See if the horses are put-to.

Drugget.

Mercy on me! in my old days to hear this.

Enter Mrs. Drugget.

Mrs. Drugget.

Deliver me! I am all over in such a tremble. Sir Charles, I shall break my heart if there is any thing amiss.

Sir Charles.

Madam, I am very sorry, for your sake; but to live with her is impossible.

Mrs. Drugget.

My poor dear girl! what can she have done?

Sir Charles.

What all her sex can do: it needs no explanation: the very spirit of them all.

Drugget

Ay! I see how it is.---She is bringing foul disgrace upon us. This comes of her marrying a man of fashion.

Sir Charles.

Fashion, Sir! that should have instructed her better. She might have been sensible of her happiness. Whatever you may think of the fortune you gave her, my rank in life claims respect; claims obedience, attention, truth, and love, from one raised in the world as she has been by an alliance with me.

Drugget.

And, let me tell you, however you may eſtimate your quality, my daughter is dear to me.

Sir Charles.

And, Sir, my character is dear to me. It ſhall never be in her power to expoſe me.

Drugget.

Yet you muſt give me leave to tell you——

Sir Charles.

I won't hear a word.

Drugget.

Not in behalf of my own daughter?

Sir Charles.

Nothing can excuſe her. It is to no purpoſe. She has married above her; and if that circumſtance makes the lady forget herſelf, ſhe at leaſt ſhall ſee that I can, and will ſupport my own dignity.

Drugget.

But, Sir, I have a right to aſk—

Mrs. Drugget.

Patience, my dear, be a little calm.

Drugget.

Mrs. Drugget, do you have patience. I muſt and will enquire.

Mrs. Drugget.

Don't be so hasty, my love; have some respect for Sir Charles's rank; don't be violent with a man of his fashion.

Drugget.

Hold your tongue, woman, I say: hold your tongue. You are not a person of fashion at least. My daughter was ever a good girl.

Sir Charles.

I have found her out.

Drugget.

Oh! then its all over, and it does not signify arguing about it.

Mrs. Drugget.

That ever I should live to see this hour! How the unfortunate girl could take such wickedness in her head, I can't imagine. I'll go and speak to the unhappy creature this moment. [*Exit.*

Sir Charles.

She stands detected now: detected in her truest colours.

Drugget.

Well, grievous as it may be, let me hear the circumstances of this unhappy business.

Sir Charles.

Mr. Drugget, I have not leisure now. Her behaviour has been so exasperating, that I shall make the best

best of my way to town. My mind is fixed. She sees me no more, and so, your servant, Sir. [*Exit.*

DRUGGET.

What a calamity has here befallen us! A good girl, and so well disposed! But the evil communication of high life, and fashionable vices, turned her heart to folly.

Enter LOVELACE.

LOVELACE.

Joy! joy! Mr. Drugget, I give you joy.

DRUGGET.

Don't insult me, Sir; I desire you won't.

LOVELACE.

Insult you, Sir! Is there any thing insulting, my dear Sir, if I take the liberty to congratulate you on the approaching——

DRUGGET.

There! there! the manners of high life for you! He wishes me joy on the approaching ruin of my daughter. She is to be in the fashion! Mr. Lovelace, you shall have no daughter of mine.

LOVELACE.

My dear Sir, never bear malice. I have reconsidered the thing, and curse catch me, if I don't think your notion of the Guildhall giants, and the court of Aldermen in hornbeam——

F f f 2 DRUG-

Drugget.

Well! well! well! there may be people at the court end of the town in hornbeam too.

Lovelace.

Yes, faith, ſo there may; and I believe I could help you to a tolerable collection. However, with your daughter I am ready to venture.

Drugget.

But I am not ready. I'll not venture my girl with you. No more daughters of mine ſhall have their minds depraved by polite vices.

Lovelace.

Strike me ſtupid, if I underſtand one word of all this.

Enter Woodley.

Drugget.

Mr. Woodley, you ſhall have Nancy to your wife, as I promiſed you: take her to-morrow morning.

Woodley.

Sir, I have not words to expreſs——

Lovelace.

What the devil is the matter with the old haberdaſher now?

Drugget.

And hark ye, Mr. Woodley; I'll make you a preſent for your garden, of a coronation dinner in greens,

greens, with the champion riding on horseback, and the sword will be full grown before April next.

Woodley.

I shall receive it, Sir, as your favour.

Drugget.

Ay, ay! I see my error in wanting an alliance with great folks. I had rather have you, Mr. Woodley, for my son-in-law, than any courtly fop of 'em all. Is this man gone? Is Sir Charles Rackett gone?

Woodley.

Not yet: he makes a bawling yonder for his horses. I'll step and call him to you. [*Exit.*

Drugget.

Do so; do so, Mr. Woodley. I am out of all patience. I am out of my senses. I must see him once more. Mr. Lovelace, neither you nor any person of fashion, shall ruin another child of mine.
[*Exit.*

Lovelace.

Droll this! damn'd droll! And every syllable of it Greek to me. The queer old putt is as whimsical in his notions of life as of gardening. If this be the case, I shall brush, and leave him to his exotics.
[*Exit.*

Enter Lady Rackett, Mrs. Drugget, *and* Dimity.

Lady Rackett.

A cruel, barbarous man! to quarrel in this unaccountable

countable manner; to alarm the whole house, and to expose me and himself too.

Mrs. Drugget.

Oh! child! I never thought it would have come to this. Your shame will not end here; it will be all over St. James's parish by to-morrow morning.

Lady Rackett.

Well, if it must be so, there is one comfort still: the story will tell more to his disgrace than mine.

Dimity.

As I'm a sinner, and so it will, Madam. He deserves what he has met with.

Mrs. Drugget.

Dimity, don't you encourage her. You shock me to hear you speak so. I did not think you had been so hardened.

Lady Rackett.

Hardened do you call it? I have lived in the world to very little purpose, if such trifles as these are to disturb my rest.

Mrs. Drugget.

You wicked girl! do you call it a trifle to be guilty of falsehood to your husband's bed?

Lady Rackett.

How!—— (*turns short, and stares at her*)

Dimity.

That! that's a mere trifle indeed. I have been in

as good places as any body, and not a creature minds it now.

Mrs. Drugget.

My Lady Rackett, my Lady Rackett, I never could think to see you come to this deplorable shame.

Lady Rackett.

Surely the base man has not been capable of laying any thing of that sort to my charge? (*aside*) All this is unaccountable to me—ha! ha!—it is ridiculous beyond measure.

Dimity.

That's right, Madam: laugh at it; you served him right.

Mrs. Drugget.

Charlotte! Charlotte! I'm astonished at your wickedness.

Lady Rackett.

Well, I protest and vow I don't comprehend all this. Has Sir Charles accused me of any impropriety in my conduct?

Mrs. Drugget.

Oh! too true, he has: he has found you out, and you have behaved basely, he says.

Lady Rackett.

Madam!

Mrs. Drugget.

You have fallen into frailty, like many others of your sex, he says; and he is resolved to come to a separation directly.

Lady Rackett.

Why then if he is so base a wretch as to dishonour me in that manner, his heart shall ache before I live with him again.

Dimity.

Hold to that, Ma'am, and let his head ache into the bargain.

Mrs. Drugget.

Your poor father heard it as well as I.

Lady Rackett.

Then let your doors be open for him this very moment; let him return to London. If he does not, I'll lock myself up, and the false one shan't approach me, though he were to whine on his knees at my very door. A base, injurious man! [*Exit.*

Mrs. Drugget.

Dimity, do let us follow, and hear what she has to say for herself. [*Exit.*

Dimity.

She has excuse enough I warrant her. What a noise is here indeed! I have lived in polite families, where there was no such bustle made about nothing. [*Exit.*

Enter

Enter Sir Charles *and* Drugget.

SIR CHARLES.
It is in vain, Sir, my resolution is taken.

DRUGGET.
Well, but consider, I am her father. Indulge me only till we hear what the girl has to say in her defence.

SIR CHARLES.
She can have nothing to say: no excuse can palliate such behaviour.

DRUGGET.
Don't be too positive: there may be some mistake.

SIR CHARLES.
No, Sir, no; there can be no mistake. Did not I see her, hear her myself?

DRUGGET.
Lackaday! then I am an unfortunate man!

SIR CHARLES.
She will be unfortunate too: with all my heart. She may thank herself. She might have been happy, had she been so disposed.

DRUGGET.
Why truly, I think she might.

Enter Mrs. DRUGGET.

MRS. DRUGGET.

I wifh you would moderate your anger a little, and let us talk over this affair with temper. My daughter denies every tittle of your charge.

SIR CHARLES.

Denies it! denies it!

MRS. DRUGGET.

She does indeed.

SIR CHARLES.

And that aggravates her fault.

MRS. DRUGGET.

She vows that you never found her out in any thing that was wrong.

SIR CHARLES.

She does not allow it to be wrong then! Madam, I tell you again, I know her thoroughly. I have found her out : I am now acquainted with her character. I am to be deceived no more.

MRS. DRUGGET.

Then you are in oppofite ftories. She fwears, my dear Mr. Drugget, the poor girl fwears fhe never was guilty of the fmalleft infidelity to her hufband in her born days.

SIR CHARLES.

And what then? What if fhe does fay fo?

Mrs.

Mrs. Drugget.

And if she says truly, it is hard her character should be blown upon without just cause.

Sir Charles.

And is she therefore to behave ill in other respects? I never charged her with infidelity to me, Madam: there I allow her innocent.

Drugget.

And did not you charge her then?

Sir Charles.

No, Sir, I never dreamt of such a thing.

Drugget.

Why then, if she is innocent, let me tell you, you are a scandalous person.

Mrs. Drugget.

Prithee, my dear—

Drugget.

Be quiet; though he is a man of quality, I will tell him of it. Did not I fine for sheriff?—Yes, you are a scandalous person to defame an honest man's daughter.

Sir Charles.

What have you taken into your head now?

Drugget.

You charged her with falsehood to your bed.

SIR CHARLES.
No—never—never.

DRUGGET.
I ſay you did.

SIR CHARLES.
And I ſay no, no.

DRUGGET.
But I ſay you did; you called yourſelf a cuckold.
Did not he, wife?

Mrs. DRUGGET.
Yes, Lovey, I am witneſs.

SIR CHARLES.
Abſurd! I ſaid no ſuch thing.

DRUGGET.
But I aver you did.

Mrs. DRUGGET.
You did, indeed, Sir.

SIR CHARLES.
But I tell you no, poſitively no.

DRUGGET *and* Mrs. DRUGGET.
And I ſay, yes, poſitively yes.

SIR CHARLES.
'Sdeath, this is all madneſs.

Drugget.
You said that she followed the ways of most of her sex.

Sir Charles.
I said so, and what then?

Drugget.
There he owns it; owns that he called himself a cuckold, and without rhyme or reason into the bargain.

Sir Charles.
I never owned any such thing.

Drugget.
You owned it even now—now—now—now—

Mrs. Drugget.
This very moment.

Sir Charles.
No, no; I tell you, no.

Drugget.
This instant.—Prove it: make your words good: shew me your horns, and if you can't, it is worse than suicide to call yourself a cuckold, without proof.

Enter Dimity. (*in a fit of laughing*)

Dimity.
What do you think it was all about? Ha! ha! the whole secret is come out, ha! ha! It was all about a game of cards—Ho! ho! ho!

Drug-

DRUGGET.

A game of cards!

DIMITY. (*laughing*)

It was all about a club and a diamond. *(runs out laughing)*

DRUGGET.

And was that all, Sir Charles?

SIR CHARLES.

And enough too, Sir.

DRUGGET.

And was that what you found her out in?

SIR CHARLES.

I can't bear to be contradicted, when I am clear that I am in the right.

DRUGGET.

I never heard of such a heap of nonsense in all my life. Woodley shall marry Nancy.

Mrs. DRUGGET.

Don't be in a hurry, my love, this will all be made up.

DRUGGET.

Why does he not go and beg her pardon then?

Sir Charles.

I beg her pardon! I won't debase myself to any of you. I shan't forgive her, you may rest assured.
            [*Exit.*

Drugget.

Now there, there's a pretty fellow for you.

Mrs. Drugget.

I'll step and prevail on my Lady Rackett to speak to him: all this will be set right.   [*Exit.*

Drugget.

A ridiculous fop! I am glad it is no worse, however.—He must go and talk scandal of himself, as if the town did not abound with people ready enough to take that trouble off his hands.

Enter Nancy.

Drugget.

So, Nancy—you seem in confusion, my girl!

Nancy.

How can one help it, with all this noise in the house? And you are going to marry me as ill as my sister. I hate Mr. Lovelace.

Drugget.

Why so, child?

Nancy.

I know these people of quality despise us all out

of pride, and would be glad to marry us out of avarice.

DRUGGET.

The girl's right,

NANCY.

They marry one woman, live with another, and love only themſelves.

DRUGGET.

And then quarrel about a card.

NANCY.

I don't want to be a gay lady. I want to be happy.

DRUGGET.

And ſo you ſhall: don't fright yourſelf, child. Step to your ſiſter, bid her make herſelf eaſy: go, and comfort her, go.

NANCY.

Yes, Sir. [*Exit.*

DRUGGET.

I'll ſtep and ſettle the matter with **Mr. Woodley** this moment. *Exit.*

Scene, another Apartment,
SIR CHARLES, *with a pack of cards, at a table.*

SIR CHARLES.

Never was any thing like her behaviour. I can pick

A COMEDY.

pick out the very cards I had in my hand, and then tis as plain as the sun.—There—there—now—there—ho—damn it—no—there it was—now let me see—They had four by honours and we play'd for the odd trick,—damnation! honours were divided—ay!—honours were divided and then a trump was led, and the other side had the—confusion!—this preposterous woman has put it all out of my head [*Puts the Cards into his Pocket.*] Mighty well, Madam; I have done with you.

Enter Mrs. DRUGGET.

Mrs. DRUGGET.
Sir Charles, let me prevail. Come with me and speak to her.

SIR CHARLES.
I don't desire to see her face.

Mrs. DRUGGET.
If you were to see her all bath'd in tears, I am sure it would melt your very heart.

SIR CHARLES.
Madam it shall be my fault if ever I am treated so again. I'll have nothing to say to her [*Going, stops.*] Does she give up the point?

Mrs. DRUGGET.
She does, she agrees to any thing.

SIR CHARLES.
Does she allow that the club was the play?

Mrs. Drugget.
Just as you please : she is all submission.

Sir Charles.
Does she own that the club was not the best in the house?

Mrs. Drugget.
She does; she is willing to own it.

Sir Charles.
Then I'll step and speak to her. I never was clearer in any thing in my life.
[*Exit.*

Mrs. Drugget.
Lord love 'em, they'll make it up now, and then they'll be as happy as ever.
[*Exit.*

Enter Nancy.

Nancy.
Well! they may talk what they will of taste, and genteel life; I don't think it's natural. Give me Mr. Woodley---La! that odious thing coming this way.

Enter Lovelace.

Lovelace.
My charming little innocent, I have not seen you these three hours.

Nancy.

Nancy.

I have been very happy thefe three hours.

Lovelace.

My fweet angel, you feem difconcerted. And you neglect your pretty figure. No matter for the prefent; in a little time I fhall make you appear as graceful and as genteel as your fifter.

Nancy.

That is not what employs my thoughts, Sir.

Lovelace.

Ay! but my pretty little dear, that fhou'd engage your attention. To fet off and adorn the charms that nature has given you, fhould be the bufinefs of your life.

Nancy.

But I have learnt a new fong that contradicts what you fay, and though I am not in a very good humour for finging, yet you fhall hear it.

Lovelace.

By all means; don't check your fancy: I am all attention.

Nancy.

It expreffes my fentiments, and when you have heard them, you won't teize me any more.

SONG.

SONG.

I.

To dance, and to dress, and to flaunt it about,
To run to park, play, to assembly and rout;
To wander for ever in whim's giddy maze,
And one poor hair torture a million of ways;
To put at the glass every feature to school,
And practise their art on each fop and each fool;
Of one thing to think, and another to tell,
These, these are the manners of each giddy belle.

II.

To smile, and to simper, white teeth to display;
The time in gay follies to trifle away;
Against ev'ry virtue the bosom to steel,
And only of dress the anxieties feel;
To be at Eve's ear the insidious decoy,
The pleasure ne'er taste, but the mischief enjoy;
To boast of soft raptures they never can know,
These, these are the manners of each giddy beau.
[*Exit.*

LOVELACE.

I must have her, notwithstanding this: for tho' I am not in love, I am most confoundedly in debt.

Enter DRUGGET.

DRUGGET.

So, Mr. Lovelace! any news from above stairs? Is this absurd quarrel at an end? Have they made it up?

LOVELACE.

Oh! a mere bagatelle, Sir: these little fracas among

mong the better sort of people never last long: elegant trifles cause elegant disputes, and we come together elegantly again; as you see; for here they come, in perfect good humour.

Enter Sir Charles *and* Lady Rackett.

Sir Charles.

Mr. Drugget, I embrace you; you see me in the most perfect harmony of spirits.

Drugget.

What, all reconciled again?

Lady Rackett.

All made up, Sir. I knew how to bring the gentleman to a sense of his duty. This is the first difference, I think, we ever had, Sir Charles.

Sir Charles.

And I'll be sworn it shall be the last.

Drugget.

I am happy now, as happy as a fond father can wish. Sir Charles, I can spare you an image to put on the top of your house in London.

Sir Charles.

Infinitely oblig'd to you.

Drugget.

Well! well! It's time to retire: I am glad to see you reconciled; and now I wish you a good night, Sir Charles. Mr. Lovelace, this is your way. Fare ye well

well both. I am glad your quarrels are at an end: this way Mr. Lovelace.

[*Exeunt.* Drugget and Lovelace.

LADY RACKETT.

Ah! you are a fad man, Sir Charles, to behave to me as you have done.

SIR CHARLES.

My dear, I grant it: and fuch an abfurd quarrel too--- ha! ha!

LADY RACKETT.

Yes---ha! ha!--- about fuch a trifle.

SIR CHARLES.

It is pleafant how we could both fall into fuch an error. Ha! ha!---

LADY RACKETT.

Ridiculous beyond expreffion! Ha! ha!

SIR CHARLES.

And then the miftake your father and mother fell into!

LADY RACKETT.

That too is a diverting part of the ftory. Ha! ha----But, Sir Charles, muft I ftay and live with my father tell I grow as fantaftical as his own evergreens!

SIR CHARLES.

Nay, prithee don't remind me of my folly.

LADY

Lady Rackett.

Ah! my relations were all ſtanding behind counters, ſelling Whitechapel needles, while your family were ſpending great eſtates.

Sir Charles.

Spare my bluſhes: you ſee I am covered with confuſion.

Lady Rackett.

How could you ſay ſo indelicate a thing? I don't love you.

Sir Charles.

It was indelicate; I grant it.

Lady Rackett.

Am I a vile woman?

Sir Charles.

How can you, my angel?

Lady Rackett.

I ſhan't forgive you! I'll have you on your knees for this. (*Sings and plays with him.*)—" Go, naughty man."—Ah! Sir Charles!

Sir Charles.

The reſt of my life ſhall aim at convincing you how ſincerly I love you.

Lady Rackett. (*Sings*)

" Go, naughty man, I can't abide you"—Well! come

come, let us go to reft. *(Going.)* Ah, Sir Charles! now it's all over, the diamond was the play.

Sir Charles.

Oh no, no, no; now that one may fpeak, it was the club indeed.

Lady Rackett.

Indeed, my love, you are miftaken.

Sir Charles.

You make me laugh: but I was not miftaken: rely upon my judgement.

Lady Rackett.

You may rely upon mine: you was wrong.

Sir Charles. *(laughing.)*

Po! no, no, no fuch thing.

Lady Rackett. *(laughing.)*

But I fay, yes, yes, yes.

Sir Charles.

Oh! no, no; it is too ridiculous; don't fay any more about it, my love.

Lady Rackett. *(toying with him.)*

Don't you fay any more about it: you had better give it up, you had indeed.

Enter Footman.

Your honour's cap and flippers.

Sir

Sir Charles.

Lay down my cap, and here take thefe fhoes off. (*He takes 'em off, and leaves 'em at a diftance.*) Indeed, my Lady Rackett, you make me ready to expire with laughing. Ha! ha!

Lady Rackett.

You may laugh, but I am right notwithftanding.

Sir Charles.

How can you fay fo?

Lady Rackett.

How can you fay otherwife?

Sir Charles.

Well now mind me, my Lady Rackett, we can now talk of this matter in good humour: we can difcufs it coolly.

Lady Rackett.

So we can—and it is for that reafon I venture to fpeak to you. Are thefe the ruffles I bought for you?

Sir Charles.

They are, my dear.

Lady Rackett.

They are very pretty. But indeed you played the card wrong.

Sir Charles.

Po, there is nothing fo clear, if you will but hear me; only hear me.

Lady Rackett.
Ah! but do you hear me. The thing was thus. The adversary's club being the best in the house—

Sir Charles.
No, no, listen, to me: the affair was thus: Mr. Jenkins having never a club left—

Lady Rackett.
Mr. Jenkins finessed the club.

Sir Charles. *(peevishly)*
How can you?

Lady Rackett.
And trumps being all out——

Sir Charles.
And we playing for the odd trick——

Lady Rackett.
If you had minded your game——

Sir Charles.
And the club being the best——

Lady Rackett.
If you had led your diamond——

Sir Charles.
Mr. Jenkins would of course put on a spade.

Lady Rackett.
And so the odd trick was sure.

(both speaking very fast, and together)

SIR CHARLES.

Damnation! will you let me speak?

LADY RACKETT.

Well, to be sure, you are the strangest man.

SIR CHARLES.

Plague and torture! there is no such thing as conversing with you.

LADY RACKETT.

Very well, Sir, fly out again.

SIR CHARLES.

Look here now: here is a pack of cards. Now you shall be convinced.

LADY RACKETT.

You may talk till to-morrow, I know I am right. (*walks about.*)

SIR CHARLES.

Why then, by all that's perverse, you are the most headstrong—Can't you look here? here are the very cards.

LADY RACKETT.

Go on; you'll find it out at last.

SIR CHARLES.

Will you hold your tongue, or not? will you let me shew you?—Po! it's all nonsense. (*puts up the cards*) Come, let us go to bed. (*going*) Only stay one moment.

ment. (*Takes out the cards*) Now command yourself, and you shall have demonstration.

Lady Rackett.

It does not signify, Sir,. Your head will be clearer in the morning. I chuse to go to bed.

Sir Charles.

Stay and hear me, can't you?

Lady Rackett.

No; my head aches. I am tired of the subject.

Sir Charles.

Why then, damn the cards. There, and there, and there. (*throwing them about the room*) You may go to bed by yourself. Confusion seize me, if I stay here to be tormented a moment longer. (*Putting on his shoes.*)

Enter Dimity.

Dimity.

Did you call, Sir?

Sir Charles.

No; never, never, Madam.

Dimity. (*in a fit of laughing*)

At it again!

Lady Rackett.

Take your own way, Sir.

SIR CHARLES.

Now then I tell you once more, you are a vile woman.

DIMITY.

Law, Sir!—This is charming; I'll run and tell the old couple.

[*Exit.*

SIR CHARLES. (*ſtill putting on his ſhoes.*)

You are the moſt malicious, poſitive, nonſenſical—

LADY RACKETT.

Don't make me laugh again, Sir Charles. (*walks nd ſings.*)

SIR CHARLES.

Hell and the devil! will you ſit down quietly and let me convince you?

LADY RACKETT.

I don't chuſe to hear any more about it.

SIR CHARLES.

Why then I believe you are poſſeſſed. It is in vain to talk ſenſe and reaſon to you.

LADY RACKETT.

Thank you for your compliment, Sir—Such a man! (*with a ſneering laugh.*) I never knew the like of this. (*Sits down.*

Sir Charles.

I promiſe you, you ſhall repent of this uſage, before you have a moment of my company again. It ſhan't be in a hurry you may depend, Madam—Now ſee here — I can prove it to a demonſtration *(ſits down by her, ſhe gets up.)* Look ye there again now: the very devil muſt be in your temper. I wiſh I had never ſeen your face. I wiſh I was a thouſand miles off. Sit down but one moment.

Lady Rackett.

I am diſpos'd to walk Sir.

Sir Charles.

Why then may I periſh if ever—a blockhead, an ideot I was to marry. *(walks about.)* ſuch provoking impertinence! *(She ſits down.)* Damnation! I am ſo clear in the thing. She is not worth my notice—*(Sits down, turns his back, and looks uneaſy.)* I'll take no more pains about it. *(Pauſes for ſome time, then looks at her.)* Is it not very ſtrange, that you wont hear me?

Lady Rackett.

Sir, I am very ready to hear you.

Sir Charles

Very well then, very well; you remember how the game ſtood. *(draws his chair near her.)*

Lady Rackett.

I wiſh you would untie my necklace, it hurts me.

Sir Charles.

Why can't you liſten?

Lady

Lady Rackett.
I tell you it hurts me terribly.

Sir Charles.
Death and confusion! *(moves his chair away.)* there is no bearing this. *(looks at her angrily)* It won't take a moment, if you will but listen. *(moves towards her)* Can't you see, that by forcing the adversary's hand, Mr. Jenkins would be obliged to—

Lady Rackett.
(Moving her chair away from him.)
Mr. Jenkins had the best club, and never a diamond left.

Sir Charles. *(rising)*
Distraction! Bedlam is not so mad. Be as wrong as you please, Madam. May I never hold four by honours, may I lose every thing I play for, may fortune eternally forsake me, if I endeavour to set you right again.
[*Exit.*

Enter Mr. *and* Mrs. Drugget, Woodley, Lovelace, *and* Nancy.

Mrs. Drugget.
Gracious! what's the matter now?

Lady Rackett.
Such another man does not exist. I did not say a word to the gentleman, and yet he has been raving about the room, and storming like a whirlwind.

Drugget.

And about a club again! I heard it all. Come hither, Nancy; Mr. Woodley, she is yours for life.

Mrs. Drugget.

My dear, how can you be so passionate?

Drugget.

It shall be so. Take her for life, Mr. Woodley.

Woodley.

My whole life shall be devoted to her happiness

Lovelace.

The devil! and so I am to be left in the lurch in this manner, am I?

Lady Rackett.

Oh! this is only one of those polite disputes which people of quality, who have nothing else to differ about, must always be liable to. This will be made up to morrow.

Drugget.

Never tell me: it is too late now. Mr. Woodley, I recommend my girl to your care. I shall have nothing now to think of, but my greens, and my images, and my shrubbery. Though, mercy on all married folks, say I!—for these wranglings are, I am afraid, What they must all come to.

A COMEDY.

Lady Rackett. (*comes forward.*)

*W*HAT we muſt all come to ? What ? Come to
 what ?
Muſt broils and quarrels be the marriage lot ?
If that's the wife, deep meaning of our poet,
The man's a fool! a blockhead! and I'll ſhew it.

What could induce him in an age ſo nice,
So fam'd for virtue, ſo refin'd from vice,
To form a plan ſo trivial, falſe, and low ?
As if a belle could quarrel with a beau :
As if there were in theſe thrice happy days,
One who from nature, or from reaſon ſtrays !
There's no croſs huſband now ; no wrangling wife,
The man is downright ignorant of life.

'Tis the millennium this : devoid of guile,
Fair gentle Truth, and white rob'd Candour ſmile.
From every breaſt the ſordid love of gold
Is baniſh'd quite ; no boroughs now are ſold !
Pray tell me, Sirs—(for I don't know, I vow,)
Pray, is there ſuch a thing as Gaming now ?
Do peers make laws againſt that giant Vice,
And then at Arthur's break them in a trice ?
No, no ; our lives are virtuous all, auſtere and hard ;
Pray, ladies—do you ever ſee a card ?
Thoſe empty boxes ſhew you don't love plays ;
The managers, poor ſouls ! get nothing now a days.
If here you come—by chance—but once a week,
The pit can witneſs that you never ſpeak.
Penſive Attention ſits with decent mien ;
No paint, no naked ſhoulders to be ſeen !

And yet this grave, this moral, pious age,
May learn one uſeful leſſon from the ſtage.

Shun ſtrife, ye fair, and once a conteſt o'er,
Wake to a blaze the dying flame no more.
From fierce debate fly all the tender loves,
And Venus cries, " coachman, put-to my doves."
The genial bed no blooming Grace prepares,
" And ev'ry day ſhall be a day of cares."

End of the SECOND VOLUME.

For Product Safety Concerns and Information please contact our EU representative GPSR@taylorandfrancis.com
Taylor & Francis Verlag GmbH, Kaufingerstraße 24, 80331 München, Germany

www.ingramcontent.com/pod-product-compliance
Lightning Source LLC
Chambersburg PA
CBHW071234300426
44116CB00008B/1025